The Helio Courier C/STOL Aircraft

The Helio Courier Ultra C/STOL Aircraft

An Illustrated Developmental History

FRANK JOSEPH ROWE

McFarland & Company, Inc., Publishers
Jefferson, North Carolina, and London

The present work is a reprint of the illustrated case bound edition of The Helio Courier Ultra C/STOL Aircraft: An Illustrated Developmental History, first published in 2006 by McFarland.

LIBRARY OF CONGRESS CATALOGUING-IN-PUBLICATION DATA

Rowe, Frank Joseph.
　　The Helio Courier Ultra C/STOL aircraft : an illustrated developmental history / Frank Joseph Rowe.
　　　p.　　cm.
　　Includes bibliographical references and index.

ISBN 978-0-7864-7719-7
softcover : 50# alkaline paper

　　1. Helio Courier aircraft — History.　2. Short take-off and landing aircraft — History.　3. Private planes — History. I. Title.
　　TL686.H45R69　2013
　　629.133'340426 — dc22　　　　　　　　　　　　2005034172

BRITISH LIBRARY CATALOGUING DATA ARE AVAILABLE

© 2006 Frank Joseph Rowe. All rights reserved

No part of this book may be reproduced or transmitted in any form or by any means, electronic or mechanical, including photocopying or recording, or by any information storage and retrieval system, without permission in writing from the publisher.

Front cover: *(top)* H-370 Courier (Bob Casebeer); *(bottom)* HST-550 Stallion (Central Arkansas Library System/Aerospace Branch and the Arkansas Aviation Historical Society)

Manufactured in the United States of America

McFarland & Company, Inc., Publishers
　Box 611, Jefferson, North Carolina 28640
　　www.mcfarlandpub.com

To Lynn L. Bollinger
and Otto C. Koppen,
whose vision and commitment
continue to serve the world

With special appreciation to
Bob Casebeer (former Vice President
of Manufacturing, Helio Aircraft Company),
Paul E. Davis (former Technical Representative —
Cambodia, Helio Aircraft Company),
without whose help this book would not have been possible.

And to my wife, Patricia Irene Rowe,
who believed in this effort throughout the years.

Acknowledgments

Dale Armstrong
Former General Manager, Helio Aircraft Co.

Lynn Bollinger
Former Chairman, Helio Aircraft Co., G.A.C.

Regina Burns
Archives Div., U.S. Army Aviation Museum
Fort Rucker, Alabama

Bob Casebeer
Former Vice President of Manufacturing,
Helio Aircraft Co.

Commonwealth of Massachusetts
Secretary of State Office

Eual Conditt
FAA, Wichita Aircraft Certification Office

Paul Davis
Former Helio Stallion tech. rep. (Cambodia)
Helio Aircraft Co.

Teresa Day
Director, Kansas Aviation Museum

Ken Dayer
Assistant Manager/Curator
Jay Miller Collection
Arkansas Aviation Historical Society

Gene DeGruson
Special Collections
Pittsburg State University, Kansas

Bob Devine
Former structures engineer, Helio Aircraft Co.
Bedford, Massachusetts

Jon W. Dwight & David Maytag
Helio Enterprises, Inc./Helio Aircraft, LLC

Dave Ellis
Institute of Aviation Research
Wichita State University

Tom Ensign
Advanced Design
Cessna Aircraft Company

Richard L. Erwin, M.D., P.A.
Newton, Kansas

Experimental Aircraft Association (EAA)
Archives Division

FAA Department of Statistics
Washington, D.C.

Fiona Hale, Librarian
National Aviation Museum, Archives Dept.
Ottawa, Ontario, Canada

Terry Heffield
JAARS, Inc.

Kate Igoe
Archives Division
National Air and Space Museum,
Smithsonian Institute

Kansas State Historical Society
Archives Division

Robert Kimnach
Former President, Helio Aircraft Co., G.A.C.

Howard Levy
Library of Congress
Archives Division

Arthur Lightbody
JAARS, Inc.

Nathan Mackey
Heliocourier.net

Margaret Martin-Heaton
Institute Archives and Special Collections
Massachusetts Institute of Technology (MIT)

Clark Masters

Acknowledgments

Edward T. McNally
Former President, McNally Manufacturing

Dave Menard
Research Division, United States
Air Force Museum
Wright Patterson Air Force Base

Larry Montgomery
Former tech. rep., Helio Aircraft Co.
Larmont Aviation
Spartanburg, South Carolina

Teresa Night
U.S. Patent & Trademark Office
Washington, D.C.

William J. Ostapctuck

Larry J. Powell
Business Relations Director
City of Pittsburg, Kansas

Kenneth J. Quimby
Arkansas Aviation Historical Society

David Ramsdale
Aviation Operations Manager
JAARS, Inc.

Brett Stolle
United States Air Forces Museum
Wright Patterson Air Force Base

Miriam Stoner
AOPA Publications

Gerald Tremain

Contents

Acknowledgments	vii
Preface	xi

1. **Chasing the Sun**   1
   Helio Progenitors

2. **Dawn of the "Tennis Court Airplane"**   27
   Early Helio Prototypes

3. **Geared for Success**   49
   Main Production Models and Variants, 1954–1974

4. **Litterbugs and Black Ops**   86
   Military Versions of the Helio Courier

5. **Above and Beyond**   106
   Turbo-Charged Helios and Concept Aircraft

6. **Twilight of the Courier**   147
   The Last Production Helio Courier Models
   and Concept Aircraft, 1983–1985

7. **Couriers of the Word**   160
   JAARS Helio Operations

8. **Epilogue**   171
   Plans for Future Helio Production

Appendix 1: Data Specification Sheets	173
Appendix 2: Helio Aircraft Models and Production Totals	215
Notes	217
Bibliography	221
Index	225

Preface

Say the words "Helio Courier" to any seasoned tail-wheel pilot, and there is a reasonably good chance that he or she will pause and then, with carefully measured words, recall with amazement bordering on incredulity the astonishing capabilities of this outstanding C/STOL (Controlled/Short Take Off and Landing) aircraft. Throughout the years, legions of stories have circulated about the confirmed as well as rumored feats of this workhorse aircraft and its crews. In fact, the Helio line of aircraft seems to be surrounded at times by the kind of mystique that is usually reserved for all but a very few outstanding aircraft.

Sitting idly on a ramp, the Helio seems innocuous enough, its overall conventional tail-dragger looks belying its incredible performance capabilities. Its overall commonplace appearance seems to confound, as well as fortify, the myths and legends that have become a part of the Helio legacy.

Conceived as a "stall-proof/spin-proof everyman's safety-plane" initially intended to revolutionize general aviation, the Helio not only defied contemporary flight practices and challenged CAA regulations, it also set a standard for STOL/slow-speed-maneuvering flight that has never since been completely equaled by a fixed wing aircraft.

From the steamy Amazon jungle in South America to the Arctic remoteness of polar expeditions, from clandestine CIA and Special Forces operative bases in Southeast Asia to corporate flight departments of the Western world, the Helio line of C/STOL aircraft has distinguished itself as one of the world's finest and most versatile aircraft.

Research for a book on the Helio Courier originally stemmed from another book project, *Borne on the South Wind: A Century of Kansas Aviation*. Helio Aircraft Company's manufacturing plant (Mid States Manufacturing) was located in Pittsburg, Kansas, and so was one of the many aircraft manufacturing companies listed in that work. While researching that book I encountered a sizeable amount of conflicting data, historical gaps, and generally enough frustration to offer incentive to try to reconstruct a reasonably accurate and cohesive history.

I chose to focus my research primarily on a developmental history, rather than a field history, due to a current lack of available material that gives a detailed and accurate accounting of how and why the original concept evolved into final production form. In this respect, the developmental history traces the genesis of Helio aircraft design/evolution, target markets, performance goals and certification through production maturity. I have not completely dismissed field history in terms of how the Helio Courier (and its stable mate, the Stallion) has been utilized by its owners/operators. Indeed, it would be impossible to discuss the Helio without touching briefly on field use by organizations such as the military and humanitarian outreach programs.

This work on the Helio Courier is organized by chapters covering distinct phases of Helio Courier development.

As unique and impressive as the Helio Courier is, it certainly is not without its historical predecessors. With this in mind, I chose to start with a brief summary (chapter 1, "Chasing the Sun—Helio Progenitors") of some of the more noteworthy attempts to build aircraft offering significantly improved safety and performance that preceded the Helio. It was these earlier efforts that set the stage for the Helio Courier concept.

In chapter 2 ("Dawn of the 'Tennis Court Airplane'—Early Helio Prototypes"), we explore the original concept, design goals, target markets and prototype testing that preceded full-scale production. This was an exciting time of inspired innovation, exacting work, and trial and error as well as serendipitous happenstances that all contributed to the development of an aircraft that would offer astounding capability and performance.

The transition from early concept prototyping to full scale production certainly brought a myriad of challenges, considering the significant extent of departure from conventional design/operation as well as a philosophical "misfit" with CAA certification. Throughout chapter 3 ("Geared for Success—Main Production Models and Variants, 1954–1974") we study the development of production aircraft from 1954 through 1974.

As the stellar-performing Helio Courier was a relatively complex and expensive machine to own and operate, it's not surprising that the military became its major customer. Because a significant amount of Helio legacy is rooted in military development and application, chapter 4 ("Litterbugs and Black Ops—Military Versions of the Helio Courier") focuses on the evolution of the Helio Courier for military use by conventional as well as unconventional (Special Operations) forces.

As unique and promising as the original Helio Courier was, its success spurred on the development of advanced concepts that sought to further capitalize on the aircraft's already superb safety and performance capabilities. Chapter 5 ("Above and Beyond—Turbo-Charged Helios and Concept Aircraft") captures these efforts. Some of these, for example the H-500 Twin and the HST-550A/AU-24A-HE Stallion, were turbocharged limited production aircraft, while many others were fanciful yet intriguing "paper airplanes" that never made it off the Helio drawing boards.

Chapter 6 ("Twilight of the Courier—The Last Production Helio Courier Models and Concept Aircraft, 1983–1985") documents the development of the last (as of this work's publication date) Helio Couriers from 1983 through 1985.

If Helio lore is a direct by-product of its unique use, then it would be fitting to discuss the Helio as utilized in humanitarian outreach programs. The Helio Courier is (when flown to its full performance capabilities) an "extreme machine" that excels in extreme environments and circumstances. Chapter 7 ("Couriers of the Word — JAARS Helio Operations") documents how one such outreach program in particular (JAARS, Inc., of Waxhaw, North Carolina) has adapted and utilized the Helios throughout the world's most extreme climates and work environments.

Finally, chapter 8 ("Epilogue — Plans for Future Helio Production") reflects on the past and present and examines possible future Helio development.

Much of the research for the book was pieced together from recorded interviews, independent archival data and primary source news articles, as supplemented by company annual reports and FAA type design specifications. A tremendous amount of information has been gleaned from discussions with former Helio company officials. Much original Helio Aircraft Company material — drawings, reports, general data and historical information — has, unfortunately, been lost through time due to various circumstances, including a flood in 1956 at the Bedford, Massachusetts, headquarters. Files also went missing during the many times the company changed ownership. That said, while initially frustrating, it is with a certain amount of satisfaction that an overall history has resulted from the contributions of so many sources.

While this work is intended to be comprehensive there are undoubtedly additional facts, stories and data that have not been yet discovered. It is my hope that publication of this work will bring forth those stories to be shared and archived.

Finally, any written history concerning the Helio Courier should ideally be supplemented with the actual experience of witnessing a demonstration of this aircraft's ultra C/STOL performance capabilities. While rarely seen, it is a truly amazing sight to behold.

I hope that this history, gleaned from former company officers, workers, owners/operators, and archives, will provide an expanded perspective on the visions of its principal leadership, the development of the company, and its impressive series of C/STOL machines.

Frank Joseph Rowe
Wichita, Kansas
January 2006

1. Chasing the Sun
Helio Progenitors

Well sports fans, how does this grab you? The Helio Courier Mark II can maintain a TAS of 28 MPH while in a 43 degree nose-high attitude and be fully controllable! It can take off in 300 feet and land to a stop in 245 feet! Firewall the throttle and it'll pull away at over 160 MPH!—Barry Schiff, *AOPA Pilot*

There have been many design innovations in aircraft technology during the last 25 years or so, but nothing has ever really come along to quite match the superbly designed Helio Courier which first flew some thirty-one years ago.—Ed Davis, *Air Progress*, November 1994

Come along with us as we wring out a nearly "impossible" plane, the fantastic Helio Courier. On wheels or floats, it's "WOW"!—Gene Smith, *Air Progress*, December 1968

When the issue is not how fast, but how slow, can an airplane fly, this gaunt, spindle-shanked Ichabod Crane of the air world is a thing of pure beauty. The Helio dooms-day demonstration normally comes near the beginning of the flight. The airplane, an outsized toothpick with the wing of a condor, is snagged by its propeller three points off zenith, the tail waggling below.—Richard Weeghman, *Flying*, August 1969

Helio Courier's performance is the stuff of legends. They've been known to land on taxi-ways or cross-wise on the runway on windy days, freak out people in their cars by flying alongside the road slower than the automobile traffic and indulge in all kinds of mischievous behavior. In fact, Helio Couriers are so much fun, we wonder how they can possibly be legal.—Ron Grable, Plane Pilot, July 1973

Between 1955 and the present day, the reader of general aviation trade periodicals might occasionally happen upon rave reviews such as these for the Helio Courier C/STOL aircraft, usually wedged between the seemingly endless yearly updates for yet another mundane and efficient version of what was usually a Beech, a Cessna or a Piper.

To fully appreciate the Helio's STOL and safety credentials, it is essential to be familiar with its earliest progenitors and the circumstances that brought about the Helio's existence. Ever since the earliest aviators struggled to master, not to mention understand, the forces acting upon their fragile powered kites, there has been a desire for craft that possessed an increased margin of safety (primarily from stall and spin) while maintaining a respectable standard of performance (high cruise speed).

Many of these long-standing safety concerns as viewed by pilots were understandable: during the early 1900s few potential pilots (and a sizeable number of high-time veteran pilots) fully understood the flight dynamics and limitations of an aircraft's wing in the invisible, ever changing ocean of air.

Flying has always involved a certain amount of calculated risk. Because the Helio was designed from the outset to address these risks and to reform general aviation air travel as an "everyman's safety plane" (rather than the specialized niche aircraft that it became), it seems appropriate to review the factors that have contributed to pilot safety concerns. These factors would to a great extent be addressed in the ultimate production form of the Helio, as well as its predecessors and contemporaries.

Many of aviators' long-standing fears concerning safety issues have been verified by accident statistics. As noted by Hugh DeHaven, serious evaluation of aviation crash data did not exist during the 1920s and 1930s. It was not until DeHaven spearheaded the development of this field in the 1940s that any widespread consideration was given to production safety enhancements. Organizations such as the CAB (Civil Aeronautics Board) and the NTSB (National Transportation Safety Board), as well as several comprehensive books, have tabulated, analyzed and clearly charted the contributing factors to general aviation accidents as experienced during each phase of aircraft operation (static, taxi, takeoff/initial climb, in-flight and approach/ landing).

An expanded, in-depth, year-to-year statistical study of all the possible categories/ causes of general aviation accidents is outside the scope of this work (NTSB records list approximately 60 "types of accidents"). A brief study of the statistical data derived from records maintained by the CAB (1948 through 1965), the NTSB (1965 to present), and the AOPA Air Safety Foundation in regard to primary categories/causes of general aviation accidents* reveals the following averaged patterns[1]:

Primary Categories of Accidents

Accidents due to pilot error: 80 percent
Accidents to weather: 12 percent
Accidents due to airframe/powerplant & systems failure unrelated to pilot error: 5 percent
Accidents due to airport/airway congestion-related factors: 3 percent

Some of the specific accident cause/factors for each of these primary categories are:

---

*"Aircraft accident" as defined by the NTSB: An occurrence associated with operation of an aircraft which takes place between the time any person boards aircraft with the intention of flight until such time as all such persons have disembarked, in which any person suffers death or serious injury as a result of being in or upon the aircraft or by direct contact with the aircraft or anything attached thereto, or the aircraft receives *substantial damage*.[2] (Note: "Substantial Damage," as defined by the NTSB prior to Jan. 1, 1968, entails damage or structural failure to aircraft of 12,500 lbs. max. certificated takeoff weight or less which is reasonably estimated to cost $300 or more to repair. Effective Jan. 1, 1968, "substantial damage" was redefined as damage or structural failure which adversely affects the structural strength, performance or flight characteristics of an aircraft, and which would require major repair or replacement of the affected component. The max. certificated takeoff weight of 12,500 lbs. was deleted from the revised definition.)

Specific Cause/Factors of Accidents

Pilot Error: Failure to obtain or maintain flying speed (stall, spin, mush), mismanagement of fuel, improper operation of powerplant and related systems, improper operation of landing gear. Flying VFR into IFR conditions, improper IFR operation, inadequate preflight, failure to maintain directional control.

Weather: Unexpected and unfavorable wind conditions (turbulence), low ceilings, & ice.

Airframe/Powerplant: Engine failure/fire, premature fatigue/failure of load-bearing structure of aircraft.

Airport/Airway: Confusing taxi and/or runway markings, runway incursions/faulty clearances/instructions through ATC mismanagement, dangerous approaches/obstructions.

An additional review of the data on general aviation accidents as experienced throughout each phase of aircraft operation (static, taxi, takeoff/initial climb, in-flight and approach/landing) reveals the following[3]:

Accidents: By Phase of Operation

Static & Taxi: 4 percent
Takeoff/InitialClimb: 22 percent
In-flight: 19 percent
Approach/Landing: 55 percent

With the exception of an occasional and short term upwards or downwards deviation in the annual causes of general aviation accidents, the weighted statistical importance of certain accident prone areas is as valid today as it was when the concept of the Helio Courier was first being mulled over.

It is clear enough that, in lieu of trying to legislate common sense among the pilot population, a reasonable solution would be to design aircraft possessing safety features that would ultimately help curb the roughly 80 percent pilot error accident figure while remaining affordable with reasonable performance. Depending on the source of accident statistics cited, and how the source interprets the term "pilot error," the figure can rise to approximately 90 percent. Adding still more confusion to "pilot error causes" are the ambiguities through time over the possibilities of "design-induced" pilot error, in which a physical component in or of the aircraft is deemed of poor design and therefore predisposes the pilot to err. In this respect, the term "human error" is starting to creep into, and in certain instances wholly displace the term "pilot error" in, the more modern statistical vocabulary. Add to this the current prevailing trend to assess pilot judgment in accidents to have been diminished by other people's actions and interests, and the "pilot error" category begins to take on monumental proportions as THE CAUSE for safety reform.

In spite of our modem tendency to view error as possibly being a "shared" commodity (whether design-induced or otherwise), it is the pilot who has been chartered with the ultimate authority, and who must pay the final price. In an environment that generates multiple opportunities for error — be it the capricious vagaries of weather, an incomplete understanding of the capabilities of the aircraft, or simply a sensory overload in a situation requiring a near instant and correct response — pilot error has usually been the focus for safety enhancements through time (particularly during the high risk phase of take off and landing).

Ultimately, the Helio Courier was envisioned and designed to address all four of the primary categories of general aviation accidents, with a reasonably high cruise speed performance to complement its spectacular low speed capability, but unfortunately with an initially unforeseen purchase price that was too high to attract and sustain wide acceptance in the civilian marketplace.

It might be worthwhile to recall that early in the twentieth century general aviation enjoyed a relatively low mortality rate following accidents (this in spite of the infant stage in development of airports, navigational aids and accurate weather forecasting/ dissemination as well as suspect reliability of powerplants). This can be directly attributed to the wholesale use of pastures for airstrips and low minimum landing speeds. With wing loadings averaging 6 to 10 pounds per square foot, and typical landing speeds in the range of 35 to 45 MPH, any mishap during the high risk phases of operation (takeoff and landing) were likely not to be fatal. Gradually, as airframes were aerodynamically cleaned up and mated to ever more potent powerplants, and as airports evolved to the point where takeoffs and landings were made on hard surfaces with a fixed heading, accidents became more numerous with a higher degree of severity in aircraft damage and human carnage.

Perhaps one of the most noteworthy early attempts to address safety issues was the Guggenheim Safe Aircraft Competition of 1929. The roots of this event can be traced to January 1926, when Daniel Guggenheim established the Daniel Guggenheim Fund for the Promotion of Aeronautics, along with a sum of $2,500,000 to underwrite projects. Harry F. Guggenheim, president of the fund, determined that the most pressing need of aviation was to advance the means to secure safety in flying. While several grants were made available to American universities to further aeronautical education, perhaps the crowning achievement was the announcement of the Safe Aircraft Competition. The competition's purpose to produce an aeroplane that would eliminate stall-spin accidents during slow speed flight, while maintaining respectable high speed and practical load carrying capability.

Specifically, the major requirements for aircraft to be submitted for final flight testing were as follows[4]:

1. Demonstrate a minimum low, level, and controlled speed of 35 MPH (max).
2. Demonstrate a glide for 3 minutes with power off and airspeed not to exceed 38 MPH.
3. Demonstrate a maximum speed of 110 MPH.
4. Demonstrate ability to take off within 300'.
5. Demonstrate ability to stop upon landing within 300'.
6. Demonstrate ability to clear upon takeoff a 35' obstacle within 500'.
7. Demonstrate ability to clear upon landing a 35' obstacle within 300'.
8. Demonstrate an ability to fly at 45 to 100 MPH for 5 minutes with "hands off."

Curtiss Tanager — The first aircraft to focus on comprehensive safety enhancements. National Air and Space Museum, Smithsonian Institute (SI NEG NO. A50412A).

    9. Demonstrate ability to perform a steep glide at no more than 40 MPH (power off), with elevator control pulled back to limit, under full control.
    10. Demonstrate capability to carry 2 people for 3 hours.
    11. Demonstrate payload capability of 5 lbs. per horsepower.

    Initially 27 aircraft were entered for the June 19 through October 31, 1929, competitive trials held at Mitchell Field, Long Island. The winner of the fly-off would receive a prize of $100,000. General attrition (including the dropping out of the only two autogyros) brought this field down to the following 7 aircraft:

1. Brunner-Winkle (biplane)
2. Cunningham-Hall (inverted sesquiplane)
3. Curtiss Tanager (sesquiplane)
4. Fleet
5. Ford-Leigh Safety Wing
6. Handley Page (biplane)
7. Taylor Bros. Chummy (monoplane)

    Most of the entries made use of various combinations of slots, spoilers and flaps, with an equally varying degree of efficiency. Unique within the field were two machines that made use of mechanisms to achieve variable camber, and thereby delay stalling angle. The Vincent Burnelli all metal monoplane not only featured variable camber, but also by way of "wing sleeve" was able to vary its chord. Also noteworthy for its variable camber wing, although not among the final 7 competitors, was the Schroeder-Wentworth monoplane.
    In the end, the Curtiss Model 54 Tanager was declared the winner, as none of the other entrants were able to completely pass all of the qualification tests. The Tan-

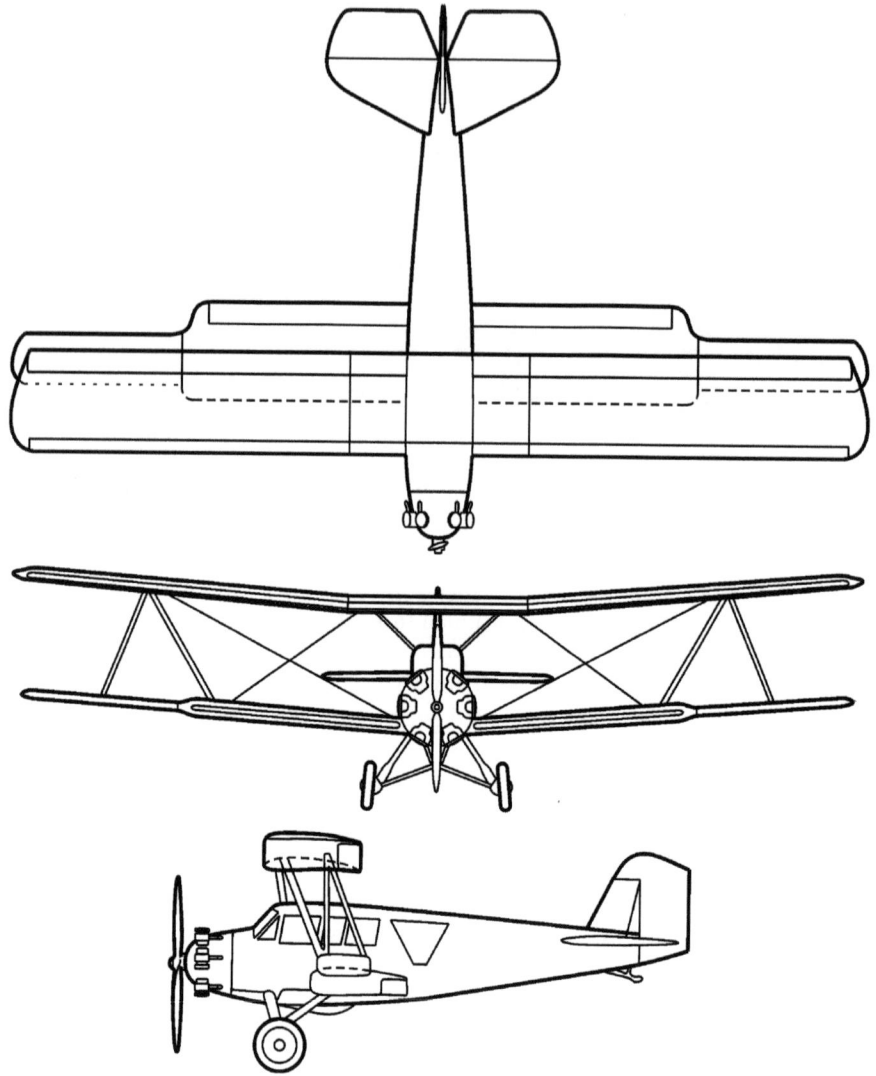

Curtiss Tanager — 3-View.

ager, a cabin biplane, featured full-span trailing edge flaps (accounting for a 33 percent increase in lift) as well as full-span Handley Page automatic leading edge slats (accounting for a 50 percent increase in lift). In addition, floating ailerons were installed on the lower wingtips. The floating ailerons (ailerons that are allowed to pivot freely with respect to the relative wind, and which the pilot controls by displacing one aileron with respect to another and not to the plane) enabled the pilot to command full lateral control of the aircraft at minimum airspeed with almost no yawing effect. In addition, the notion that the rudder should be taken away from the unskilled pilot was incorporated into the design, as the Tanager's aileron did not need correcting by rudder for turns. Long-stroke oleo landing gear with approximately one foot of travel allowed the aircraft to absorb high-sink-rate landings.

As noted in the February 8, 1930, edition of *Aviation* magazine[5]:

> The Tanager has been landed repeatedly by completely stalling it at varying heights up to 200′—stabilizer and elevator all the way tail heavy and held in these positions. When this is done the plane settles in a landing position, does not pick up speed, and lands itself with no more shock in the cabin than accompanies a normal landing in the usual type of craft. True, the ground comes up so fast that one expects the wheels to come right through the wings the first time it is done, but the landing gear is designed to cushion the shock of this gliding condition if started at any altitude.

As designed under the guidance of Curtiss chief engineer T. P. Wright and Robert Osborne, some of the Tanager's performance statistics for the Guggenheim competition were as follows[6]:

Wing Loading: 8.5 lbs./sq. ft.
Min. flying speed: 30.6 MPH
High speed: 112 MPH
Gross Weight: 2841 lbs.
Powerplant: 176 HP Challenger

As technically impressive as the Tanager was, the newspaper editorials were less than glowing, with writers expressing frustration that nothing more radical than some new-fangled form of "lateral control" should surface from such an all-out high-dollar assault on improving flying safety. Indeed, fate seemed to conspire to undo what strides were made during this effort. No sooner had the Curtiss Tanager been declared the winner than the Handley Page contingent filed suit for the equivalent of the $100,000 in prize money, for patent infringement of its leading-edge-slat design. In 1930 the Tanager, once thought of as heralding a new generation of nearly "foolproof" aircraft designs, was destroyed in a fire while parked on a grass strip. What few hopes remained for general aviation safety reform stemming from the Guggenheim contest were to be completely extinguished in short order from the effects of the Great Depression. While certain concepts may have held promise, they all were to prove too costly to produce during the following era, when the prevailing trend for general aviation manufacturers was to scrape by with production of cheap, relatively light weight (yet in certain circumstances aerodynamically novel) "flivver" type aircraft. Models such as the American Eagle Eaglet, Aeronca C-2, Rearwin Junior, and Taylor E-2, as well as various forms of primary gliders, evolved to suit the less-than-well-heeled pilot.

Unique to the era in which the Guggenheim competition took place was the emergence of the autogyro as a possible means to improve general aviation safety. While never displacing the fixed wing aircraft in sales, the autogiro—pioneered as early as 1923 by Juan de la Cierva of Spain—deserves consideration. Cierva proposed the autogyro as a means of combating the stalling tendencies of fixed wing aircraft, as evidenced in his first successful design, the Cierva C.4 of 1923.

The autogyro achieved flight by using a conventional prop/powerplant to obtain forward speed and free-spinning overhead rotor blades to supply lift by way of "autorotation" (a flight condition in which lift is obtained by a relative airflow from the front and below, and by which the blades rotate into the relative wind).

On average, the autogyro is capable of maintaining slow speed flight of approx-

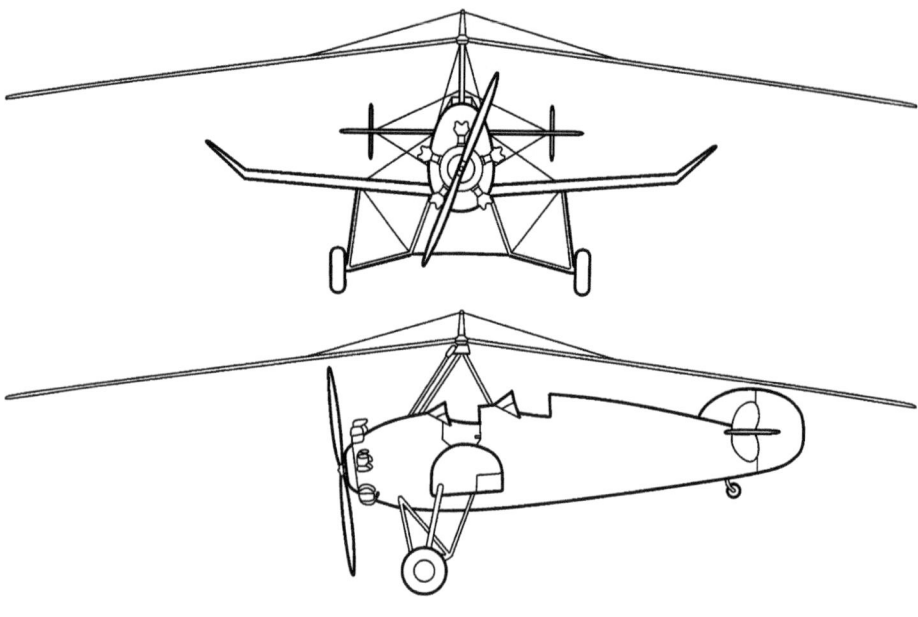

Autogyro.

imately 20 to 25 MPH, near vertical takeoff, and in emergency situations a near-vertical controlled descent with full auto-rotation for a safe landing.

Evolutionary design improvements, including articulated blade design, cyclic pitch control, and the provision of a drive shaft to temporarily pre-spin the rotor blades while on the ground to provide a near-vertical "jump takeoff," gave the autogyro very impressive performance. Unfortunately, certain issues (limited range, unpredictable bouts of ground resonance, and restricted load carrying capabilities due to a narrow CG travel) combined to limit sales largely to "sportsman flyers" and corporate promotional campaigns rather than pure utilitarian needs.

In the United States, autogyros built through licensing agreements with Cierva included Pitcairn, Kellet and Buhl, while other worldwide manufacturing continued by way of AVRO and DeHavilland of Great Britain, Focke-Wulf of Germany and Kamov of Russia.

For a time, the military looked at the autogyro as a possible observation platform, and several airmail carriers toyed with the notion of using the autogyro as an addition to their fleets. Such was the novelty and promise of the autogyros that on April 22, 1931, President Herbert Hoover presented the Collier Trophy for the "greatest achievement in aviation" to Harold Pitcairn. As if to underscore the significance of this recognition, one of Pitcairn's autogyros actually landed at the White House for the awards presentation. Indeed, it seemed that for a while autogyros were in the headlines everywhere, with celebrity flyers from Amelia Earhart to Frank Hawks setting records and giving rave testimonials to this revolutionary means of safe air travel.

Much of the groundwork to refine the autogyro (in spite of its limited capabilities) was to translate directly to the production and wide-scale acceptance of the helicopter. In 1936, Juan de la Cierva died in a DC2 crash in London. Ironically, his death

Lanier Vacu-Plane. National Air and Space Museum, Smithsonian Institute (SI NEG NO. A4388).

marks the approximate time of transition in which the first successful helicopters were being developed, which would ultimately eclipse in the public's mind the contribution of the autogyros.

Efforts to build a safer aircraft were not restricted to just a clever combination of existing boundary-layer control devices (e.g., leading-edge slats, slots and slotted flaps). Edward H. Lanier (who amassed a tidy sum of money as the inventor of the ice cream cone) parlayed his profits into a series of evolutionary aircraft designs that featured his "Vacu-Cell" concept.

Inspired by the Wright brothers, Lanier started his aircraft venture in 1907. Lanier believed that as long as aircraft operation required large areas for takeoff/landing and a considerable amount of skill, most of the public would remain spectators rather than become part of the small, elite band that served as the pilot base. He further shared the belief espoused by the famous Louis Blériot that the wings of an aircraft should ideally be designed to allow an aircraft to descend in the manner of a parachute.

Lanier's vision of an aircraft that possessed high lift capability, stability, and reasonable control at low speeds materialized as the Lanier Vacu-Plane. Built in 1935 with assistance from students at the University of Miami, the Vacu-Plane featured an airfoil with an open area (Vacu-Cell) where the top surface of the wing is normally located.

This opening created a vacuum of reported substantial strength to create lift, while stub wings were located outboard of the Vacu-Cell (vacuum section) as a means to locate ailerons. Performance was recorded to be impressive; powered by a 36 HP Aeronca engine, the plane had a top speed of 110 MPH and a landing speed of 28 MPH.

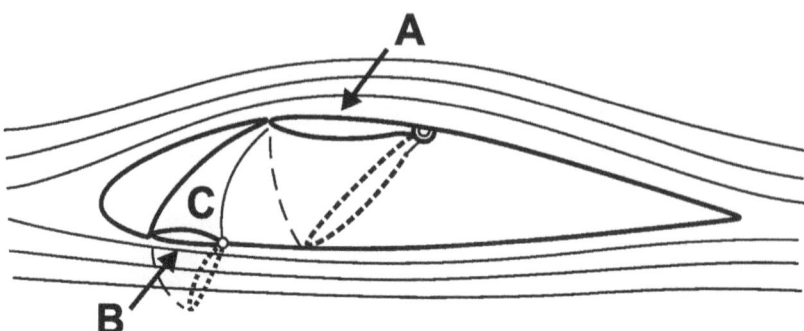

Cruising, the airfoil's six sets of upper surface vanes (A) are closed, as are the lower vanes (B.) When closed, the lower vanes cover the mouth of the venturi-shaped air passage (C) in the wing. At this setting, the wing resembles a conventional airfoil.

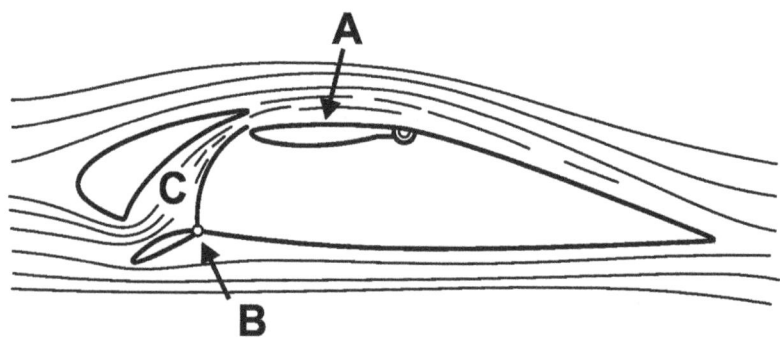

For Take-off, vanes A and B are opened slightly. Air is directed into the venturi passage, spurting out at increased pressure and speed. A slight vacuum cell is formed by depression of the top vane, creating a negative pressure area and providing lift.

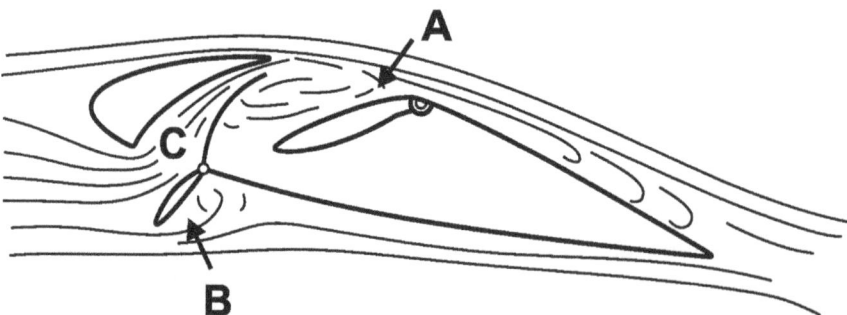

For landing, exaggerated openings are required as the plane loses forward speed. The venturi maintains airflow over the top of the wing at greater than stall velocity. The vacu-cell created by maximum depression of vane A provides more than normal lift.

Although Edward H. Lanier died just prior to the end of World War II, his son Edward M. Lanier would resurrect and modify the principle during the 1940s with the debut of the Lanier Paraplane. The airfoil used in the Paraplane differed from that of the earlier Lanier Vacu-Plane (which was designed as a fixed-position, constantly open air chamber to produce substantial negative air pressure) in that six moveable vanes on top of the wing could be closed or opened at the discretion of the pilot, thereby varying lift. Production models were envisioned to have three predetermined settings to vary the opening size of the vanes in relation to the takeoff, cruise and landing phases of flight. In addition to the relatively high degree of lift generated from the inboard cells, the outboard cells served as slots to provide high-pressure airflow to ailerons in order to maintain effective control at slow speed.

As powered by a 90-HP Continental engine, the Paraplane had a speed range of 30 to 120 MPH. Takeoff could be achieved in less than 200 feet; a fully controlled landing was possible while holding full aft stick, with the aircraft settling in at an approximate 45 degree angle.

Although at least three prototype Paraplanes were built and successfully flown, mass production was never seriously considered due to high production costs. Rather, an unsuccessful attempt was made to license the patents to other manufacturers.

Another equally novel attempt to design a safer aircraft through innovative boundary-layer control was the series of aircraft collectively known as the "Custer Channel Wing" design. Legend has it that, during a particularly nasty storm, Willard R. Custer witnessed a barn roof being wrenched from its supporting walls and blown clear away by the fierce winds.

Custer marveled at this awesome display of wind, and it caused him to challenge the conventional wisdom of how best to generate useable lift in aircraft. Custer deduced that the barn roof flew off due to the speed of the rushing wind over it, not because it acted like an airfoil (although a poor one) flying due to moving through the air. From this close encounter with nature's fury emerged the theory that Custer would champion for the rest of his life and that would draw lifelong skeptical reviews from many of his peers. Specifically, Custer submitted that it was preferable to generate lift by moving the air over the airfoil, rather than by moving the airfoil through the air.

The overall design that Custer chose to achieve this would prove to be one of the most distinctive visual profiles yet conceived for an aircraft (although its ultimate failure to be mass produced would relegate it to being one of the more obscure).

The engines in each of Custer's successive designs were all center mounted inside a semi-circular channel section of the wing, the channel portion of the wing itself being comprised of an NACA 4418 airfoil. The propellers were located in a pusher-type configuration in order to draw high velocity air through the channel, thereby creating a higher degree of lift than is normally achieved in conventional winged aircraft (*Jane's Aircraft* annual for 1955–1956 lists a power-on lift coefficient of 5 for the Custer model CCW-5 as compared to 3 for the closest high lift conventional aircraft).[7]

The Channel Wing also featured two sets of ailerons. One set was located out-

Opposite: Lanier Vacu-Plane airfoil.

board of the channel for use during normal flight, while another set was located inboard of the channel to provide effective control for STOL flight mode. Control was further enhanced by being able to alter the in-flight pitch of the propeller and/or engine RPM.

Custer's first aircraft, the model CCW-1, first flew in November 1942 and was powered by two 75-HP Lycoming engines. Like the elder Lanier, Willard Custer would benefit from the assistance of his own son, Harold Custer, to carry on development. The Channel Wing was developed up to the model CCW-5, which during the late 1950s/early 1960s was contemplated as a full production aircraft with help from Noorduyn Aircraft of Canada.

Typical performance statistics for the CCW-5 included a maximum speed of 200 MPH and a minimum speed of 35 MPH when powered by two 260-HP Continental engines. Takeoffs of between 50' and 200' and landing runs of 300' were common, while it was also not uncommon for the channel-wing to demonstrate near-hover flight in mild wind conditions.

In spite of impressive flight demonstrations in which the channel-wing aircraft performed feats that ordinarily would have put the pilot of a more conventional aircraft at dire risk, economics and conservative attitudes ultimately derailed the enthusiasm for mass production. Perhaps it is fitting to note that Custer's notion of creating

Custer Channel Wing — Instantly recognizable on any ramp. National Air and Space Museum, Smithsonian Institute (SI NEG NO. 86-5556).

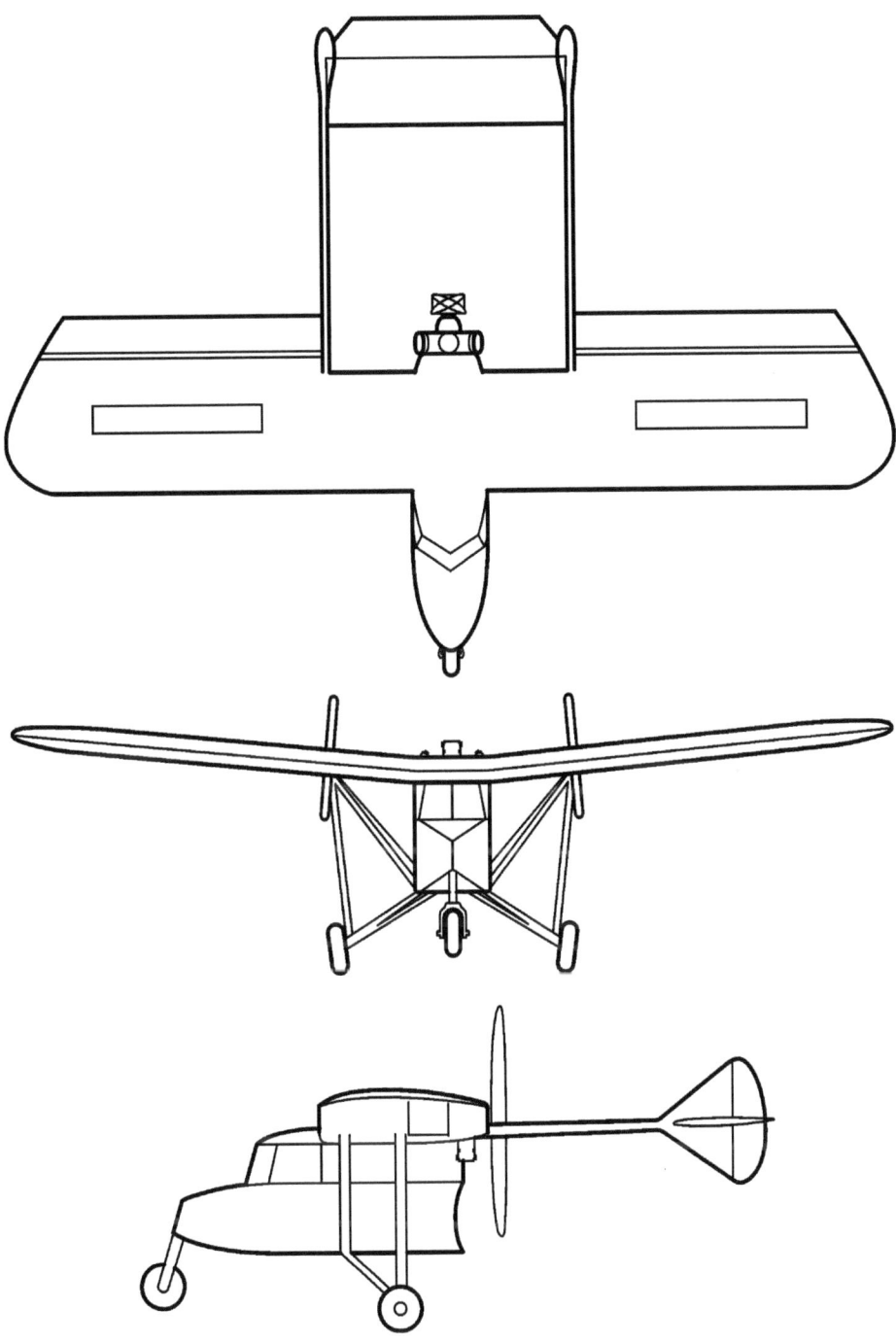

Weick Model W1—3-View.

"powered lift" still commands serious consideration, as evidenced by the Boeing YC-14 (and McDonnell-Douglas YC-15) medium STOL transport prototypes first flown in 1976. While dispensing with Custer's channel sections, the Boeing prototypes did make use of the basic concept of creating powered lift by using two General Electric turbofans mounted well ahead of the wing to blow high-speed air over the top surface of the wing. (The YC-15 used blown flaps, which went into production as the C-17.) This modern form of powered lifting (dubbed "USB"—Upper-Surface Blowing) as used on the Boeing YC-14 embodied principles that can be traced to the early inspirations of Willard Custer and his literal "barn storm" experience.

If the Lanier and Custer machines received a less-than-lukewarm reception from market forces, then the efforts of Fred E. Weick and his creations, the models W1/W1A and Ercoupe, can be classified as some of the more stellar campaigns to field aircraft with improved safety features.

Prior to the success of the Ercoupe, Fred Weick introduced his model W1 (1933) and model W1A (1935) aircraft. It was the homely looking W1 series that set the standards by which the Bureau of Air Commerce would judge entrants (15 in all) in its safety oriented personal plane competition of 1935.

Being of a pusher design, the W1/W1A demonstrated superior flight characteristics in that they would not stall/spin, and they possessed much improved ground handling without the propensity for ground loops or nose-overs. Major differences between the W1 and W1A were that a trailing-edge glide-control flap (W1A) eventually replaced a fixed leading-edge airfoil (W1). The wings on the W1A were further modified to incorporate an NACA slot-lip aileron for improved lateral control for low speed/high angle of attack. An elevator/aileron combination two-control system was installed on the W1A, with restricted elevator travel to eliminate stalls from excessively high angles of attack.

In 1933, the Bureau of Air Commerce re-instituted a version of the Guggenheim Safe Aircraft Competition, with general specifications for the contest gleaned from the highly successful W1/W1A aircraft. As overseen by Eugene Vidal, Director of the Aeronautics Division, Department of Commerce, some of the more noteworthy Light Plane Contest criteria required the winning aircraft design to be able to attain the following[8]:

- Max. speed of 110 MPH.
- Minimum controlled flying speed of 35 MPH.
- Clear upon takeoff a 35' obstacle from a standing start 800' away (no wind, at sea level).
- Clear a 35' obstacle during landing and stop within 400' (no wind, at sea level).
- No tendency to ground loop.
- No tendency to side-slip or spin (in both power-on and power-off flight).
- Landing gear must be capable of withstanding repeated vertical drops onto the ground at a velocity of 20" per second without damage.
- Capable of turning using up to 20 degrees of banking without use of rudder and without skidding or slipping.
- Improved pilot visibility (per cones of vision as expanded upon in original rules).

1. Chasing the Sun

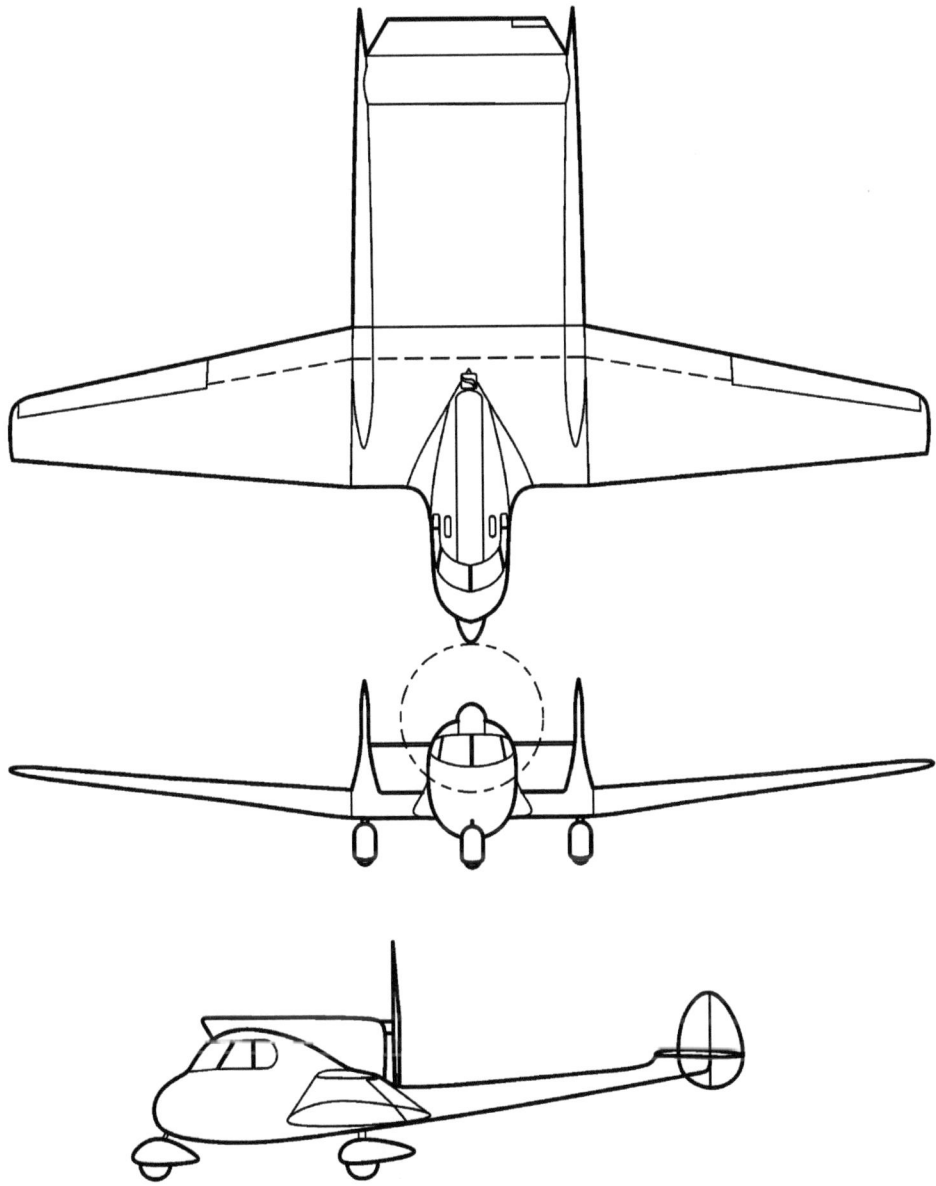

Hammond Model Y — 3-View.

- Engine to be rated at not over 100 HP.
- Engine not to require servicing at less than 50 hours' interval.
- Engine should be able to use aviation and automobile grade fuels.
- Cost of production version of aircraft to meet a retail price of $700 per aircraft.

Although the W1/W1A served as the "role model" for the contest, it would be Dean Hammond's equally homely looking design, the Model Y pusher prop aircraft, which would win the contest (this aircraft would later be re-designated the Stearman-Hammond Model Y-1S).

As originally designed by Dean Hammond and Carl Haddon, the production version that was influenced by Lloyd Stearman (at the request of the Bureau of Air Commerce) was powered by a 150-HP, 4-cylinder Menasco. The pusher prop was fenced off between twin tail booms for ground safety concerns. Differential ailerons provided 35 degrees up and 15 degrees down deflection without need for rudder. Split flaps could be deployed between 40 and 60 degrees, and elevator was restricted to 10 degrees up and 22 degrees down travel.

Although the well-intentioned aim of the Bureau of Air Commerce contest was to stimulate affordable, safe aircraft for mass production, the end result just about parallels the fate of the Guggenheim competition. The Hammond Model Y, for all its laudable safety features, wound up selling for between three and five thousand dollars instead of the seven hundred dollars listed in the contest specifications, at a time when the effects of the Depression were still influencing how the buying public spent its hard-found cash. It's no wonder that, aside from a handful that went to the Bureau for its inspectors' use, hardly any were sold to the public. Further working against the Hammond Y was an undercurrent of unease at the notion of filling the skies with possibly hundreds or thousands of Hammond Ys (or its equivalents) piloted by novices with no more flight training than the Hammond factory's recommended 1 to 3 hours' worth.

Weick's inventive genius would surface again with an aircraft of much more lasting influence in the form of the Ercoupe. Belying its relatively sleek, modern appearance, the embryonic Ercoupe can be traced back to the early work done with the models W1/W1A. Weick joined Henry Berliner at ERCO (Engineering and Research Corporation) in the 1930s. First flight of the Ercoupe (Model 310) occurred in October 1937, with the first production model (Model 415C) receiving its type certificate in March 1940.

Weick's philosophy in creating the Ercoupe was to develop a safer aircraft by making pilot input as simple as possible and physically eliminating any chance for the aircraft's wing to become stalled, thereby eliminating the dreaded spin.

One of the primary safety features for which the Ercoupe is known (standard in early models, and later an option) is the elimination of rudder pedals. A "two control" system was designed in which an interconnect between the ailerons and rudder permitted patently safe coordinated turns, while at the same time preventing a cross-controls situation. Elevator travel was also limited to approximately 12 degrees (later increased to 13 degrees to improve landing flares) to prevent the wing from reaching and exceeding the critical angle of attack. All input was made through an automobile-type steering wheel, with the pilot's feet resting on nothing but the floor. Lack of an independent means of operating the rudder necessitated that the engine be offset to counter P-factor upon takeoff. It also required that larger amounts of aileron deflection be factored into the design to overcome the adverse yaw conditions that usually are neutralized through the use of rudder alone. The engine was further canted at a downward angle, and the wing was set at a zero degree incidence to help keep the aircraft on the ground in gusty conditions. Weick incorporated tricycle landing gear on the Ercoupe (a first on mass-produced civil aircraft) to elim-

Ercoupe — The first aircraft certified by the CAB as characteristically incapable of spinning. National Air and Space Museum, Smithsonian Institute (SI NEG NO. 96-10521).

inate the ground loops and nose-overs that were a frequent nemesis of contemporary aircraft. Among the many unique innovations of the Ercoupe is the distinction of being among the first aircraft to use RATO (Rocket Assisted Takeoff)—another radical yet effective way to reduce takeoff distance!

The nose gear could be steered by the pilot through turning the control wheel automobile style. The main gear was allowed a moderate amount of swivel in order to handle mild crosswind conditions. Along with a rather stout semi-monocoque metal forward section and a full monocoque aft fuselage for structural integrity, the Ercoupe also afforded the pilot outstanding outward visibility by means of a bubble-top canopy. Powered initially by a 65-HP Continental engine (later models used 75, 85 and 90 HP), typical performance yielded a top speed of around 117 MPH and a landing speed of 45 MPH. Takeoff distance over a 50' obstacle was a lackluster 2,375' with a 590' ground roll, while landing over the same height obstacle was 1,750' with a 750' rollout.

As with any aircraft design, compromises were necessary. When combined with the unique innovations found on the Ercoupe, those compromises and their resultant impact on performance limitations drew their share of critics. Noteworthy among the many legitimate complaints were that without independent rudder control the pilot was unable to perform a forward slip during a steep approach, thereby limiting the use of short field landings; also, the lack of independent rudder control caused the aircraft to be flown in a "crab" during landing approaches, requiring the swiveling main landing gear.

The "two-control" system also tended to be confusing to veteran pilots, who found it hard to overcome the habits acquired in years of flying a conventionally rigged "three-control" aircraft. This situation was further compounded by federal regulations that put a license restriction on pilots of Ercoupes who had not demonstrated competency in a conventional aircraft. If a pilot got his training in a ruddered aircraft, there would be no restriction when flying an Ercoupe. Adding to all of this, while flying at slow speeds the Ercoupe had a tendency to develop a relatively high sink rate that, if not checked, could lead to a potentially serious accident.

Although the Ercoupe initially sold quite well, market forces would ultimately erode its appeal. Despite close to 6,000 copies having been produced by five different manufacturers (ERCO, Forney, Air Products, Alon and Mooney), the Ercoupe and its descendants could not in the long run displace the sales of the more conventional aircraft. At a time when faster, four-place aircraft with superior utility were becoming more in demand (the Ercoupe had a very limited useful load/payload capability of about 500 lbs./400 lbs. respectively), Weick's safety plane became less sought after, especially at higher and higher prices. Paradoxically, the Ercoupe was deemed by an ever-increasing pilot population to be almost too easy to fly, relegating it to a less-than-desirable ownership status. To its credit, Fred Weick's design was, in its short heyday, proof at a reasonable price that an aircraft with safety enhancements could be a modest success. The fact that examples are still sought after and flown by pilots with certain physical limiting disabilities (e.g., paraplegics) gives added testimony to the simplicity that was designed into this unique machine. Perhaps the most lasting testimony to the Ercoupe's impact on safety is the fact that the superb inherent

General Skyfarer—The second aircraft certified by the CAB as incapable of spinning. National Air and Space Museum, Smithsonian Institute (SI NEG NO. 96-15096).

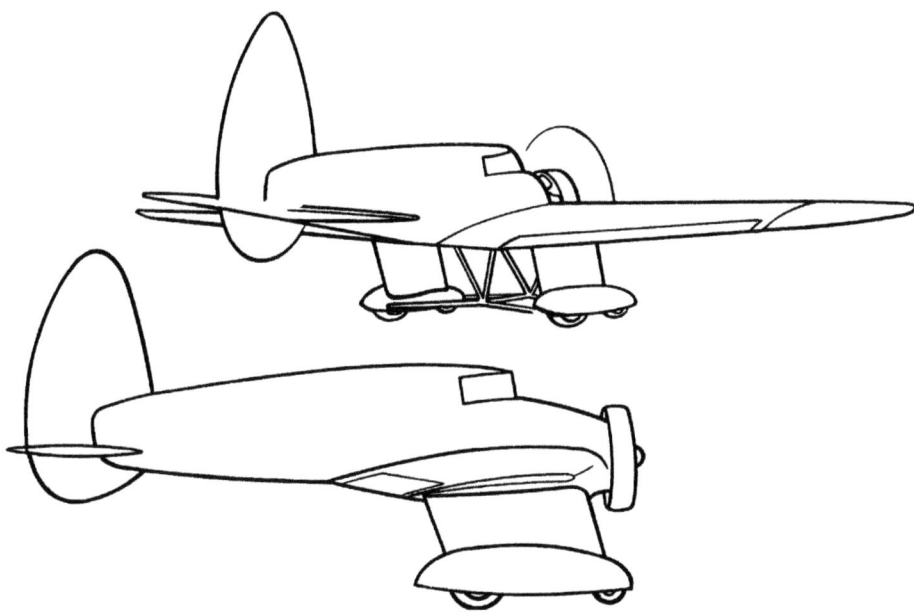

Koppen 1934 "safety airplane" concept drawing.

dynamic stability of its tricycle landing gear can be found on the vast majority of general aviation aircraft to date.

Developed during the same approximate time period as the first production Ercoupe, the Model G-180 Skyfarer was the only other aircraft certified at that time by the Civil Aeronautics Board as being incapable of spinning. Designed by MIT graduate Otto Koppen, the Skyfarer was an aircraft designed to provide nearly "foolproof" flight for novices by way of using a simplied two-control system, much like the Ercoupe. Koppen's experience prior to the Skyfarer included a stint with Henry Ford in development of the 1926 Ford "Flivver," as well as research for a safety oriented monoplane (1934) featuring dual tandem landing gear as an answer to ground loops, as well as a two-control rudderless system (aileron/elevator) sporting a vertical stabilizer of monumental proportion.

Rather than the aileron/rudder interconnect as was featured on the Ercoupe, the Skyfarer utilized an aileron/elevator interconnect, a system considered practical as long as the aircraft design provided for adequate levels of directional stability. Two fixed vertical fins (sans rudders and associated pedals) provided lateral stability and underscored Koppen's contention that "*the only purpose of a rudder is to cover up the mistakes of the designer.*"[9] Control input was accomplished in a similar fashion to the Ercoupe via a single control wheel, which was also used to steer the nose wheel.

Powered by a 75-HP geared Lycoming, the Skyfarer had a maximum speed of 100 MPH and a minimum speed of 44 MPH (with flaps). With a relatively low wing loading of 11.1 lbs./sq. ft., the Skyfarer was capable of a takeoff run of 300' and a landing run of 100'. While capable of producing nearly perfect coordinated flight, the Skyfarer shared the Ercoupe's lack of utility as well as its inability to perform the much-valued slip.

The ancestry of the Helio Courier (also designed by Koppen) can be partially traced to the strong welded steel tubing center cabin truss and use of the geared engine of the short-lived little Skyfarer.

The notion of an aircraft that embodied many of the superior flight characteristics found in aircraft that evolved out of the safe-aircraft competitions of the 1930s, but with improved levels of utility, was certainly not lost on the military air powers of the world. In fact, practical development was indeed hastened by the relatively limitless commitment of research funding by nations seeking various forms of aerial advantage. Such was the case of the Fieseler Fi-156 Storch ("Stork").

Designed in 1935 by Reinhold Mewes and Victor Maugsch of Fieseler-Flugzeugbau G.M.B.H., the Fi-156 evolved from the Fieseler F5 and Fi-97 trainer/aerobatic aircraft. Featuring full-span leading edge slots, slotted flaps and a wing with a wing loading of 9.8 lbs./sq. ft., the Storch could very easily land in a distance no longer than its wingspan. Outer sections of its hinged trailing edge served as a statically balanced and slotted aileron. In order to maintain longitudinal control at very low speeds (to counter strong nose-down pitching moments during flap use) the elevator on the Storch incorporated a fixed external slat (located beneath the horizontal tail and at the hinge line of the elevators) to avoid stalling out the tail under such low speed loading. To complement the Storch's superb flight characteristics, the ground handling capabilities were enhanced by wings that could be folded back for storage and transport.

As powered by a 240-HP Argus inverted V-8 engine, the Storch possessed a maximum speed of 109 MPH and a minimum flying speed of around 32 MPH. Swinging a fixed, two-bladed wooden prop of a little over eight and a half feet in diameter, the Storch was able to develop significant amounts of thrust at low speeds for takeoff from confined spaces.

This 3-seat cabin monoplane was capable of clearing on takeoff a 50' obstacle within 318 feet as well as landing over the same obstacle and coming to a halt within

Fieseler Storch—An extremely distinctive and capable STOL machine with wartime heritage.

300 feet. Aiding in the utility use of the Storch was its long-stroke (16" of travel) steel-spring/oil-damped landing gear/undercarriage that permitted the Storch to absorb landing impact from a very high descent rate.

As used by Germany's Luftwaffe of World War II, the Storch was employed primarily as a staff transport (perhaps most notably by Generalfeldmarschalls Erwin Rommel and Albert Kesselring as a Type C-1), observation platform (C-2), multi-purpose/utility craft (C-3) and to a lesser extent a light bomber carrying three 110-pound bombs (C-5) or a 298-pound depth charge. Although the Storch was outfitted with a single rearwards firing MG 15 machine gun, its slow-speed capability was also relied upon as a defensive measure that permitted the crew to elude much faster and more unwieldy fighter aircraft.

Of the approximately 2,500 Fieseler Storchs built during the war, perhaps none is more famous than the one piloted by Hauptmann Heinrich Gerlach. Gerlach coaxed a crippled and overloaded Storch aloft in the successful 1943 rescue of Benito Mussolini (Operation Eiche). As directed by SS Captain Otto Skorzeny, the Storch barely became airborne with its VIP cargo from a rock-studded, windless strip on the highest mountain in Italy (the Gran Sasso d'Italia, at 6,500 feet elevation).

The tactical worth of having an STOL liaison-type aircraft like the Storch to round out the inventory of wartime aircraft was clearly not lost on the Allied forces of World War II. Indeed, during a brief visit to the 1938 National Air Races, a Storch was scrutinized very closely at Wright Field by U.S. authorities. On that occasion, a comparison flight test against a Kellett autogyro demonstrated the Storch's superior performance and in very short order prompted the U.S. government to launch a program to develop its own counterpart of this remarkable aircraft.

As specified by the U.S. Army Air Force, a request for a two-seat Army co-operation (observation) monoplane intended for infantry liaison, artillery spotting and short-range reconnaissance was quickly drafted. Emphasis was placed upon the new aircraft's ability to land and take off in very short spaces as well as possessing a decent high speed. Answering the design competition were the Stinson YO-49, Bellanca YO-50 and the Ryan YO-51.

Developed in 1940, the Stinson YO-49 (with a 13" stretch, known as the YO-49A, later as the L1 Vigilant series) was perhaps the most successful of the entrants, with approximately 324 built. Powered by a 295-HP Lycoming R-680-9 engine, the YO-49 could achieve respectable slow speed flight by way of full-span automatic leading edge slots as well as pilot actuated slotted trailing edge flaps. Top speed was 122 MPH with a crew of two seated in tandem order.

Also built in 1940 was the Bellanca entrant, known as the YO-50. Powered by a 450-HP inverted V-12 Ranger engine, only three prototype test aircraft were built. Full-span leading edge slots with slotted flaps providing the necessary high lift.

Rounding out the competition was the Ryan YO-51 Dragonfly, of which also only three ships were built. Powered by a 420-HP Pratt & Whitney nine-cylinder Wasp Junior radial engine, the Ryan entry made do with large Fowler-type slotted flaps as well as leading edge slots. If the Ryan YO-51 did not take top honors in the competition, it certainly deserves honorable mention as the one aircraft that came closest in appearance to the Fi-156, with its wide-track pyramid type undercarriage and V-strutted wing supports.

Stinson YO-49 — All-metal monoplane designed for artillery spotting, reconnaissance and liaison duties. National Museum of the United States Air Force.

Bellance YO-50 — Observation monoplane as evaluated by the U.S. Army Air Corps. National Museum of the United States Air Force.

Within as short a period of time as it took to develop these three observation aircraft, they would be replaced by the less complicated and lighter Aeroncas, Cubs, Taylorcrafts and Stinsons. It was found that incorporating such relatively cost-effective and expedient modifications as adding drooping ailerons (acting in conjunction with flaps) on the Stinson L-5s and adding wing spoilers to improve short-field landings on Taylorcraft L-2s was much more effective in meeting strategic wartime production requirements.

While a Ryan YO-51 might have been easily capable of demonstrating a slow speed flight of 30 MPH, its top speed of 130 MPH based upon the output of a 420-HP engine was utterly unacceptable for application to civilian aircraft. Even the Storch, with a conservative top speed of 109 MPH based on a 240-HP engine, was pushing the envelope of practicality for widespread acceptance for civilian usage. Though a clearly effective and justifiable expense in wartime, military STOL aircraft—even one such as Great Britain's Prestwick Pioneer (an early contemporary

Ryan YO-51 "Dragonfly"— 2-seat Army co-operation monoplane as pitted against the YO-49 and YO-50. National Museum of the United States Air Force.

Ryan YO-51— Featuring an extensive system of flaps and slots for impressive short-field work. National Museum of the United States Air Force.

of the Helio) with a top speed of 145 MPH based on a 520-HP Alvis engine — were beyond the resources of the general public.

Although the U.S. military was able to achieve respectable results with the light "grasshopper" liaison aircraft during the war (Cubs, Taylorcrafts, etc.), inter-service rivalries would surface during the immediate postwar years with the Air Force and Army each developing its own STOL aircraft. The machines developed would revert to the same type of logic used in producing the pre-war YO series of aircraft: relatively complex airframes with complicated high-lift devices mated to disproportionately powerful engines.

The Army placed its faith in the Boeing L-15 Scout two-place liaison aircraft, with 12 aircraft built from 1947 to 1948. Powered by a 125-HP Lycoming engine, the L-15

Boeing L-15 Scout — Produced by Boeing Wichita, and capable of being disassembled and towed by a vehicle in the field. Boeing Wichita/Kansas Aviation Museum.

Convair L-13 — Outstanding liaison aircraft. Kansas Aviation Museum.

had a top speed of around 100 MPH (cruising at 80 MPH) and a minimum slow speed of approximately 40 MPH. Certainly unique in appearance, the L-15 featured a tubular tail boom that minimized the mass of conventional rear fuselage construction. STOL was accomplished using a 270-square-foot wing area including full-span trailing edge "flaperons" (a combination of flaps and ailerons) mounted below and aft of the wing. Turns during low-speed flight were accomplished by curved spoilers that rotated out of the upper wing, effectively destroying the lift over that portion of the wing to roll the aircraft. The flap located opposite the spoiler was simultaneously deflected downward to enhance the roll rate. Attached to the tubular tail boom was a horizontal tail composed of an inverted wing section with slotted elevators to provide the longitudinal control necessary for slow speed flight on aircraft with powerful flaps. To round out the novelty of this aircraft, it could be quickly assembled and disassembled for delivery by truck or cargo aircraft anywhere in the world.

The Air Force's choice for a new STOL aircraft was the Consolidated Vultee (Convair) L-13. Powered by a 245-HP Franklin flat-six engine, the L-13 had a top speed of 115 MPH (cruising at 92 MPH) and a slow speed of 43 MPH. A partially slotted leading edge, double slotted ailerons (18.8 square feet each) and powerful slotted flaps (25 square feet each) aided in the L-13's STOL capabilities. Like the Storch's, the L-13's cabin windows canted outward at the top for superior outward vision. With about 300 L-13s built, the aircraft was a modest success, but like the Boeing L-15 it too fell short in the areas of control and stability. Both suffered from the seemingly eternal nemesis of the cost and complexity of building such machines. For all their promise, both machines flirted with, but could never truly claim to be able to meet, the generally accepted STOL standard of being able to land and takeoff within 500 feet over a 50-foot obstacle with practical control and stability. (The L-15 required approximately 600 feet for takeoff over a 50-foot obstacle, and the L-13 required 561 feet for the same takeoff, illustrating the rule that it is much harder to depart from a short space than to land in one.)

In the face of questionable performance in return for a sizeable investment, the remaining L-15s were relegated to use in Alaska with the U.S. Fish and Wildlife Service, and the more numerous L-13s continued in a rather low-profile role with various National Guard units. Eventually, because of their numbers, attempts were made by several firms to salvage the L-13 by installing modifications to improve its lackluster STOL performance for use in the private sector. The Associated Explorer (1955) was an L-13 with a supercharged 450-HP R-985 Wasp Junior engine. Additional modifications included redesign of the stabilizer to include about one-third more area and a larger, sturdier landing gear. Similar conversions used 300-HP Lycoming radials with rework to the vertical stabilizers (Centaur 101 and Caribbean Traders Husky Mk II).

Though STOL aircraft development programs like the L-13 and L-15 appeared to preoccupy military mind of the 1940s and '50s, they were not perceived as the final frontier for STOL/boundary control systems. In fact, experiments were carried out with a "jet-pump" powered forced-air system for controlling the boundary layer in an attempt to achieve higher levels of lift with reduced drag.

Flight test research for the Office of Naval Research was contracted to the Cessna Aircraft Company of Wichita, Kansas, in January 1951. This contract was primarily undertaken to substantiate research claims stemming from the proposed development of a boundary-layer-control version of the German Arado Model 232B medium transport aircraft of World War II (as a possible replacement for the Junkers Ju-52/3m). One of these experimental aircraft was modified by the Germans to allow air to be sucked through the leading edge of the main wing, and then blown via a hydrogen peroxide pump out over the trailing edge, thereby effecting improved lift capabilities.

Actual flight tests by Cessna were made with a highly modified Cessna Model 170A. The resultant experimental aircraft and its derivatives, designated models 309A,

B, and C, used a small AirResearch APU-type gas turbine (and other forms of power) to suck air in through an inboard section of the flap, pump the air span-wise, and eject the compressed air out through an outboard slotted section of flap, thereby energizing the boundary layer so that flow separation was significantly reduced and maximum lift coefficient was dramatically improved. Other modes for blowing air, such as an engine driven generator to supply electricity for fans in the wings, as well as dry chemical reactions to supply a gaseous airflow, were also tried with varying success.

In comparative tests of the Model 309 against a stock Model 170A, Cessna noted that a 40 percent savings in takeoff ground run was achieved, while the Model 309 would come to a complete stop within four lengths of the aircraft upon landing.

Unique in concept, the actual test aircraft, with turbine and all necessary hardware installed, was hopelessly overweight: with the pilot on board there was no utility left. A refined version was envisioned which was based upon the principle that a certain amount of power derived from a purpose-built engine could in fact provide the basis for improved lift while affording a practical useful load.

Even a cursory review of this chapter reveals the diverse means available, prior and concurrent to the development of the Helio C/STOL aircraft, to improve flight safety in the air as well as on the ground. Whether some combination of controlled, automatic or blown slot as located on the leading edge or trailing edge, linked or unlinked to some form of spoiler, aileron or elevator, with or without rudder, with tricycle gear or castering conventional, a wide variety of control devices was well tested and available for consideration for the preliminary design of the Helio aircraft in the late 1940s/early 1950s.

Perhaps the prevailing sentiment toward STOL/safety development was best captured in an article written by Cy Caldwell in the October 1938 issue of *Aero Digest*: "It's an odd thing about these airplanes designed to be safe at all speeds, unspinable, unbounceable, unbreakable, unsaleable — they all look funny. Some day some genius will incorporate the excellent safety features of such craft in something that more nearly resembles an airplane."[10]

With flaps the size of proverbial barn doors as well as other equally odd-looking high-lift appendages deployed, a host of gangly contraptions— Storchs and Paraplanes, L-13s and Dragonflies— awed as well as confounded crowds as they clawed their way into the air at alarmingly high angles of attack as if chasing the sun across the sky.

With only the limited, yet inspired, success of the little Ercoupe as a precedent, it would be up to the Helio series of C/STOL aircraft to take up and expand on the considerable challenge of introducing an STOL/safety plane of reasonable utility at a truly affordable price.

2. Dawn of the "Tennis Court Airplane"
Early Helio Prototypes

The Helioplane-Two, Helioplane-Four and Model 391

"With this brief flight, impromptu and unheralded, the air age became available for the average man.

On this morning of April 8, 1949—mark it down—the first really safe small airplane for private civilian flying became a reality."—Saville R. Davis, *Christian Science Monitor*, May 16, 1949

"For the first time the aviation industry has created an airplane that can operate from a tiny one-way strip less than a block long right in the heart of built-up areas—and at the same time is sufficiently quiet to arouse no objection from its neighbors. It is as easy to fly as any other three-control lightplane and can be flown and maneuvered at less than 30 M.P.H. with no risk of stalling."—John C. Ross, *Flying*, June 1949

"...If Koppen's design can take off in less than 100 feet with only 85 hp and can maintain good control at less than 30 MPH, a revolutionary technical advance will have been made in light plane performance."—*Aviation Week*, May 16, 1949

"A revolutionary performing highly safe personal airplane with jack rabbit takeoff but with approach stability well below the stalling speed of all present day light aircraft has made successful flights at the Norwood, Mass., airport."—Albert D. Hughes, *Skyways*, July 1950

With test pilot Jack Phillips aboard, the Helio test mule, known as the "Helioplane-Two," debuted during a rainy (and unplanned) test hop at the old Canton, Massachusetts, airport on April 8, 1949. With this low key, sparsely attended inaugural flight began yet another crusade to provide the world with an answer to the vexing problems of safe flight.

The setting for the origins of the Helio is perhaps as unique and unexpected as the aircraft's performance is startlingly impressive. Rather than emerging from one of the traditional meccas of general aviation manufacture such as Wichita, Kansas, the Helio was the progeny of a remote and elite Boston brain-trust drawn from the revered halls of Harvard University and the Massachusetts Institute of Technology.

Its visionaries were Dr. Lynn Bollinger (Professor of Business Administration, Harvard Business School) and Dr. Otto C. Koppen (Professor of Aeronautics, MIT).

While it is fair to say that the Helio Courier was the result of the engineering genius and personal motivation of Otto Koppen as applied to the guidelines set down by Lynn Bollinger, it was Bollinger whose market analysis provided the business foundation and impetus to move the project forward toward reality.

Lynn Bollinger, a former airline pilot and FBO operator, had for many years been a critic of the complacency with which general aviation manufacturers had addressed the market. Indeed, in 1945, Bollinger had teamed up with fellow Harvard associate Arthur H. Tully Jr. to survey 180 FBOs (Fixed Base Operators) as to possible improvements in personal plane operating requirements. The result of this exhaustive effort was formally published by the Harvard Business School as "Personal Aircraft Business at Airports." In this study, Bollinger and Tully predicted that, in spite of the industry-wide accepted estimate of a 300,000-airplane market (during the immediate post–World War II time frame), perhaps only around 38,000 personal aircraft might be sold, and also that following this initial boom sales would taper off dramatically. This would prove to be extremely prophetic: approximately 35,000 aircraft were shipped in 1946, with a decline to 15,594 in 1947. The "slump of 1948" was to be felt for many years to come, with annual aircraft sales averaging a disappointing 5,000 units.

Bollinger and Tully further surmised that the reason for this drop in sales would be due to an "unfortunate pattern of limited utility into which the personal aircraft industry had been frozen." Specifically, Bollinger and Tully cited a lack of utility due to excessively high landing speed and takeoff run requirements. Bollinger contended that the primary problem involving general aviation aircraft was the inaccessibility of existing airports.[1] Bollinger expounded on this theory in a 1949 *Aviation Week* article, stating: "With outlying airports, it has been determined that 300 miles is generally about the minimum distance which can be flown to save time. But on a trip of that distance it is cheaper to use the airlines. Secondly ... the weather becomes ... too unpredictable. To solve the problem, there would have to be airports located close to community centers, making trips practical over much shorter distances."[2]

To compound the problem of the inaccessibility of many airports and airstrips, Bollinger noted that objection to aircraft noise by residents near landing fields, as well as aircraft safety enhancement concerns of pilots, were imperatives that had to be addressed. As a final note, Bollinger declared in a sweeping and perhaps all too general statement, that currently, customers are putting a higher priority on transportation needs, rather than for a mere sporting recreation.[3]

As an answer to this industry induced malaise, Bollinger submitted initially that a new aircraft must be designed to possess the following three requirements:[4]

1. The new aircraft must be designed to use a one way airstrip not more than 900 feet long (between 50-foot obstacle at either end), or, not more than 600 feet long if not obstacles are present.

2. The new aircraft must possess safety enhancements that are in accordance with the latest findings.

3. The new aircraft must be sufficiently quiet to allow it to be used at airports that have residential homes adjacent to them.

While contemporary aircraft fell somewhat short in their ability to address the first requirement, particularly upon takeoff while carrying any useful load (typical for the era, a 1946 Cessna Model 140 required 1,850 ft to clear a 50-foot obstacle upon takeoff and 1,530 ft. to clear the same obstacle upon landing), it was the lack of progress in safety enhancements that Bollinger deemed in dire need of attention.

Bollinger was a disciple of the teachings of Hugh DeHaven, widely regarded as one of the first proponents of using a comprehensive and systematic approach of statistical analysis to push safety upgrades in aviation. As director of crash-injury research at Cornell University Medical College, New York, beginning in 1942, DeHaven released his findings and recommendations on a periodic basis starting in 1943. The major safety recommendations cited by DeHaven, and in many instances, championed by Bollinger as a part of the guidelines that influenced the design of the Helio Courier, are as follows:[5]

1. Design forward fuselage and cabin structures to resist crash loads as well as flight and landing loads.

2. Design aircraft structures to absorb energy by progressive collapse.

3. Design tubular structure to bend and fall outwardly away from occupants.

4. Locate the pilot and passenger seats as far aft in the fuselage as possible behind the wing.

5. Locate fuel tanks in, or on, the wings-not between the firewall and the instrument panel.

6. Provide space between the instrument panel and forward section to permit forward displacement of the panel and instrument cases.

7. Design the instrument panel to be free of sharp rigid edges in range of the pilot's head.

8. Fabricate the instrument panel of ductile material or use an energy-absorbing shield on the panel face.

9. Mount instrument cases on shear pins or as low on the panel as possible.

10. Provide shoulder harness, safety belts, seats and seat anchorages of sufficient strength to resist failure up to the point of cabin collapse.

In addition to DeHaven's recommended structural improvements as listed above, Bollinger believed that much could be done to reduce the sensory overload on the pilot by simplifying engine and flight control demands. Bollinger believed that his new aircraft design should automatically make as many adjustments as possible to reduce pilot/design-induced error. Bollinger hoped that through a cleverly designed control system, pre-calculated to yield the instantaneous and optimal synchronization of control usually found only in the hands of an expert pilot, flying would become a much more attractive proposition to the safety-conscious public. Harking back to the concept of the Ercoupe, Koppen and Bollinger envisioned an aircraft that would be as simple and uncomplicated to operate as an automobile. Both men believed that an average person should be able to enter the cockpit, warm up the engine, open the throttle and simply fly away without the tedious checklist routine.

At this point, it might be worthwhile to note that, while theoretically laudable, the pursuit of advances in aviation safety has not always garnered the results intended, nor has it always translated well into the sales ledgers of aircraft manufacturers. Indeed, although mandated in the Air Commerce Act of 1926, the use of safety belts was at times believed to cause abdominal and spinal injuries. This notion led some pilots to initially discard their belts or actually unfasten them just prior to impact upon crashing. In 1948, Beech Aircraft Company of Wichita, Kansas, became the first large-scale general aviation manufacturer to evaluate and install shoulder strap restraints in its line of Bonanzas, Travel-Airs and Twin Bonanzas. Initially factory-installed as standard equipment, the shoulder harness restraint was later made optional as "the owners not only refused to use the restraint systems but many actually requested the removal of the shoulder restraints."[6] There were performance penalties (increased weight/increased cost) from beefing up aircraft structures in the name of safety enhancement. It would appear that the increased utility of the Helio concept was what Bollinger would rely on to capture sales, with safety as an added bonus.

While Otto Koppen would officially join the Helio effort about 1946, Koppen had worked previously with Bollinger in a project to find ways to reduce the noise emissions of light aircraft. Sponsored with NACA (National Advisory Committee for Aeronautics) funds, the Aeronautical Research Foundation was loaned aircraft, engines and support instrumentation to carry out noise reduction experiments.

Much of the flight testing was conducted in and around Boston suburbs such as Dedham, Massachusetts. There were promising results: Koppen noted that they were able to reduce the noise of their experimental aircraft to about 60 decibels, so much so that "it was so quiet that we had to stop taking measurements when a car came down the road."[7] During this period, the alliance between the two academics Bollinger and Koppen was further strengthened by their shared conviction about the value of an aircraft of not only much improved noise reduction, but also of significantly improved utility and safety.

Fresh with a degree from MIT in general science (graduated 1924) Otto Carl Koppen spent 3 years working on the engineering staff of the Ford Motor Company. While much of Koppen's interest would over the years be focussed on improving the in-flight stability and control of light aircraft, it was the nimble and somewhat conventional Ford "Flivver" (named after the Model T) that would be his first project to receive acclaim. Asked by Henry Ford to develop an inexpensive single-place aircraft that anyone could fly, the 27-year-old Koppen's only strict specification from Mr. Ford was that it "must fit in my office."[8] Built in secret, the Flivver debuted on July 31, 1926 (Ford's 63rd birthday). With only two prototypes built, the Flivver project foundered on February 25, 1928, with the untimely death of test pilot Harry Brooks as he attempted to set an endurance/distance record in the number two Flivver from Dearborn, Michigan, to Miami. A plugged fuel vent was alleged to be the only evidence of trouble. Koppen would partner with William B. Stout on shared development of the famed Ford Tri-motor until Fairchild Aviation Corporation lured him away. A subsequent tour as vice president and chief engineer of General Aircraft Corporation (first at Weston, Massachusetts, and later Astoria, New York) yielded the nearly fool-proof General Skyfarer as described in chapter one. Shackled by the ban on civil aircraft development during World War II, the Skyfarer would serve as an interim project whose ancestry would lead to the Helio Courier.

Due to his state-of-the-art practical knowledge, the veteran input of Koppen was formally enlisted in the mid–1940s by Bollinger to update and expand on his earlier design goals of what would eventually become the Helio Courier.

As envisioned by Bollinger and Koppen, the overall objective for their high-wing utility monoplane was to retain the current cruise speed, payload and the power of contemporary light aircraft while additionally being able to maintain safe low-speed flight and to be able to perform takeoffs and landings in less than 100 feet.[9]

The more specific design goals were:[10]

1. Aircraft to possess the capability of at least 30-MPH slow speed flight while remaining fully controllable.
2. Aircraft to be stall/spin proof.
3. Aircraft to be capable of quick takeoff and climb at full gross weight and no wind conditions in 100 feet or less and to be able to clear a 50-foot obstacle in less than 300 feet from standing start.
4. Aircraft must be able to land within 100 feet.
5. Aircraft must possess a cruising speed above 100 MPH.
6. Aircraft must possess low noise level (at least comparable with automobile).
7. Aircraft must possess improved structural integrity of airframe and interior.
8. Aircraft targeted to sell for approximately $500 more than current conventional light aircraft.

To achieve these design/performance goals, Koppen expertly combined several existing designs in a manner and to a degree that had never yet been accomplished. As Koppen noted: "You understand, none of the devices-or even, I guess, the ideas-on the airplane are mine, I just pick them here and there and everywhere and just try to get the best combination to get the best design. It's not an invention."[11]

The prototype aircraft, officially referred to by Koppen as the "Proof of Concept" aircraft, was to evolve from a Piper Vagabond. Money to finance the fledgling project came from Bollinger, Koppen, and Charles A. Rheinstrom (a vice president of American Airlines), each of whom contributed $6,000, for a grand total of $18,000. The cabin section of a Piper Vagabond, its wing panels, control parts and horizontal tail were purchased to be reconfigured to Koppen's highly modified design.

Construction of the initial Proof of Concept aircraft was carried out late in 1948 at E. W. Wiggins Airways, an FBO located some 15 miles southwest of Boston at Norwood, Massachusetts. Koppen and Bollinger persuaded its president, Joseph Garside, of the plane's potential. Subsequently, a sympathetic Garside provided much needed material and labor at cost, and in some cases for free.

Modifications to the Piper Vagabond were quite extensive, with only the cabin frame tubing, wing struts, spar, windshield and rudder pedals remaining from the original purchased parts. According to Koppen, "it is all new from the cabin back, and from the firewall forward."[12] Approximately 45 inches was added to the airframe from the cabin to the tail, while the original door was dropped in favor of one on each side in a staggered layout (one alongside the pilot and the other aft of the co-

Piper Vagabond — 3-View.

pilot to improve cabin structural integrity). The main landing gear was moved well forward and featured Goodyear crosswind landing gear. The extreme forward position of the main gear permitted the aircraft to be flown at maximum allowable forward CG (center of gravity) to the point that, even when landed with brakes locked, the aircraft could not be nosed over. The main gear also featured a small diameter, high-pressure variation pneumatic strut with about one foot of travel (14 inches of wheel-strut travel before flexing 9 inches).

An all-welded steel tube cabin safety frame was provided in order to insure superior margins of survivability in the event of an accident. In total, approximately 150 pounds of extra weight was added in airframe reinforcement.

Power was initially reported to be provided by a Continental A65 65-HP, four cylinder, horizontally opposed, air cooled engine; however, long-term flight testing was accomplished with a Continental C-85 85-HP, four cylinder, horizontally opposed, air cooled and fuel-injected engine. Fuel injection was decided on as an improvement in order to drastically reduce chances of engine failure and carburetor heat control distractions in the cockpit. Power was supplied to a relatively enormous nine-foot diameter, wide-bladed Aeromatic propeller. A reduction drive system con-

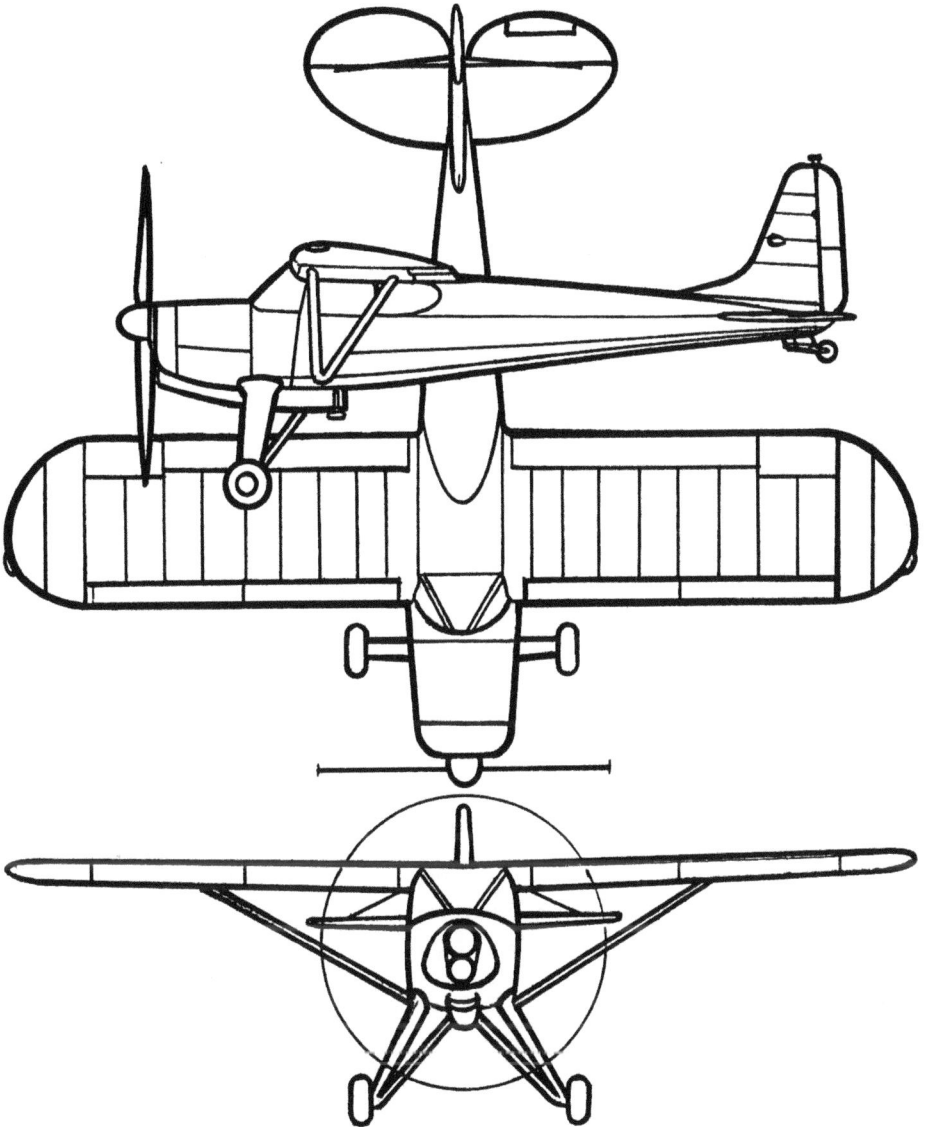

Helio Proof of Concept aircraft — 3-View.

sisting of ten automotive V-belts transferred power to the propeller in a ratio of 2.3 to 1. The use of the V-belts was believed to aid in reducing noise transmission compared to a conventional cogged gear system, as well as reducing the considerable weight penalty of using a conventional and elaborate reduction gearbox.

The propeller was attached to a constant-speed hub, which turned at 1,200 RPM. At this RPM, propeller tip speed could be reduced so as to not generate excessive noise.

The selection of a nine-foot prop mated to an 85-HP engine can be attributed to Koppen's "Magic Formula" for superior short-roll takeoff ability. Koppen's formula was that "if you take the prop diameter in feet and square it, and then divide by the horsepower, the result should be 1 (or very close to it)."[13]

As Koppen noted, many current conventional aircraft were quite capable of landing in a relatively small area, however, those same aircraft did not develop enough forward thrust to overcome the drag of flaps to takeoff again, thereby limiting their usefulness.

This was not necessarily a new idea, as Koppen had applied this formula to the Ford Flivver, which had excellent takeoff ability. With a six-foot prop and 35 HP, the Flivver came very close to matching the ideal ratio according to Koppen's "Magic Formula."

In the case of the Helio Proof of Concept aircraft, with a nine-foot prop and 85 horsepower, the resulting ratio would yield an equally impressive (although on a much grander scale) final number very close to the ideal of "1":

$$\frac{9^2}{85} = \frac{81}{85} = 0.95$$

Although it proved quite successful in the Proof of Concept aircraft (as flight tested by pilot Jack W. Phillips, along with lead mechanic Dave Everest), and was eventually to see production, this "magic formula" was taken to extreme in a short lived experiment in which the four-place prototype was fitted with an absolutely massive 11-foot prop, mated to a 145-HP Continental engine:

$$\frac{11^2}{145} = \frac{121}{145} = 0.83$$

As testimony to this extreme experiment, one day while flight testing the prop inadvertently went into flat pitch and nearly sent the pilot through the windscreen due to the colossal equivalent flat-plate area of the prop alone. A disbelieving representative from the prop manufacturer was sent out to flight test the aircraft again. With the prop engineer on board, the aircraft was set in a fast glide and the prop once more reverted to flat pitch. Apparently the prop representative was severely shaken by the incident and, according to Koppen, "he just disappeared! We never heard from him again!"[14]

One of the challenges of using such a large propeller (in the case of the Proof of Concept aircraft's final nine-foot prop) was that the CAA regulations stipulated that there must be at least nine inches of clearance between the prop tip (prop in a vertical alignment) and the ground with the aircraft in a level position and shocks completely compressed. The Proof of Concept aircraft actually had negative one-and-one-half inches of clearance, so that the prop tip would theoretically have dug into the ground one and one-half inches.

Koppen informed the CAA about this situation, but advised them that due to the aircraft's unique and stable takeoff and landing nature (for takeoff the tail wheel was always the last off the ground, and upon landing the main gear struts were always at full extension to keep the prop tip clear) this should not be a problem. The CAA dispatched four test pilots to prove otherwise. Koppen noted that the CAA pilots tried

2. Dawn of the "Tennis Court Airplane"

Lynn Bollinger and oversized propeller on Proof of Concept aircraft.

in vain to bend the prop by trying to land with the fuselage level, and then by coming in tail high (the aircraft simply bounced and then the tail whipped down). Ultimately, by the end of the day the CAA told Koppen that "if he could make the aircraft that way, we'll buy it!"[15]

To overcome the inherent tendency of an aircraft to suddenly climb when engine power is quickly applied, Koppen had the angle at which the engine was mounted depressed by 4 percent in order not to startle an inexperienced pilot.

To provide the necessary high lift needed for STOL capability, as well as for stall/spin prevention, Koppen utilized Handley Page leading edge slats (again, not a new feature since they were invented in 1923) along the full length of the leading edge. The slats operate automatically, sliding in and out of the mother wing (a NACA 23012 wing section similar to that used on the P-51 Mustang) by way of roller guides. When not needed (high speed/cruise) the slats retract into the leading edge of the otherwise very aerodynamically clean wing through the effect of high pressure against the slats themselves. When needed most (slow speed/landing), the slats deploy as the angle of attack of the wing increases, and the center of pressure moves forward on the wing to suck the slats open. This allowed Koppen to provide maximum lift coefficient with minimum drag coefficient (that is, to offer the greatest lift for the least drag), thereby resulting in an aircraft with both incredible low speed and a reasonable high speed potential. The slats retract to an aerodynamically clean state as the aircraft accelerates; the center of pressure on the wing moves aft and ram air pressure exerts pressure to close the slat. With the slats deployed, approximately 64 percent of the lift generated is from the slats themselves, while the angle of attack at which the wing would normally stall doubles. Bollinger stated that "since it is completely stall-proof, it is also spin-proof. At 30 MPH, the wing is 14 degrees from stalling angle-further from stall than a Cub in normal flight."[16]

Full span, single slotted flaps were integrated into the trailing edge of the wing to provide much-needed extra lift. The extra lift is obtained as high-pressure air from below the wing streams through the flat slot, thereby energizing the airflow adhesion. In order to fulfill the design criteria for full span flaps, the ailerons and flap mechanisms were combined. A crank mechanism, located in the cockpit, was used to lower both ailerons (the ailerons otherwise being conventionally operated by the control stick). Once the ailerons were lowered to act as flaps, aileron deflection was from the preset position of the flaps. In order to overcome adverse yaw conditions as well as to provide the type of coordinated turn input that only an expert pilot could deliver, Koppen designed a synchronized rudder-aileron interconnect system. The rudder was of a split type, in which the lower portion was interconnected to the aileron control, and thereby operated independent of any rudder pedal input, while the upper portion of the rudder operated via rudder pedal input in the conventional manner.

All of these features that contributed to the Proof of Concept aircraft's superior slow-speed capability were envisioned as a vital part of the improved safety aspect.

Koppen and Bollinger believed that, from a survivability standpoint, the Helio aircraft was likely to produce much more favorable outcomes after a forced landing due to engine failure or rapidly closing weather ceilings than current offerings in the general aviation field.

In the event of an engine failure at an approximate altitude of 1,000 feet, the Helio was claimed to be able to glide for two miles before it would have to land. This would translate to a circular flight path with a four-mile diameter. It was suggested that by squaring the radius the pilot would have over 12 square miles available to locate an acceptable landing area.

In the event of potentially hazardous flying conditions such as lowered weather ceilings or darkness, the Helio could be landed on a patch of ground that most conventional light aircraft would not dare even contemplate. If the Helio had to make a forced landing and tangled with some obstruction, the aircraft, by virtue of its rel-

2. Dawn of the "Tennis Court Airplane"

Original Helioplane prototype aircraft. National Air and Space Museum, Smithsonian Institute (SI NEG NO. A51463).

atively slow approach and landing speed, would still provide superior odds of survivability to its occupants.

Koppen and Bollinger point out that published crash investigation research clearly indicates that because the force of impact (energy) increases (proportionally) as the square of the speed (velocity), crash survivability favorably increases as a result of the slower flying speeds of the Helio. To put this concept into numbers, for an aircraft traveling at 60 MPH upon impact, the crash is four times as severe as one in which the aircraft is traveling at 30 MPH.

A contemporary yardstick for setting safe landing speed criteria, and one which was embraced by Koppen and Bollinger, was the findings of Hugh DeHaven. He asserted that, for aircraft traveling at 40 MPH or less, the resultant shock-absorbent capabilities of an aircraft posed a relatively negligible risk to the occupants. Conversely, as landing speeds increased above this 40-MPH figure, the potential risks for not surviving the crash increased very sharply.

In an extreme emergency in which absolutely no suitable landing patch was available, Koppen and Bollinger advised that the Helio could, at very slow speed/high angle of attack, be settled down at a rate of descent less than that of a parachutist and with very good chances for survival.

Since its performance capabilities were similar to those of a helicopter, it would be understandable to compare the Helio with various rotorcraft of the period. In fact, the name Helioplane (as well as Helio Courier and all of its derivative Helio namesakes) was coined by its creators to suggest that this new aircraft combined the virtues of the helicopter's landing and slow flight speed with the relatively high speed and simplicity of contemporary conventional aircraft. Koppen states that "the Helio offers 88 percent of the flight performance characteristics of a helicopter, while doing away

Side view — Helio prototype. Howard Levy Collection, National Air and Space Museum, Smithsonian Institute (SI NEG NO. 98-15836).

Helio demonstration using a tennis court for an airstrip.

with the helicopter's complex mechanisms that are subject to wear and costly, time consuming adjustment."[17] To be fair, at the time of the Helioplane's design, the practical development of the helicopter for non-military use was still much in its infancy; utility, reliability, ease of operation and cost had yet to be deemed acceptable for widespread civilian sales.

To showcase the Helioplane's STOL/safety capability (as well as to entice investors) the aircraft was flown from the tennis courts located alongside Harvard Stadium (hence two of the Helio's many monikers: the "Tennis Court Airplane," or "Tennis Court Special"). It was also flown from the MIT athletic field along Massachusetts Avenue.

Test pilot Jack Phillips recalled that his most rewarding flight was the public debut of the Helioplane at the MIT athletic field. With the goal posts taken down, the Helioplane started its takeoff run and-to the astonishment of the crowd-lifted off at the 30-yard line (90 feet)!

The outstanding STOL/safety improvements of the Helioplane let it use short landing strips which are tucked into many small communities. It also had a much quieter operational noise range. This was accomplished to forestall objections by homeowners living near, or in some cases adjacent to, the landing strip. The use of the geared-down prop to reduce tip speed "sonic noise" was the primary means of noise reduction, but an external exhaust silencer was also designed to eliminate any possible remaining noise objections from the public. The silencer, or "hush box" as Koppen dubbed it, was unlike most standard mufflers with their baffles and attendant back-pressure problems. It essentially was a combination free-flow type of insulated expansion chamber and jet-augmented engine cooler, measuring approximately nine inches in diameter and about three feet long.

In practice, exhaust gases exiting the engine were fed through a venturi-type passageway and on out the chamber. This process was based upon an "air pump" principle for efficiently ejecting exhaust gases (hence another name for this apparatus: an "ejector tube"). Koppen noted that ordinarily it might take 2½ percent of the engine's power to cool the engine. With the ejector tube, he could now "use energy that is ordinarily thrown away in that the velocity of the exhaust gas can suck cooling air through to the engine as well."[18] Of particular benefit was the envisioned improvement in providing adequate engine airflow at the very low airspeeds at which the Helio Courier excelled.

With its many unique and promising features, the Helio Proof of Concept aircraft was certainly not without its initial wrinkles to be ironed out: in particular, its less than stellar ability to perform acceptable turns. In the words of Otto Koppen: "we had this ideal arrangement, and it calculated beautifully. The airplane made perfect turns on the drafting board, but when we flew it, it didn't turn at all! The adverse yaw was defeating it. We only flew it a couple of times, and that's that!"[19] In place of the less than satisfactory "flaperons," true ailerons were eventually fitted as an evolutionary development to the Proof of Concept aircraft; these ailerons were designed to droop in conjunction with the now-separate flaps, aileron deflection being from the preset position of the flap.

As a further refinement, in place of the less than spectacular split-rudder/drooping-aileron arrangement, Koppen ultimately settled on using a form of spoiler (as tested by the NACA), combined with a somewhat more conventional tail set-up, to accomplish turns. Koppen rejected the use of a "conventional" spoiler for roll control due to it' inherent problem with the lag time between when control input was made and when roll was actually accomplished. Despite its occasional use in aircraft such as the Mitsubishi Mu-2, Koppen classified the spoiler as "a nasty kind of control" for use in general aviation aircraft.[20]

The "new" form of roll control Koppen used was termed an interceptor (a British invention) and was operated in conjunction with the leading edge automatic slat (another British invention). Whereas traditional spoilers tend to be located in a more aft position on the wing, typically between the rear spar and the trailing edge of the wing's upper surface, the interceptor was located just aft of the leading edge slat gap. In actual use, the interceptor was used to block (or "intercept") the high velocity flow of the air through either the left hand or right hand slat gap. Hence, the portion of the lift (64 percent) normally generated by a section of the leading edge slat would disappear, yielding a significant rolling moment without any lag whatsoever.

In a letter dated August 27, 1963, to Philip Hopkins, director of the National Air Museum, Smithsonian Institution Lynn Bollinger noted that "the most unique factor of the Helio design was the use of a lateral control roll augmentor which is physically similar to a spoiler in appearance and construction, but which is aerodynamically placed so that it controls the flow of air through the slat gap and thus the pressure pattern for the leading edge slat, over and above its less important function as a spoiler."[21] As adamant as Koppen and Bollinger were in insisting that the device be called an "interceptor" or a "lateral control roll augmenter," it is perhaps understandable that these terms never really caught on, and that most people just referred to them as simply "spoilers."

The interceptor concept consisted of four curved blades (two on the left-hand wing and two on the right-hand wing) installed at the approximate location of the maximum wing camber just aft of the outboard slats. The interceptors were actuated by cables and pulleys connected to the control wheel and ailerons. With the control wheel in a neutral position, the interceptor blades were in a retracted position within the wing. In this retracted position, the blades were recessed approximately half an inch below the wing surface so as to avoid unwanted operation at high speeds when minimal aileron deflection is called for.

When the differential interceptors are deployed through large amounts of control-wheel input at slow flight speeds (large aileron deflection in order to maintain a level flight attitude), the result is very effective, not to mention disconcerting to the low-hour Helio pilot. As described in the March 1984 issue of *Flying* magazine, during a flight test of a Helio H-800 (one of the last Helio models, although still utilizing the same interceptor-type control as used on the early prototypes), the following observation was made concerning the use of the interceptors: "It is uncomfortable: the Helio rocks back and forth while you slam the wheel from stop to stop, trying to level the airplane. Large roll inputs at slow speed defy everything I've learned about controlling airplanes in slow flight, but it works in the Helio. Veteran Helio pilots say you get used to the unusual roll characteristics, apparently caused by low dihedral effect, but it takes many hours."[22]

Bollinger noted that a pilot with zero previous time in a Helio required between 5 and 10 hours of experience in the Helio just to begin to feel comfortable with the interceptors. Indeed, considering that the interceptors were designed to give a minimum wing tip vertical velocity on the order of 10 feet per second, it is quite clear that the system would prove almost alarmingly effective in uninitiated hands. Describing the system, Koppen advises that "a separation control is not like an angle of attack control, it's a brutal thing."[23]

HELIO WING LIFT
PRESSURE DISTRIBUTION PATTERN

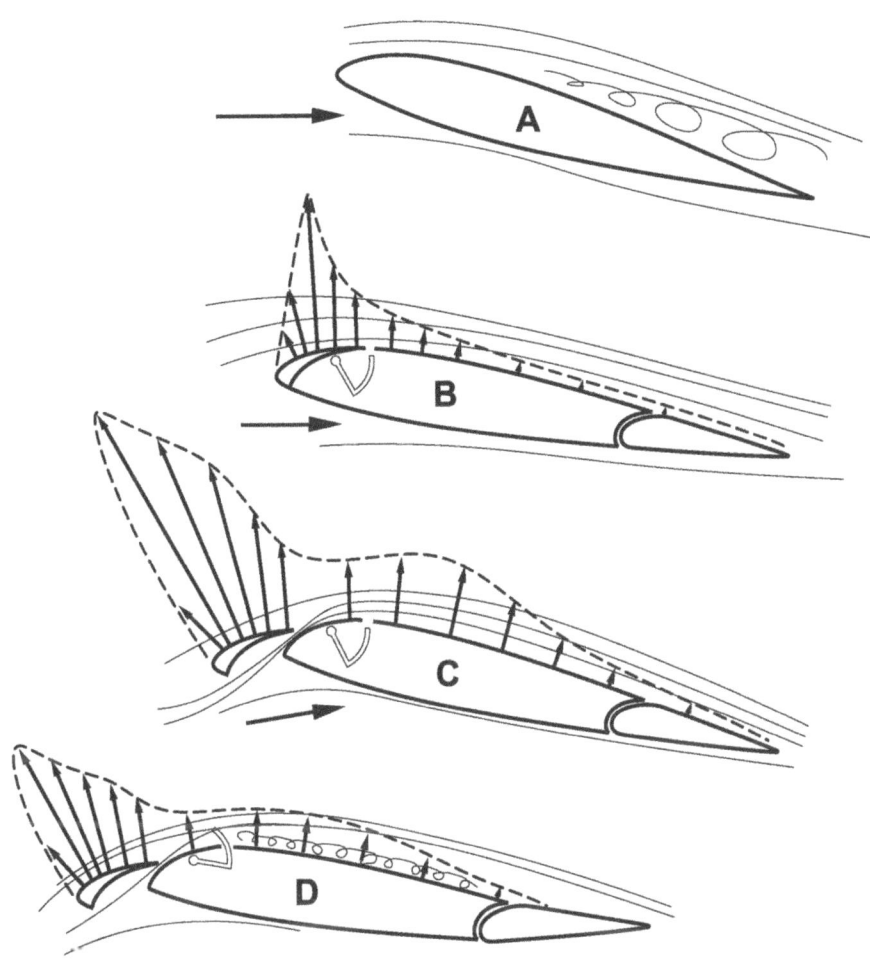

A. Conventional Wing (15 Degree AOA)
B. Slatted Wing, Closed (9 Degree AOA)
C. Slatted Wing, Open (20 Degree AOA)
D. Slatted Wing with Interceptor Deployed

Helio aircraft airfoil sections. Bob Casebeer.

In retrospect, it can be argued that controlling an aircraft at slow speeds with interceptors in this manner is a departure from the original design goal of an aircraft that anyone could fly safely from the start. Some would argue that it would be preferable to deal with an adverse yaw condition than to wrestle with extreme control-wheel inputs. Regardless, the interceptor system would prove extremely effective once mastered by new pilots.

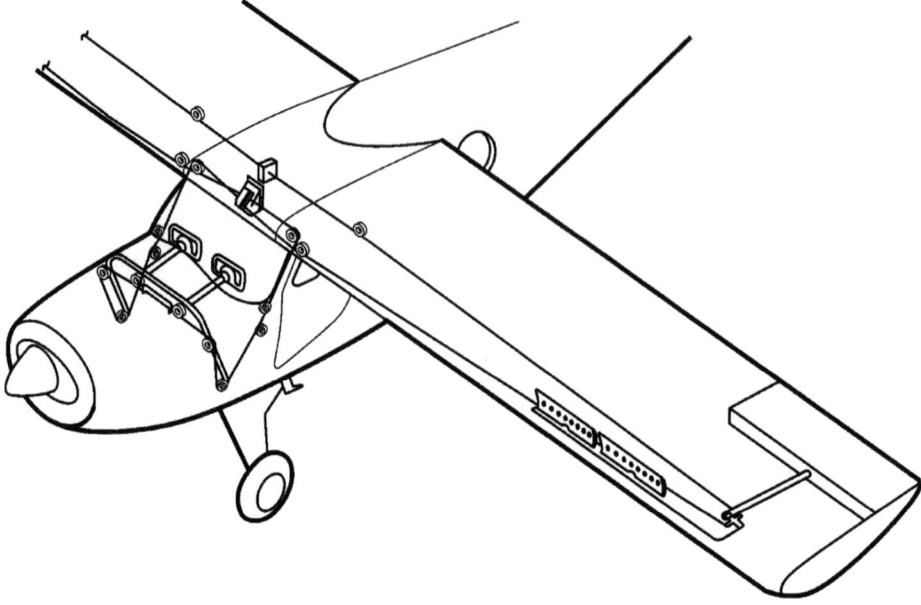

Top: Helio aileron and interceptor control system. Bob Casebeer. *Bottom:* Aileron types.

Conventional-Type Aileron

Frise-Type Aileron

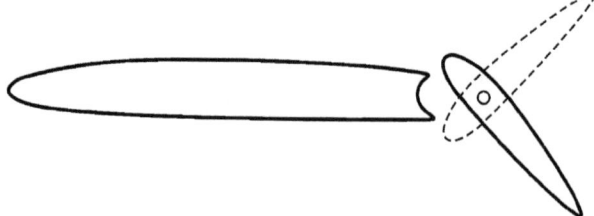

Further refinements to the control system included the ultimate use of Frise-type large-chord ailerons. The Frise-type ailerons were adopted because the revised flap system still occupied a considerable portion (66 percent) of the trailing edge of the wing, leaving precious little real estate for an aileron of much worth. The Frise ailerons also offered a superior degree of stability about the vertical axis due to the design's inherent ability to almost completely negate adverse yaw (in fact, it yielded a proverse yaw condition). Ordinarily, an adverse yaw condition is created due to the greater drag produced by the downward-deflected aileron while banking. To overcome this, the Frise aileron is designed with an offset hinge axis, which allows a portion of the leading edge of the aileron to move in the opposite direction to the main surface of the rest of the aileron.

Thus, the drag created by leading edge of the aileron while protruding into the airflow is adequate to neutralize the drag effect of the opposite "down aileron." The Frise ailerons used on the Helio were of a fabric-covered (non-nitrated/fire retardant) Duralumin-framed construction. Even on early through late production Helios using metal-skinned fuselages and wings, fabric-covered Frise ailerons were used; otherwise, lead weight would have had to be fitted as a mass balance (to deter the possible onset of flutter) to the leading edge to counter the otherwise large mass of aluminum that would be located aft of the hinge-point axis. In the few instances where certain Helio aircraft have been refitted with non-OEM, metal-covered ailerons, it has been noted that overall useful load is reduced by approximately 8 pounds.

During the certification flight tests the CAA noted that, while the ailerons operated as expected, they felt that control feel was on the light side. Otto Koppen states that "I never saw an airplane with too light ailerons! How in the world do you change the aileron hinge moment without spending any money? The routine way of doing it would be to change the leading edge balance, put more aerodynamic balance on it, or change the gearing between the aileron and wheel.... Something expensive. Luckily I thought of the idea of a piece of string over the top of the aileron at the trailing edge. I had somebody go into the storeroom and get a ball of string and we glued it right there ... on the top of the aileron at the trailing edge, right across the aileron! They flew it and said okay, we'll buy that. Make it like that!"[24]

While the improvised use of string may raise eyebrows, its effectiveness in yielding better perceived control-surface feedback has proven acceptable with reasonable field service wear. While it was used on almost all models of Helios, it is not uncommon to find Helios in the field without the string installed after having had their ailerons renovated by an unsuspecting craftsman.

By the end of 1949, Lynn Bollinger decided to proceed with plans to further refine and ultimately market the Helioplane. Refinements were sorted out with a version touted as the "Helioplane-Four" (N74151) and three true prototypes (soon to be re-christened "Courier," and then "Helio Courier") based largely on the success of the Proof of Concept aircraft. As the Helioplane-Four name suggests, the prototypes would reflect greater utility than the Proof of Concept aircraft in that they would all be four-seat executive versions. Construction of the prototypes was started in early 1950 at the development shops located at Norwood-Canton Airport, Massachusetts. The prototypes were completed with refinements being incorporated on

Helio prototype N71451—the Helioplane-Four. National Air and Space Museum, Smithsonian Institute (SI NEG NO. 96-10534).

an ongoing basis. The major differences between the final version of the Proof of Concept (Helioplane-Two) and the final version of the prototype (Helioplane-Four), is that the Helioplane-Four prototype included the following features:

Improvements Found on the Helioplane-Four

    Fully Cantilevered Wings—lighter, stronger, with less drag. Cantilevered wings also permitted easier access for loading and unloading, as well as aiding in improved vision from the cockpit.

    Four-Place Seating—to increase market appeal over two place seating.

    Continental C-145-4 Engine (V-belt geared)—to maintain acceptable performance with the added weight of two additional occupied seats.

    Length/Span Increases—proportionally larger than in the Proof of Concept aircraft, with a 6.5-foot increase in wingspan and a 4.9-foot increase in length.

    Shortened Prop—from a 108" prop on the Proof of Concept aircraft to a seven-inch-shorter Hartzell two-blade constant speed prop.

    Stabilator—a fully flying stabilator replaced the more conventional horizontal stabilizer and elevator system. The all-moveable horizontal tailplane was cited to possess approximately 40 percent less weight and drag than a conventional two-piece horizontal tail, and was fitted with an anti-servo trim tab. Some sources credit the Helio with being the first mass-produced civilian general aviation aircraft to incorporate this type of control surface.

    Larger Vertical Tail Fin/Rudder—perhaps one of the most recognizable features of all Helios from the three prototypes on was the greatly enlarged vertical tail, designed to provide ample surface to ensure stability and a positive/effective response

2. Dawn of the "Tennis Court Airplane"

Helio prototype N4164D — Pre-production prototype. National Air and Space Museum, Smithsonian Institute (SI NEG NO. 96-10520).

to rudder control input down to the minimum speed range of approximately 28 MPH.

Passenger Windows—the eventual addition to the prototypes of two round windows, one located just aft of each existing square cabin window, would prove to be one of the distinguishing visual trademarks of early-built Helios. The "portholes" were used up until 1969, when they were replaced on the H-295 Series 1400 with more up-to-date square windows in order to give the aircraft a more svelte appearance. However, the 1969 makeover of the windows seemed actually to give the Helio a more ordinary appearance; if any thing, it is a largely shared opinion that it detracted from the aircraft's uniqueness.

A comparison of the general/performance specifications for the final version of the original Proof of Concept aircraft and the prototype Helioplane-Four is as follows:

General Specifications

Proof of Concept (The Helioplane-Two)		Prototype (The Helioplane-Four)	
Length	22.4 feet	Length	27.3 feet
Span	28.6 feet	Span	35.0 feet
Height	UNKNOWN	Height	8.0 feet
Wing Area	150 sq. ft.	Wing Area	207 sq. ft.
Wing Loading	9 lbs./sq. ft.	Wing Loading	13 lbs./sq. ft.
Flap Area	UNKNOWN	Flap Area	31.0 sq. ft.
Aileron Area	UNKNOWN	Aileron Area	17.8 sq. ft.
Vertical Fin Area	UNKNOWN	Vertical Fin Area	13.6 sq. ft.

	Proof of Concept (The Helioplane-Two)		Prototype (The Helioplane-Four)
Rudder Area	UNKNOWN	Rudder Area	6.4 sq. ft.
Horizontal Stab. Area	UNKNOWN	Stabilator Area	30.0 sq. ft.
Elevator Area	UNKNOWN	Power Plant	145 HP Continental
Power Plant	85 HP Continental	Prop	101" Hartzell
Prop	108" Aeromatic	Fuel Capacity	52 Gallons
Fuel Capacity	UNKNOWN	Empty Weight	1,800 lbs.
Empty Weight	745 lbs.	GWT	3,000 lbs.
GWT	1,250 lbs.	Useful Load	1,200 lbs.
Useful Load	505 lbs.	Cruising Speed	124.6 MPM
Cruising Speed	UNKNOWN	Top Speed	145 MPH
Top Speed	115 MPH	Minimum Speed (power on)	33 MPH
Minimum Speed (power on)	27 MPH initial	Initial Rate of Climb	1,000 FPM
Rate of Climb	UNKNOWN	Service Ceiling	17,800 feet
Service Ceiling	UNKNOWN	Range	UNKNOWN
Range	UNKNOWN	Dist. to Clear 50' Obstacle	UNKNOWN
Dist. to Clear 50' Obstacle	300 feet	T.O. & Landing Distance	100 feet
T.O. & Landing Distance	UNKNOWN		

Note: While the Proof of Concept aircraft is in the collection of the National Air & Space Museum, Smithsonian Institution the three prototypes no longer exist. One of them was destroyed in a flight test incident, the others were scrapped. Much information-early original drawings, data, and flight test history-was lost in a hurricane-caused flood in August 1955 at the company headquarters in Norwood, Massachusetts. All data listed for the above aircraft is gleaned from sketchy magazine articles of the period, or were estimated through extrapolation and regenerated drawings.

One of the three pre-production aircraft (based on the Helioplane-Four) was extensively modified to accept a more commercially available powerplant and prop. This aircraft, re-designated the Model H-391, was procured for Army evaluation in 1952 (Serial 52-2540) and assigned the military designation of YL-24. ("Y" denoted that it was currently undergoing the operational testing phase for possible acceptance by the military, and "L" stood for liaison-type aircraft.) It was this aircraft that would be the immediate predecessor of the production Model H-391B. Certification was applied for (to CAR Part 3) on May 1, 1951, and would be received (Type Certificate 1A8) on August 5, 1953, as the eighth airplane to be certified by Region 1, CAA.

Primary differences between the Helioplane-Four prototype and the H-391 are as follows:

Improvements found on Model H-391 (YL-24)

Revised Nose Cowl— H-391 used aerodynamically improved nose cowl sheetmetal.

Landing Over 50' Barrier

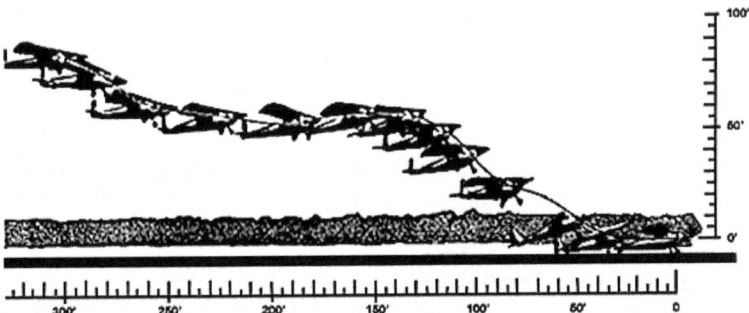

Take-off Over 50' Barrier

Helio takeoff and landing diagram. Bob Casebeer.

Powerplant-H-391 was powered by a Lycoming GO-435-C2 six-cylinder horizontally opposed air-cooled geared engine of 260 HP swinging a Hartzell 101" prop. Immediate prototypes used Continental C-145-4 engines of 145 HP.

Dimensions and Performance-Overall dimensions were slightly larger than the immediately preceding prototype, while performance was enhanced with 115 extra horsepower.

Model H-391 (YL-24)

Length	30.0 feet
Span	39.0 feet
Height	8.8 feet
Empty Weight	1,800 lbs.
GWT	3,000 lbs.
Useful Load	1,200 lbs.
Wing Loading	13 lbs./sq. ft.
Cruising Speed	142 MPH
Top Speed	160 MPH
Minimum Speed (power on)	30 MPH
Minimum Speed (power off)	41 MPH
Initial Rate of Climb	1,100 FPM
Service Ceiling	25,000 feet
Range	600 Miles
Dist. to Clear 50' Obstacle	500 feet
T.O. & Landing Distance	220 feet

With the completion of the H-391, the Helio Aircraft Corporation, under the guidance of Lynn Bollinger as chairman, R. C. Utley as president, and Dr. Otto Koppen as vice president, was on the verge of realizing its dream of not only developing a radically improved aircraft in terms of substantial margins of safety and utility, but also completely revolutionizing air travel for the masses with its latest version of the fabled "everyman's airplane."

3. Geared for Success
Main Production Models and Variants, 1954–1974

Models H-391B, H-392, H-395, H-395A, H-250, H-295 (1200), H-295 (1400) and HT-295

> "From the time I saw the Helio H-295, I knew if it flew as good as it looked then I was hooked. The salesman had given me the full pitch and I concluded he was either the biggest liar I'd had ever met or I'd been living in the dark ages for the last twelve years of my flying career."—Ed Davis, *Air Progress*, November 1994

> "'And done a hundred things you have not dreamed of; wheeled and soared and swung-high in the sunlit silence; and hovering there, I've chased the shouting wind along and flung my eager craft through footless halls of air....' Flying the Helio Super Courier, in the continuation of *Rotor and Wing*'s Pilot Evaluations, we had the same feelings as those expressed in these immortal lines written by an RCAF pilot more than 20 years ago during the Battle of Britain.... The Courier has been called poetry in motion by some pilots. It doesn't really 'hover there,' but it seems to come pretty close."—Jim Kissick, *Rotor & Wing*, April 1969

Efforts to manufacture the first true production model, the H-391B, became a somewhat frustrating odyssey. The fitful start can perhaps be attributed to the two academics' idealism and nearly blind faith in the concept of an aircraft whose flight characteristics and control input ran counter to practically all long-standing conventional wisdom and which would allow almost anyone to land and takeoff just about anywhere within almost obscenely short distances for which the CAA had practically no regulations.

Several years would pass after the first press releases were issued for the "Helioplane-Two" that announced production versions within a very short time (press release dated Sunday, May 15, 1949: "It will be ready for commercial production within a year").[1] Before actual production started, the Helio project would test the resolve of both Koppen and Bollinger, as challenges from the CAA and other forces would gradually reshape the market strategy and focus of the project. It was in the face of these obstacles, the original concept of an "everyman's" safety plane would have to undergo a rather sobering transformation in order to ensure some form of practical use and return on investment.

Attempts to manufacture the Helio predate by several years the first actual manufacture of the H-391B; limited quantities were built by Fleet Manufacturing of Canada in 1954, then at the McNally facilities in Pittsburg, Kansas, in 1955.

During the preliminary development of the original Helioplane-Two, Koppen and Bollinger entertained the idea of presenting the project for consideration of financial backing to several U.S. government agencies, specifically the NACA, the CAA, and the military.

Although the top man at the CAA was impressed by the novel aircraft, T. P. Wright pointed out that the U.S. Congress would not allocate money for the development of light aircraft.

Koppen and Bollinger received a similar reaction from the NACA, whose development projects were based upon "pure research," rather than "applied research" as would have been the case for the Helioplane-Two.

While reaction from the military was more promising, representatives of the armed forces suggested that they seek development funding from the private sector.

It was reported that Koppen and Bollinger also approached several unspecified light plane manufacturers; however, these companies were apparently satisfied with how their own product line was selling without such a revolutionary new aircraft.

With further promising plans for development of the four-place Helioplane-Four, a glimmer of hope emerged with the announcement in early March 1950 that John Lawler, president of Aeronca Aircraft Corporation of Middletown, Ohio, would sign contract arrangements for licensing rights to manufacture the Helioplane-Four. Helio Aircraft Corporation would handle all sales and distribution from its Norwood, Massachusetts, headquarters. Bollinger noted that Aeronca was "selected" to build the Helio because of "their excellent production facilities, skilled workers and a reputation for dependable workmanship."[2] For its part, Aeronca expressed enthusiasm for the Helio project due to the aircraft's previously unheard-of utility for business and pleasure. Amidst all of the expected hype and mutual compliments was the cold business reality that by 1950 the "sales slump of 1948" for light aircraft had firmly entrenched itself, and Aeronca was willing to gamble on introducing an aircraft like the Helio that just might generate much-needed sales. Aeronca would, however, still cover itself by continuing production of its own two-place "Tandem" and four-place "Sedan." At that time, plans were to expect certification of the Helioplane-Four by July 1950, with production of components for the first batch of 25 aircraft to follow shortly afterwards. The first batch of components would then be shipped to Norwood for final assembly, flight testing and delivery. Following successful completion of these 25 aircraft, final assembly would be relocated back to Aeronca for continued production.

Aeronca's commitment to the plan appears to have been in earnest, with financing for the new program reported to have come from a Reconstruction Finance Corporation Loan matched by the community of Middletown. There was an issue of $400,000 of new "prior participating preferred stock," and-most importantly for Aeronca-approximately one million dollars' worth of claims from "preferred creditors" (accounting for some 80 of the company's creditor claims) was to have been written off, with the creditors receiving 200,000 shares of the new preferred stock. It was further reported that one-third of Aeronca's own distributor network had by early 1950 received down payments worth over $400,000 for the aircraft.[3]

In the meantime, Helio Aircraft Corporation was hard at work putting the finishing touches on a service plan that would ensure customer satisfaction for the new Helio owners and perhaps entice more people to become customers. In a Report to Stockholders dated May 15, 1950, Chairman Lynn L. Bollinger stated a plan to consign initial sales to a select few geographic areas (principally Detroit and Chicago) in which a service center would be created. This would be accomplished before any Helios would be delivered to the areas, with future service centers to be expanded in due order. It was reasoned that the Helio owner would have no responsibility for maintenance, save for fuel and oil; all other details would be covered under a service contract with the service center. The contract would be an all-inclusive service and maintenance "policy" at a fixed fee. Bollinger noted that the effectiveness of the policy would be to a certain extent dependent upon the warranty agreement to be arranged with the engine manufacturer. The service center operator would be paid a fee for each Helio in his territory, and subsequently be held responsible for its service record. The service center would also be held responsible for compliance with any service bulletins as well as periodic inspections and services-without added charge to the owner.

Bollinger further noted that much of this plan was based upon a new and innovative approach used by certain manufacturers of automobiles and agricultural equipment to maintain customer satisfaction and loyalty. He stated "Basically our distribution policy is designed to relieve the user of his customary service and maintenance headaches. A flexible, open-minded attitude and much effort will be needed in developing a strong sales-service pattern. We may make mistakes as we try new approaches, but the weaknesses of the old system call for a change, and in view of the new uses and markets opened by Helioplane characteristics, we have an unparalleled opportunity for improvement in the industry's marketing practices."[4]

The May 15, 1950, Report to Stockholders also detailed a seven-point plan of policy involving bringing the Helioplane to market, those seven points being:

1. Financing
2. Engineering and Certification
3. Production
4. Design
5. Pricing
6. Distribution
7. Competitive Objectives

While the detailed points of policy concerning (1) Financing, (2) Engineering and Certification, (3) Production, (4) Design and (6) Distribution have been covered, it is items (5) Pricing and (7) Competitive Objectives that warrant a closer look.

Under the topic of pricing, it was proposed that the Helioplane-Four be a high quality, executive-type airplane initially priced somewhere between $7,000 and

$9,000. This pales somewhat in comparison to the earlier and highly suspect estimate in the May 15, 1949, Press Release that the Helio would be marketed at approximately $500 more than a "comparable aircraft" ("comparable aircraft" being envisioned as costing in the neighborhood of $3,000 in 1949), thereby setting the price of the Helio at around $3,500. This target price may have been a little off the mark, considering that a basic 1949 Cessna Model 170A (with Continental C-145-2 engine) cost $5,995.

Bollinger began to hedge on the original idea of building an affordable safety plane for the masses exactly one year from that first press release of May 15, 1949. In the Stockholder's Report of May 15, 1950, Bollinger noted that:

> The unique safety and performance qualities of the Helioplane do, of course, also make it an ideal vehicle for the lower-priced, personal and agricultural markets. We are well aware that a larger market for a four-place airplane lies in the under $5,000 price range. In fact, some of the flying public may be disappointed that the first Helioplanes are not priced in that category.
>
> Aircraft manufacture costs, however, are greatly affected by volume, and at present day volume of aircraft usage a choice must be made between dependable quality or low cost. While we are confident that the utility of the Helioplane will eventually build a volume market, the fact remains that such a market does not now exist.
>
> We have therefore chosen the alternative of building a high quality vehicle, and shall enter the lower price markets only as the volume permits without compromise on dependability. We believe the executive market is the best initially because these users tend to recognize the value and can afford to pay for real safety.
>
> Meanwhile, realistic pricing permits many construction details, which will pay major dividends in terms of ruggedness, reliability and a real safety record.
>
> For example, certain highly resilient heat-treated tubing in the cabin-a new safety feature-adds to cost without affecting appearance or performance. The owner will never know the difference unless he is involved in a mishap-then he will be very grateful. The leading-edge slats on the wing are solely for safety, through elimination of the stall-spin hazard. The flying skill is literally built into the wing-rather than remaining dependent upon piloting ability. Apart from its advanced performance and safety, the Helioplane-Four will be comparable in structural refinement to other four-place aircraft selling in the $12,000 and higher category.

In regards to product development and upgrades, Bollinger stated that

> ...the initial price of the Helioplane is predicated not on a mass market, but nevertheless in expectation of substantial orders. If these fail to materialize, it may later become necessary to raise the price-as has been the experience with many new aircraft. On the other hand, if Helioplane sales exceed our estimate-and we have tried to be conservative-the price should come down. Our primary initial market will be the business and executive user. Later, we hope, it may also prove possible to provide a dependable vehicle for the "average" pocket book. The only market for which we believe a lower cost model may prove practical in the near future lies in agricultural and remote region areas, where users are willing to sacrifice speed, comfort and other features for economy. The possibility of a stripped-down model for this market is still being explored.[5]

In March 1951, the initial price for the Helioplane-Four was again adjusted upwards, reflecting the clearer reality of manufacture: the first 100 aircraft would be priced at $9,800 each (for comparison purposes a 1951 Cessna Model 170A was then selling for $6,495). These first 100 aircraft were to be used for market testing and exploration of new uses. Most were to have been sold primarily to business users in a few key industrial areas where full service facilities would be available (an exception being for a few aircraft to be placed in remote areas where new uses might be explored).

Ultimately, by the time the Helio Courier actually became available to the public in 1954 as the Model H-391B, the aircraft would rocket in price to $24,500 (a 1954 Cessna Model 170B was listing at that time for $8,500). At that price, the Helio was destined for only special niche markets such as the military, law enforcement agencies, a few well-heeled individuals and isolated corporate operators who could afford the initial steep sticker price as well as expensive maintenance fees.

Under the topic of Competitive Objectives, the virtues of a comprehensive service plan and the benefits of on-going product upgrades were underscored.

Bollinger noted: "Our objectives with respect to market introduction, service and sales may now be labeled 'idealistic.' We shall try to justify that label, and at the same time to be realistic and practical.

For the long run, we believe a strong profitable business can best be built through building customer confidence in the absolute integrity of the product and the organization behind it. We are, therefore, willing to forego quick profits for the sake of developing a service organization and service standards to match the unsurpassed engineering of the Helioplane."[6]

In regards to product development and upgrades, Bollinger stated,

> Are we running any risks of losing competitive leadership by the long period of careful testing and development? Yes-in terms of the months before others may have slow-flying aircraft on the market-and the Helioplane is evidently starting a new design trend. For the long run, however, your company should be even farther ahead because of the extra time and care taken to assure product integrity.

The first and easiest Helioplane characteristic you may expect to see copied is its slow-flight. Slow flight by itself, however, is neither new nor particularly useful. The Wright Brothers flew 26 MPH in their flimsy biplane. Slow flight is useful only when combined with quick takeoff under full load conditions plus efficient high-speed operation and stall-proof safety. The absence of any one of these means severe curtailment of utility.

Others may wish to make use of the know-how and patent claims evolved over a period of years in the Helioplane development. Your company has already licensed use of the basic data to one independent manufacturer (Fairchild). In that instance, the license does not involve participation in the personal flying business. When, however, the competitive advantages of the Helioplane's unique features have been tested on the market, we shall be ready to license their use in the personal flying field as well, should other manufacturers so desire.

The long-range opportunity in this branch of aviation should make not only room but a real need for several companies producing light aircraft with truly advanced performance. We shall do all we can both to maintain a leading position and to encourage healthy development of the entire industry.[7]

Despite an extensive and carefully crafted business plan (at least on paper), the Helio-Aeronca deal to produce the Helioplane-Four was ultimately derailed due to the untimely and far-reaching effects of the Korean War (June 25, 1950, to July 27,

1953). Bollinger noted: "We had hired three students from the Harvard Business School for the summer, and by mid-summer they'd sold over fifty. The price was right-$9,850-and I had a firm contract from Aeronca to build them for $6,750, so there was profit there.... [Aeronca] was so enthusiastic about it they were going to abandon (eventually) their own four-place and sell the Helioplane. Then came the Korean War, and Aeronca was taken over by the Air Force to build parts for B-47s and the like. They've never touched a civil airplane since. But we paid back every penny we'd taken in deposits.[8]

When asked to expand on the impact of the Korean War, Bollinger stated "We got a letter one day saying we could only use 10 percent of the aluminum we had used in the last three months. So it was either a military airplane or no airplane."[9]

Bollinger contended that

> ...following the outbreak of the Korean War, the U.S. government unwittingly changed the entire complexion of the light-plane industry. Through the Controlled Materials Plan, USAF was given the power to commandeer, in effect, the capacities of established lightplane manufacturers.
>
> Four of the seven leading light-aircraft companies, including Aeronca, were given no practical choice but to drop their light aircraft and to take on defense orders. With their strongest distributors and key airport locations then quickly absorbed by the remaining three companies, none of these four was able to re-establish itself in the post–Korean light-plane industry.
>
> Thus, after the Korean War, the U.S economy, which had previously had a surplus of experienced light plane production and distribution capabilities, then had a shortage of both. Those companies remaining in the business had all the orders they needed. None of them had reason either to assist or try to duplicate our STOL design innovation.[10]

With no U.S. light-plane manufacturer either willing or able to produce the Helio, Koppen and Bollinger were able to persuade the venerable Fleet Manufacturing, Ltd., of Fort Erie, Ontario, Canada, to supply major components for assembly at Norwood. It was envisioned that eventually Fleet would manufacture flyaway aircraft for sale in Canada and British Commonwealth countries.

At the time, Fleet appeared to be an almost ideal source (for a "foreign" business) for manufacture of the H-391B, not only from a technical expertise standpoint, but also from the fact that Fleet was well located geographically to facilitate coordination with Helio's Boston-based operations.

Since its founding in February 1929 by Major Reuben Hollis Fleet, the company (directly descended from the first aircraft company, Consolidated Aircraft Company of Buffalo, New York) had produced a series of aircraft that were well received in the field. Perhaps the most notable aircraft by Fleet were the Models 1 and 2 Fleet Finch biplanes (426 built), the PT-23 and PT-26 Fleet Cornell II monoplane trainers (1,902 built), and the Fleet Model 80 high wing, strut braced Canuck cabin monoplane (225 built).

While Fleet had performed admirably during the Second World War, mostly by building primary trainers and outer wing panels for the Lancaster bomber, the cancellation of major government defense contracts and other market vagaries of the postwar years would test its management's resources to continue to maintain a viable work force and product line. Its most recent postwar airplane, the Model 80 Canuck (first produced in 1945), would have its production terminated in 1948. To compensate for a depressed general aviation market, Fleet did what many other aircraft companies (including many U.S. light-airframe manufacturers) were doing to stay alive: diversified its product line.

A mixed bag of new products ranged from the aerodynamic Cabincar travel trailer to assembly of an urban bus for Twin Coach Corporation, ship furniture, aluminum windows and doors, doll buggies, baby cribs, office partitions, aluminum boats, refrigerators, kitchens, bars, furnace parts and toboggans for the Canadian Army. On the aviation-related side, Fleet eventually built DHC-2 Beaver fuselages for DeHavilland, as well as components such as nose-wheel drag-links for the Republic F-84 and wing panels/fuselages for the F-86 Sabre. The lapses between contracts at times were frustrating, and resulted at a point in management's having to sell tooling just to cover company paychecks.

It was in this scattered manufacturing environment that Helio approached Fleet with the prospect for the bold new Helio Courier. During 1954, Fleet Manufacturing obtained the Canadian and British Commonwealth manufacturing and sales rights to the Model H-391B, while primary emphasis would be placed on the initial manufacture of components for Helio assembly and sale in the United States.

Herman L. Eberts, president and general manager of Fleet Manufacturing, Ltd., was brought in from Canadair Limited in 1953 to reorganize and revitalize Fleet. It was under his watch that resources involving 277,000 square feet of Fleet plant facilities and approximately 850 company employees were available to handle the Helio project as begun in early 1954. Production of Fleet-built Helio Couriers for exclusive sale in Canada was announced to cost approximately $1,500 less than the U.S.-assembled counterparts, thereby costing $24,500 each (price did not cover radio, but did include standard contact flight instruments).

Production of Helio Courier components and aircraft by Fleet Manufacturing, Ltd., was on a relatively small scale, with breakdown as shown below:

- 3 airframes shipped as knockdown components for assembly at Norwood, Mass. (It was reported that the entire airframe, except for the forward section of the fuselage, was built at Fleet. Tooling for the forward section was eventually planned to be sent to Fleet for 100 airframe build-up.)
- 1 complete aircraft built as a Fleet Canadian demonstrator at Fort Erie, with constructor number C/N FML-004 (bearing registration: CF-IBF). This aircraft completed its first flight on February 1, 1955, with flight tests completed by Dennis H. Byron on Feb. 23, and with Canadian Certificate of Airworthiness 4523 issued February 23, 1955.
- 2 additional complete sets of parts (not as knockdown assemblies) delivered to Norwood, Mass., upon curtailment of program.[11]

In essence, then, six aircraft (5 accounted for in parts or assemblies that were a part of a pre-production order for components for 5 aircraft (of which all were forwarded to Norwood), and 1 actual H-391B, built and assembled on Canadian soil as a demonstrator) was the sum total of the Helio/Fleet effort.

An added benefit of having Fleet build the early H-391B components was the

The only Fleet-built H-391B (featuring special Fleet-Helio graphics on the aft fuselage) demonstrating its incredible STOL takeoff at Flushing Airport, New York. Central Arkansas Library System/Aerospace Branch and the Arkansas Aviation Historical Society.

ability to use the plastic shop and fiberglass equipment recently acquired from Canadair. With this on-site capability, Fleet designed, developed and manufactured the fiberglass laminated plastic door frames, wing tips, empennage tips and tail fairings.

As a part of the promotion of the Helio Courier in Canada, a demonstration was held for the press at Toronto's Island Airport on June 9, 1954. The Helio that was used for this demonstration was H-391B, Number 001 (N242B). Painted on each side of its aft fuselage was the following wording:

HELIO
COURIER
MANUFACTURED JOINTLY BY
HELIO AIRCRAFT CORP, NORWOOD, MASS., USA
FLEET MANUFACTURING LTD, FORT ERIE, ONTARIO, CANADA

Fleet also exhibited its role in producing the H-391B at the Canadian International Trade Fair and other venues. From 1955 to 1957, Fleet conducted an extensive campaign to reach prospective buyers in both the civil and military Canadian market, without much luck. Finally, Fleet number FML-004 (CF-IBF) was sold in 1957 to a company in Edmonton, Alberta, and with it went the last remaining vestiges of the Fleet effort for Helio sales.

It was surmised that the success of the domestically produced DeHavilland Beaver led to the downfall of the Fleet-built Courier in Canada.

Bollinger recounts the outcome of the period with Fleet: "Our company accordingly next subcontracted production of the Courier to a producer of military airframe components. That company, however, was forced to default as a result of excessive costs resulting in turn from inadequacy of complete airplane manufacturing experience. We were thereby forced to enter into the manufacturing of our own airplane–lacking only the requisite capital, the experience, the intent, the plans and the personnel!"[12]

With production at Fleet Manufacturing Ltd. quickly coming to a premature ending, a source was finally located: a company tucked away in the southeastern corner of Kansas. According to Bollinger, "Fortunately, through the availability of unexpectedly qualified personnel in the small town of Pittsburg, Kansas, together with excellent cooperation of our plant's former owner, the McNally-Pittsburg Company, Courier production became successful and efficient."[13]

The company was known as Mid States Manufacturing. It was a subsidiary of the McNally-Pittsburg Manufacturing Corporation, formed by Edward T. McNally, whose main business of building coal preparation equipment was based to a large extent on the local business of strip mining.

The origins of Mid States Manufacturing can be traced back to about 1951, when the city leaders were investigating the possibility of attracting new manufacturing business opportunities to Pittsburg. At the time, Pittsburg's major source of employment was Pittsburg State University, along with the underground and strip-mining operations that dotted the surface. The prehistoric swamps that covered these lowlands would provide ample fields of coal, as well as zinc and lead, to support the local economy for years. To underscore the scale and commitment of the mining business, one of the operations featured a mammoth strip mining power shovel weighing 11 million pounds, and capable of scooping 150 tons of coal in one bite.

Pittsburg is located in the Cherokee Lowlands that adjoin Missouri, more scenic than the stereotypical flat and sparse terrain that most people envision when they think of Kansas. A no-nonsense work ethic, stemming from the generations of hardworking immigrant miners, contrasted well with the dynamic academic environment and future promise of graduates from Pittsburg State University. Add in local lore that suggests the area had served at some point as a place of respite for organized crime factions during gang wars, and the city of Pittsburg could be viewed as a Midwest microcosm of some large east coast industrialized metropolis. The timing was right, and Pittsburg, Kansas, presented itself as a progressively evolving center of industry well suited and enthusiastic to support future Helio production.

The possibility of organizing a company to do subcontract work, building B-47 landing gear doors for Lockheed Aircraft Corporation, was discussed. A charter of incorporation was filed September 6, 1951; the company was named Mid States Manufacturing Corporation, with Edward T. McNally as chairman. Other board members were Ben J. Horton, Percy Coles, A. W. Hubbard and Raymond Letton. The contract with Lockheed Aircraft Corporation of Marietta, Georgia, was finalized on November 21, 1951. The location of the first manufacturing operations was in the basement of the Pittsburg Memorial Auditorium. This arrangement, in which the facil-

Aerial view rendition of Pittsburg, Kansas, manufacturing plant.

ities were leased from the city, was envisioned as just a temporary measure in order to get the company going. Before the end of the year, fabrication was underway with M. W. Hubbard as general manager and Dale Armstrong as superintendent.

Operations were satisfactory, with a profit being made from the B-47 subcontract work. However, with the Korean War truce, military work was eventually phased out, and other sources for products were sought.

The first mention of doing work for Helio Aircraft Corporation came from Mid States' manager of sales (and aviation enthusiast), Cliff Waterman Jr., who suggested that they should contact Helio. Subsequently, meetings were held with Lynn Bollinger to discuss specifics of a deal. The result was that a contract was negotiated in December 1954 for Mid States to build the production version of the Helio Courier. Benefits of a relatively low local labor rate, a skilled workforce, and a central location for shipping augured well for the deal.

Contract specifics called for Mid States Manufacturing Corporation to build the Model H-391B Helio Courier for a period of three years (anticipating 300 aircraft produced within that time frame) from the time that the first plane was delivered, or to April 1, 1955, whichever came first. The contract further called for Mid States to pay $70,000 for plans, drawings and tooling, with an additional loan to Helio in the amount of $20,000 to be in the form of a promissory note that was to be paid by April 1, 1958.

At a meeting held by Mid States on January 20, 1955, it was agreed to spend $60,000 to build a new assembly plant and office space (60 feet by 120 feet) at West

Fourth in Pittsburg. Tooling from Fleet Manufacturing Ltd. was loaded in a cattle truck and delivered to Pittsburg to restart fabrication and assembly operations. At this time, the plant was operating with about 100 workers. Later, the plant was to be expanded by 50 to increase production. This was accomplished in the months from October to December 1968, in which 17,000 additional square feet of plant assembly and storage space (an increase of about a third) was added. Accounting for the expansion was:

- 12,000 square feet of plant assembly area
- 3,780 square feet of warehouse area
- 960 square feet of plant facility area

Normal production capacity for 1968 was pegged at four aircraft per month. With the increased space and facilities, the new production line rates would permit eight aircraft per month, with estimated peak line flow of twelve aircraft per month, based upon a single-shift, forty-hour work week. Eventual production floor space at Pittsburg would total 45,000 square feet.

The first Helio Courier out of the Pittsburg plant flew on March 24, 1955. It was flown to the airport by Lynn Bollinger himself, though Russell White normally performed the shakedown flights. The first plane was not fabricated on site, as its components were from leftover Fleet and Norwood stockpiles. The first H-391B to be fabricated, assembled, and test-flown in Pittsburg would debut later in the month, around the 30th. Local management involved in the initial production at the Mid States facility were Verne Marsh as vice president and general manager, Dale Armstrong as production manager, Ralph Gaston of engineering and Robert Holshouser as shop superintendent

Upon completion of the first five Helios in Pittsburg, it was evident that the negotiated price to manufacture the aircraft was too much of a burden on the fledgling Mid States plant. Under the current contract, Mid States would be unable to fulfill its part if some other arrangements couldn't be made. At this time, the management of Helio was headed by Lynn Bollinger as president, Otto Koppen as vice president, Lawrence N. Smithline as general manager and chief of engineering, Lawrence W. Caton as purchasing agent, Joe Hastings as plant superintendent, and Merrill G. Hastings as factory manager.

It was then proposed that Helio Aircraft Corporation take over the Mid States plant in exchange for stock in Helio. This agreement was ratified at a meeting on July 30, 1956, at which time Mid States Manufacturing received common stock, a block of preferred stock, and promissory notes from Helio. Effective August 29, 1956, Helio Aircraft Corporation was to gain complete control and ownership of the manufacturing plant, along with the equipment and organizational resources which totaled some 150 employees. Mid States Manufacturing Corporation was renamed Mid States Division of Helio Aircraft Corporation, and the Mid States Manufacturing Corporation was from that time on simply a stockholder in Helio Aircraft Corporation, and was without an active role in its day-to-day plant operation.

On May 31, 1960, a request was filed on behalf of the Board of Directors of Mid States Manufacturing to dissolve and distribute the assets, which were forwarded to the McNally Pittsburg Corporation.

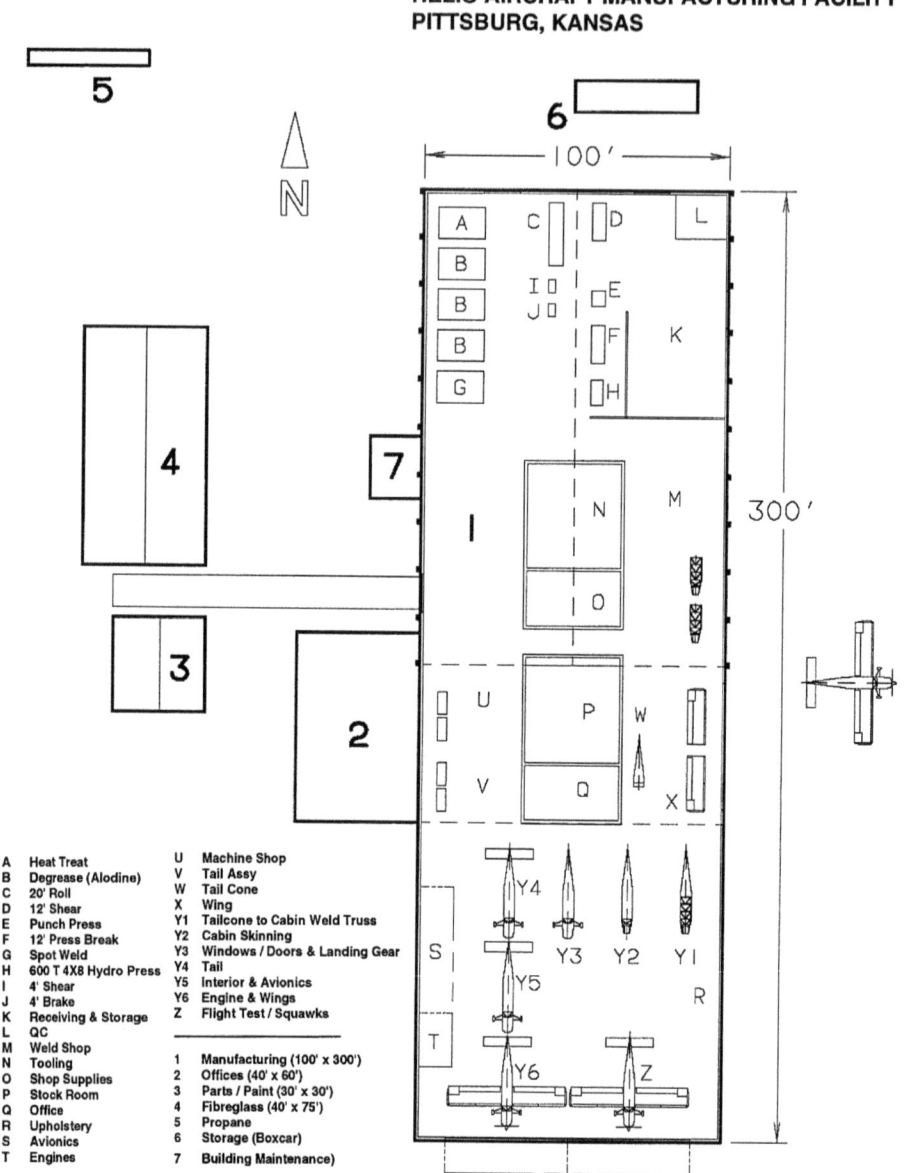

Helio Aircraft manufacturing facility layout, Pittsburg, Kansas.

Effective May 1, 1961, Helio Aircraft Corporation reacquired the mortgage it had given, and for its part, McNally Pittsburg received the land from Helio. In this final arrangement, Helio Aircraft Corporation would lease the property from McNally Pittsburg for future Helio production.

While main production would always be maintained at the Pittsburg plant, the Helio Aircraft Corporation headquarters would eventually be relocated. The company was originally based at the Boston Metropolitan Airport Norwood/Canton,

Massachusetts. That airport dated to the 1920s, and had five cinder runways. A move was made between 1963 and 1964 to the Boston suburb of Bedford. This location afforded a fully equipped aircraft development and components manufacturing facility on the civilian area of the Hanscom Air Force Base. The location was selected for its proximity to the resources of MIT and other advanced technology facilities clustered in the area.

The 30,000-square-foot building housed engineering and administrative offices, as well as a high bay area utilized as a shop to perform service and prototype assembly work. Directly behind the building was an apron that provided direct access to all of the Hanscom Air Force Base runways. Most of the prototype and limited production development flight testing, as well as the FAA certification flight testing programs, were conducted at this location.

The H-391B was produced from 1954 to 1959; in that time 102 examples were made. The experience would prove to be enlightening-in a disconcerting way-for Helio management. Certainly, while the aircraft measured up quite well in performance and quality, its success in the civilian sector was hampered by several factors. First was the extremely high cost of purchasing the aircraft, plus a certain amount of initial resistance to off-airport use. The other factor was CAA/FAA waverings over the most basic definition of what constituted an STOL aircraft and the associated landing requirements for such an aircraft. Moreover, Koppen's and Bollinger's expectations for government approval of their plans to have existing regulations revised in order to allow their new aircraft to land and takeoff just about anywhere could reasonably be considered overly optimistic.

Originally, Koppen and Bollinger envisioned the Helio as being allowed to land on business and residential property, thereby doing away at least partially with the need to use regular airports. Early on, the H-391B (particularly the Helio H-391B, N242B) was used frequently to demonstrate the benefits of STOL landings for business use.

One such demonstration was recounted by Otto Koppen: "We have a road over there which is like Silicon Valley, Route 128, where all of the electronic companies are located. And, one of our pilots took a Helio and landed over the fence of the factories and onto the grounds of every one, with the idea of selling them an aircraft. But the idea was so fixed in their minds, that an airplane belongs at an airport, period."[14]

Indeed, the 16-mm promotional film that shows this demonstration is impressive despite the lack of immediate sales. The Helio is landed over fencing with no head wind, and a 10-12 knot crosswind. The two off-airport-site businesses in the film are the Polaroid and Sylvania Electric corporations of Waltham, Massachusetts, along Route 128. Landings and takeoffs were easily accomplished within 500 feet; one of them was made with a 90° turn upon rotation to clear a bank of trees.

In May 1955 another demonstration was carried out, with extensive publicity, in which an H-391B was flown from the Pittsburg plant to the St. Louis airport. The Helio was then flown as part of an experimental short hop to demonstrate its possible use for an air taxi service from the airport to the St. Louis riverfront.

Throughout the early years of marketing the H-391B, its unique STOL and safety advantages were well presented to the public. The official marketing pitch included the following[15]:

H-391B using downtown St. Louis, Missouri, parking lot as an "airfield" during slow-speed landing demonstration. Bob Casebeer.

Time Saving and convenience is made possible through ability to use small unprepared open spaces. Factory yards, golf courses and meadows take the place of airports, thus often giving quicker point-to-point transportation than the fastest of multi-engine ships confined to outlying airports. Short hops over traffic-choked roads also become practical without the complexities of the helicopter-at a fraction of the cost and at twice the speed.

Schedule dependability heretofore attainable only with expensively equipped multi-engine airplanes and highly trained, two-man crews are made possible by the Courier's ability to proceed safely even when very low ceilings and restricted visibility may be encountered enroute. Ability to slow down without danger of stall and to turn-on-a-dime or to land almost anywhere permits safe under-the-weather travel.

Peace of mind not commonly attained in single-engine executive aircraft, especially over bad terrain or after dark, is provided through ability to descend slowly without risk of stalling and to land in very small spots. From an altitude of 1000 feet, for example, the power-off gliding range covers an approximate 12-square-mile area within which many openings of more than 75 yards are commonly available, even in mountainous terrain. The power-off rate of descent is less than that of a parachute.

Simplicity of operation reduces the skill ordinarily needed. The ability to slow down gives the inexperienced pilot ample time to re-judge and alter his flight course if the need arises. The perfect control and stability even at very slow speed also contribute to ease of flying.

Along with these points, a list of typical uses for which the Helio Courier offered unique advantages was also given:

1. Executive plant-side to plant-side transportation.
2. Inter-plant engineering liaison.
3. Sales travel, direct to small towns and outlying plants.
4. Direct service and parts for critical industrial equipment.
5. Taxi service to and from outlying terminal airports.
6. Airfreight from airport to point of usage for time-critical items.
7. Pleasure travel direct to beach, farm, golf course, mountain, etc.
8. Personnel and supplies to field operation: oil drilling, mining, highway construction, ocean fishing, pipeline construction, railroad maintenance, forestry, general construction, motion picture filming, etc.
9. Timber inspection and selection.
10. Real estate inspection, esp. industrial sites.
11. Medical supplies for emergencies and stranded groups.
12. Missionary activities in remote areas.
13. Forest dusting and pest control.
14. Wildlife surveys and census.
15. Mapping, photography and aerial surveillance.
16. Forest fire fighting and fire patrol.
17. Emergency evacuation.
18. Police and traffic surveillance.
19. Border patrol.
20. Ambulance service.
21. "Bush service" in remote areas.
22. Exploration.
23. Float and ski operations.
24. Aerial coordination of activities, such as highway operations, commercial fishing, dams and waterways dredging, construction, trucking, railroading, livestock handling, shipping, logging.
25. Commuting from summer resorts and rural areas.
26. On-the-spot news reporting and rapid film deliveries.
27. Access to remote hunting and fishing areas.
28. High-tension line inspection and service.
29. Pipeline patrol and repairs.
30. Aerial prospecting, including uranium detectors and other airborne deposit locators.
31. Agricultural: spraying, fertilizing, dusting, inspection of crops, erosion seeding, equipment service.
32. Ranch communication and supply.
33. Snow-area rescue and supply missions.
34. "Penetration" air service, i.e., government-financed pre-airliner operations.

(Military uses include: liaison, observation, low-speed patrol, communications, low altitude photo-reconnaissance, light supply work, litter evacuation and personnel transportation.)

By 1957, buyers and users of the Model H-391B included many corporate and government agencies. A partial listing:

H-391B with skis permitted the Courier to operate in cold weather and remote territories.

Union Carbide Nuclear Company of Grand Junction, Colorado; Island Creek Coal Company of Huntington, West Virginia; International Research and Development Corporation of Columbus, Ohio; Western Newspaper Union of New York City; Bostwick Prospecting Company of Shelburne, Vermont; Holland Furnace Company of Holland, Michigan; Bender Oil Operations of Bakersfield, California; Paradynamics, Inc., of St. Louis, Missouri; Rounds and Porter Lumber Company of Wichita, Kansas; Stein Lumber Company of Sacramento, California; Southern Peru Copper Co.; and Petroleum Helicopters, Inc., flying for Gulf Oil in Bolivia. Governmental agencies operating the H-391B included the Peruvian Ministry of War and the U.S. Border Patrol, as well as agencies in Canada, Brazil, Mexico and Venezuela.

In spite of these encouraging sales, the use of the Helio's STOL abilities was still being limited by a lack of regulatory commitment.

To further convince the government of the ability of STOL aircraft to fly and land in congested areas, Helio successfully completed 18 months of services tests in cooperation with the New York Port Authority, in which the Courier repeatedly landed and took off from a 400-by-200-foot standard helicopter-size landing pad. These tests, conducted in 1959 next to the ramp at Teterboro Airport, were used to demonstrate the ability of the STOL Helio Courier to use helicopter-size landing zones, thereby avoiding the congested runways of the typical metropolitan airport.

The issue of STOL regulatory definitions was never completely resolved, at least not to Lynn Bollinger's satisfaction. The lack of clear-cut policy was to haunt the company for years, and would become a factor which to a certain extent (according to Helio company thinking) curbed its sales appeal.

As Bollinger stated in a report to stockholders dated June 15, 1974:

In those early years, in the absence of any regulatory definition of "STOL," the Courier model was able to get started in the U.S. commercial market using 600 foot strips. Regulatory approval of those operations was attained by proving "equivalent safety" to an initially skeptical FAA (then CAA). Since that time, however, manufacturers of conventional airplanes have been able to persuade the FAA to specify that a "STOL" landing area should be 2000 feet or more in length. (Previously a Class 1 airport for conventional light-planes required only a 1500 foot landing area.)

Thus, the commercial utility of any truly advanced new STOL designs that can use 600-foot strips safely has been effectively blocked within the U.S. and within the many other major nations that automatically follow FAA/ ICAO standards.

To avoid being associated with that economically discredited 2000 foot "STOL" concept, in current governmental negotiations our company is now using the term "H/E (Helicopter/Equivalent) " to indicate the contrasting economic capabilities of its product.

...After the Korean War, the remaining three comfortably entrenched (existing light plane) companies did not need or desire federal regulatory acceptance of the new STOL design concept. Instead, that concept was only a threat, which might disrupt their control of key on-airport distribution locations.

At that time, the CAB held informal hearings to evaluate recommendations of the FAA (then CAA) Flight Safety Division with regard to approval of 600 foot STOL strips and the use of non-conflicting low-altitude approach lanes by advanced types of STOL aircraft such as Helio had successfully demonstrated in that type of operation.

In response, the controlling "industry consensus" was such that-despite FAA's incontrovertible tests demonstrating safety and feasibility-such an approval was termed premature "in view of rapid pending changes in the state-of-the-art."

That was fifteen years ago; the relevant state-of-the-art with light aircraft has scarcely changed since-nor has the effective domination of federal regulatory policies by protectors of the status quo. Preservation of obsolete regulatory restraints still blocks public use of truly advanced STOL aircraft services where most needed-that is, apart from active jet runways and in helicopter air-lanes apart from heavy-aircraft traffic.

During the 1950s, protectors of the light-plane status quo understandably were happy to support the helicopter industry's contention that all "spoke-to-hub" type of short-haul urban air transportation could be handled economically by the helicopter alone-without permitting STOL airplanes to get into the act. The CAB and Post Office were accordingly convinced that with only three years of steadily declining Government subsidies such helicopter services would become fully self supporting.

After 14 years of increasing helicopter subsidies, however, the Government finally realized that the basic helicopter design concept was and still remains an inherently uneconomic vehicle for most such public-transportation purposes. Nevertheless, the very real public need for truly self-supporting STOL (or H/E) services in these areas still remains obstructed.

Despite its regulatory preclusion from the principal markets for which the Helio product line was originally designed, the company was able to recover its investment and establish a modestly profitable demand by exploiting within the U.S. as well as overseas that small sector of the market where the users operate principally on their own private strips.[16]

Ultimately, the full success of the company would be compromised by a series of ill-fated decisions/circumstances, keeping the name Helio from becoming as recognizable as Cessna, Beech, Piper, or even Ercoupe or Maule. Whether it was factors such as a too-high purchase price, lack of STOL regulatory cooperation/ "conspiracy" on the part of the CAA/FAA, placing too much emphasis on potential

HELIO COMPANY ORGANIZATIONAL TIMELINE

ACTIVITY	ORGANIZATIONAL CHANGE	DATE	LOCATION	REMARKS
Early Prototype Development	Founded as Helio Aircraft Company	3/08/1948	Boston, Mass.	5,000 shares of common, no par
	Helio Aircraft Corporation	10/31/1949	Norwood, Mass.	27,000 shares of preferred, non-cum par
	Helio Aircraft Corporation (Massachusetts corp) and Midwest Aircraft Corporation become Helio Aircraft Corporation (Delaware corporation)	3/06/1950	Headquarters: Norwood, Mass. Initial works located at Fleet Manufacturing in 1954, then relocated to Pittsburg, KS, 1955	Midwest Aircraft Corporation was set up as part of an aborted Aeronca deal. The main works was located in Pittsburg, Kansas, and operated independently under contract as Mid States Manufacturing until 1956.
Bulk of Production	Helio Aircraft Corporation acquires production facilities from Mid States Manufacturing Corporation. Mid States Manufacturing becomes the Mid States Division of Helio Aircraft Corporation	8/29/1956	Headquarters: Norwood, Mass. works was located at headquarters, then relocated (1963-64) to Bedford, Mass. Works: Pittsburg, KS	
	Helio Aircraft Corporation becomes Helio Aircraft Company, a Division of the General Aircraft Corporation. Also, Transport Division of General Aircraft Corporation assigned for the Model GAC-100	4/28/1969	General Aircraft Corp. based at 822 Connecticut Ave., Washington, D.C.	Effective during April 1969, Helio Aircraft Corporation issues 284,332 shares of stock for net assets of GAC, and then changes it's name to General Aircraft Corporation.
	Helio Precision Products		Bedford, Mass.	Former head Helio office does independent research.
Temporary Halt to All Production (Dec.1974)	Helio Courier LTD (also referred to as John Roberts LTD)	1974	Works: Pittsburg, KS. Head Office and Marketing Division: Helio International, located at Cross Anchor, S. Carolina	John Roberts LTD acquires sole distributor rights, and exercises option to buy company (production rights, but not tooling). Transaction never completed due to legal dispute over tooling. Production temporarily ceases from 1975.
Very Limited Production of Models H-700 and H-800 (1981-1984)	Helio Aircraft LTD	11/08/1976	Works: Pittsburg, KS	Helio Precision Products sells assets to New York investor Allan Goldhush. Company is restructured. Sub-contract work done for Boeing. Built the models from H-700 and H-800 1981 thru 1984.
Era of Legal Disputes over Ownership	Helio Aircraft INC	8/23/1984	Works: Pittsburg, KS	Assets sold to individual investor Gary Adams. Bankruptcy declared.
	(A) CAMCORP, and then later known as (B) Aircraft Acquision Corporation, claim ownership and forms Helio Aircraft Corporation.	11/1989	CAMCORP, and later Aircraft Acquisition Corporation, based in Morgantown, West Virginia	Darius Zerbach, President *See note below for allegations and legal dispute over ownership by CAMCORP and AAC of Helio Type Certificates and legal rights.
	Helio Enterprises LLC	12/1992	Kent, Washington Tucson, Arizona	Rights and assets acquired from Gary Adams of Corser Ventures, Tulsa, Oklahoma

*Note: According to published legal paperwork, CAMCORP (Consolidated Asset Management Corporation) and it's successor, AAC (Aircraft Acquisition Corporation), had entered into a contract to purchase Helio assets in 1989, but allegedly never followed through with the terms of the contract set by the previous owners. It was alleged that the FAA had erroneously issued Helio Type Certificates to AAC. The Federal Aviation Administration (FAA) revoked the Type Certificates and awarded them to Helio Enterprises, Inc., On 8/11/1994.

Helio company organizational timeline.

military orders or safety issues, lack of advertising for the civilian sector, or even alleged misdoings on the part of certain governmental agencies, the initial promise of profitability would prove elusive, resulting in a series of management restructurings of the company in attempts to capture the success that once seemed so certain.

With its headquarters in Bedford, and works in Pittsburg, Helio would deliver the bulk of its production aircraft before 1974, when production was temporarily halted largely due to the factors noted above. The Pittsburg works would remain open with a skeleton crew to do Helio spare parts manufacture, as well as limited subcontract work for Boeing-Wichita. A series of new management groups would struggle to rekindle production, with a brief return to building H-700 and H-800 aircraft from 1983 to 1985.

Helio Aircraft Profiles

The remainder of chapter three consists of a series of profiles that detail the differences between the various main models and variants of the Helios built between 1954 and 1974. The models profiled consist of the following aircraft: H-391B, H-392, H-395, H-395A, H-250, H-295 (1200), H-295 (1400) and HT-295.

PROFILE: H-391B

The model H-391B was the first large-scale production version of the Helio Courier. Between 1954 and 1959, a total of 102 H-391Bs were constructed (H-391B serials 001-102), making it the third most widely produced model of Helio built to date. The most-produced model of Helio was the model H-295 (1200 and 1400 series) with 174 units built, followed by the model H-395 with 138 units built.

Aside from the outstanding STOL capabilities outlined in the previous chapter, the H-391B possessed several unique features that came to distinguish the aircraft in the field.

From a safety standpoint, the single feature that was of paramount importance was the network of welded chrome-moly tubing that served as a cocoon around the occupants to enhance survivability. The design was based on the assumptions that

H-391B, JAARS, Inc., N242B—("Ol' No. 1") the first production—and still active!—Helio Courier. JAARS, Inc.

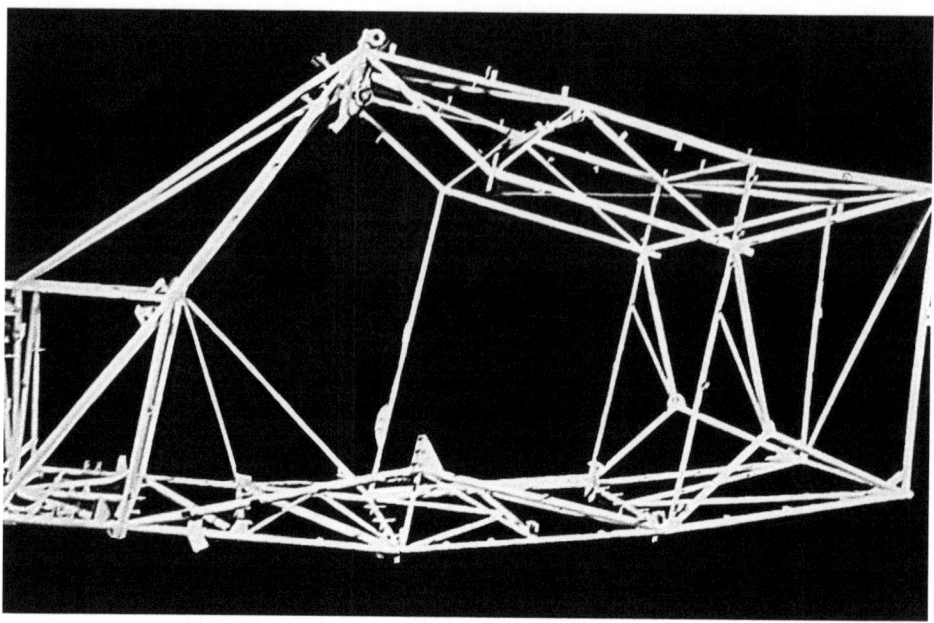

Helio safety case structure. Bob Casebeer.

this type of aircraft would probably be subjected to rough treatment, and that accidents were bound to happen. The bench type seats (rigidly installed) along with the safety cage were stressed to 15 Gs of deceleration load. To reinforce the safety cocoon, and to reduce chances of cabin deformation, the door openings were staggered: entry to the cockpit was via a left-hand door, while passengers entered through a door on the right-hand side, aft of the co-pilot's seat.

The engine mount, to which was fitted one of several versions of the geared Lycoming GO-435 series engine, was designed so that the engine would not be driven back into the cockpit in the event of an accident. Early development work on the engine mounting system included the conceptual provision that, upon impact, the engine should pitch up and over the safety cage.

Another physical characteristic worth noting was the tall main-gear undercarriage. In addition to the ability to resist nose-overs, the mounting of the long-stroke oleo-pneumatic struts was credited with yielding a certain amount of progressive deformation upon rough impact, thereby absorbing energy that would ordinarily be transmitted on up to the cabin.

The tall struts not only provide necessary ground clearance for the prop, but they also set the aircraft upon takeoff at a static ground angle that provides maximum lift.

As an option, the main gear could be outfitted with Goodyear crosswind landing gear. An instrument-panel-mounted latch was used to engage/disengage the castering gear, to which were fitted hydraulic disk brakes, actuated through toe extensions on the left-hand set of rudder pedals.

Inside the cabin, very little in the way of unusual instrumentation can be seen that would reveal the unique capabilities of the machine. Layout of the instrument

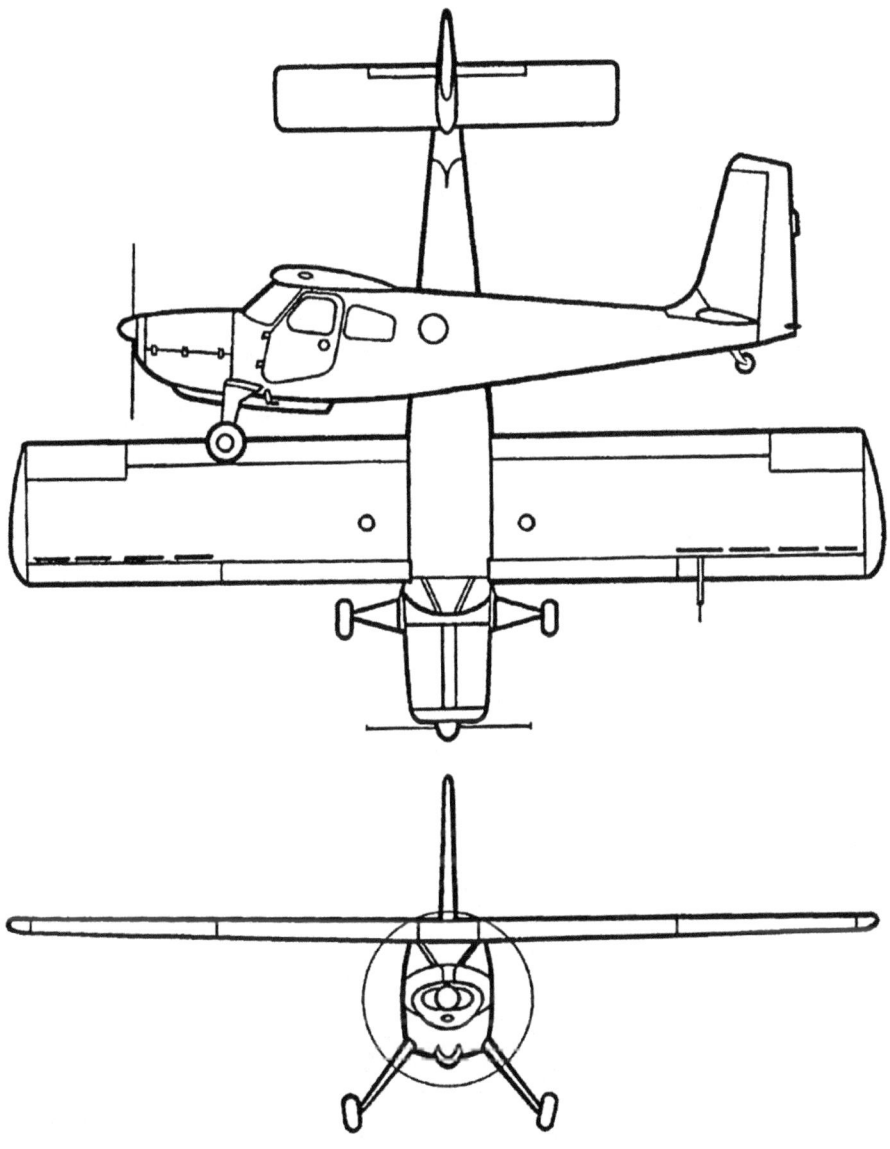

Helio H-391B — 3-View.

panel adhered to the standard of the day as set forth by the CAA, with flight instruments clustered to the left and engine monitoring gauges to the right of center. As would be expected, dual flight controls were provided.

Perhaps the only tell-tale interior indicators that this was not your ordinary aircraft were the on/off fuel selector location (centered where the co-pilot's door would normally be) and the concentric flap and elevator trim crank handles centrally located in the cockpit overhead. The larger (flap) crank required 15 turns for full (40°) flap deployment, while the smaller crank (elevator trim) had an indicator gauge located alongside the handle.

Left: Lycoming GO-435-C2 engine. National Air and Space Museum, Smithsonian Institute (SI NEG NO. 96-10522). *Right:* H-391B cross-wind landing gear allows the Courier to land with drift, permitting the wheels to automatically align with the runway up to 20° off-line.

H-391B front three-quarter view.

Located behind the aft bench-type seat is a space dedicated for either 200 pounds of baggage or installation of a fifth seat. (Although the H-391B was initially sold as a 4-place aircraft, beginning with H-391B S/N 066 a fifth seat was available as Helio P/N 391-030-902.) If necessary, the aft bench seat could be removed to provide a six-foot-long space in which cargo could be carried.

Perhaps one of the most revealing flight reviews ever penned of the Helio Courier

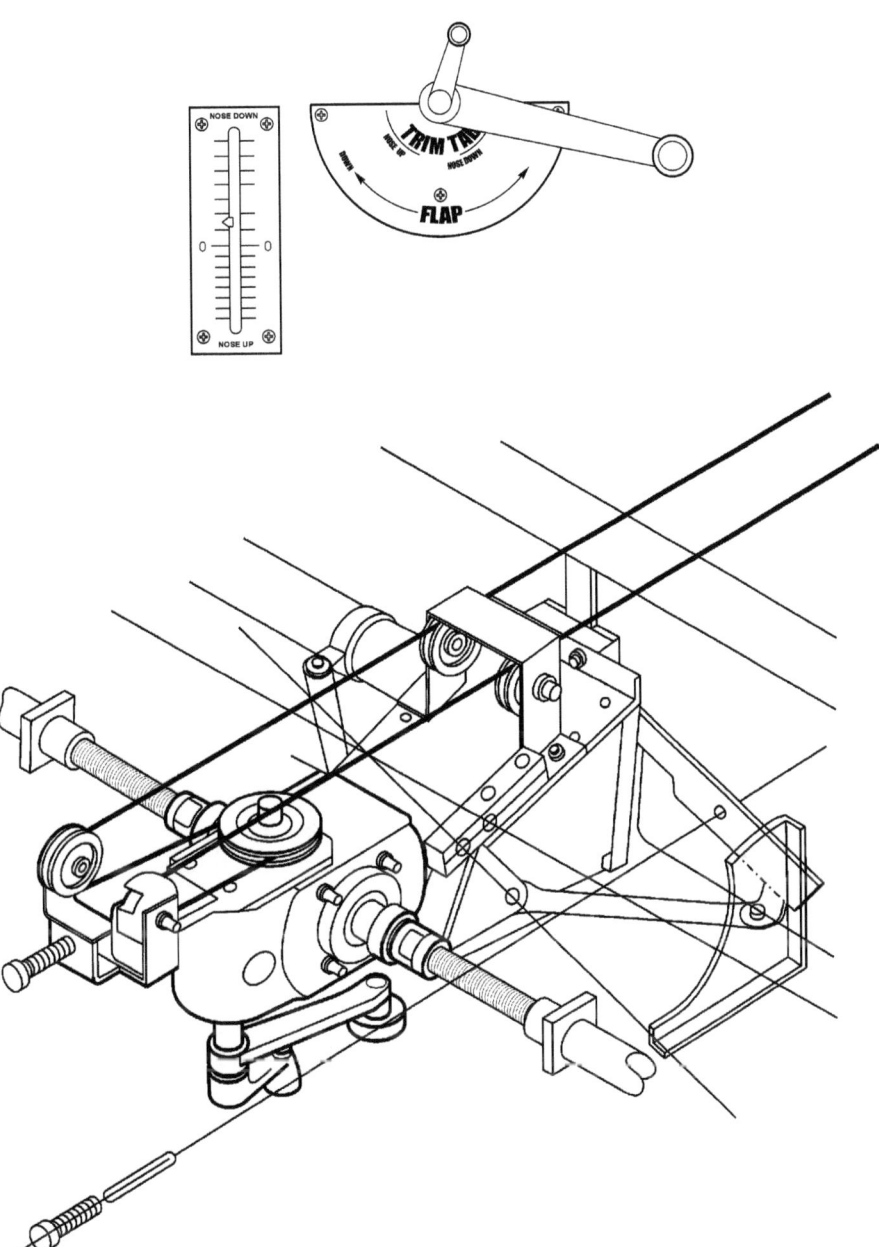

Top: Overhead flap-crank detail, with the long handle for flaps, and the short handle for trim. *Bottom:* Overhead flap crank system. Both, Bob Casebeer.

model H-391B appeared in the March 11, 1960, issue of *Aeronautics* and *Astronautics*. "Flying the V/STOL Courier," written by veteran aviation writer John Fricker, concludes:

> The Courier certainly seems completely viceless.... It is possible, however, that short landings could be made considerably more comfortable by providing the present

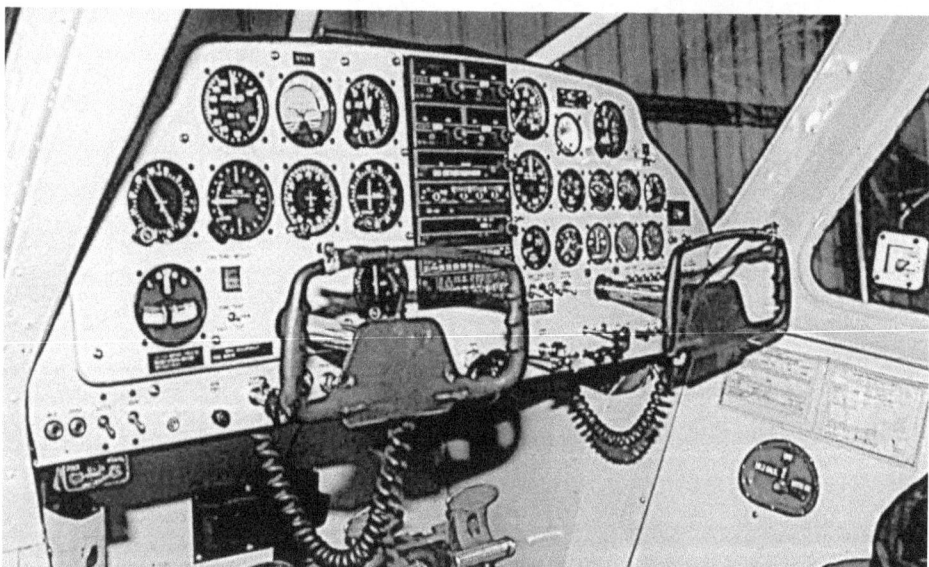

Top, left: H-391B right-hand front door detail. *Top, right:* H-391B interior cabin view — looking aft. Bob Casebeer. *Bottom:* H-391B cockpit and instrument panel view.

rather hard undercarriage with liquid-spring type of shock absorbers and low-pressure tires.

The Courier has proved itself a remarkable and successful example of design and engineering, and for the performance range which it offers its initial cost of about $30,000 f.a.f. is not high. Of this total, its manufacturers consider that its special features account for some $11,500.[17]

3. Geared for Success

Top: H-391B — The classic Helio Courier. *Bottom:* H-391B outfitted with Edo floats and capable of taking off at full gross weight of 3,000 lbs. in zero wind in less than 350 feet. Bob Casebeer.

General Specifications

Model H-391B Helio Courier

Powerplant: H-391B was powered by a Lycoming GO-435-C2 series six-cylinder, horizontally opposed, air cooled geared engine of 260 horsepower swinging a Hartzell 101" prop. Immediate predecessor (H-391) used the same basic type of engine.

Price Range: $24,000–29,500

Dimensions & Performance:

Length	30 ft.	Wing Area	231 sq. ft.
Span	39 ft.	Wing Chord	6 ft.
Height	8 ft. 10 in.	Flap Area	38.1 sq. ft.

Tailplane Span	13 ft. 4 in.	Minimum Speed (power off)	41 MPH
Dihedral	1 degree	Initial Rate of Climb	1,100 FPM
Incidence	3 degrees	Initial Climb Angle	18 degrees
Empty Weight	1,900 lbs	Service Ceiling	25,600 ft.
GWT	3,000 lbs.	Range	600 Miles
Useful Load	1,100 lbs.	T.O. Distance over 50' Obstacle	500 ft.
Wing Loading	13 lbs./sq. ft.		
Cruising Speed	157 MPH	Landing Distance over 50' Obstacle	500 ft.
Top Speed	160 MPH		
Minimum Speed (power on)	30 MPH		

Weights:

Gross, Normal	2,800 lbs.
Gross, Industrial	3,000 lbs.
Gross, Agricultural	3,500 lbs.

See Appendix 1 for further data specifications.

PROFILE: H-392

The model H-392 was built in 1957. It was essentially an H-391B that was highly modified for high altitude aerial photography/survey purposes. Although only one aircraft was built at the time, Lynn Bollinger believed that there was a market for at least 25 of this type of aircraft (with a price tag of around $45,000), noting that there were approximately 50 aerial survey companies located worldwide. Many of these firms were making do with old, expensive-to-maintain ex-military aircraft.

Work on the H-392 project was initiated after an inquiry from Compañía Aerofoto Mexicana (CAM) for a highly modified H-391B capable of performing high altitude photographic work. The fact that the Courier possessed a high/strutless wing favored its use as a photographic platform.

Main differences between a stock H-391B and the H-392 were that the Strato-Courier had a 340-HP Lycoming GSO-480-A1A6 supercharged six-cylinder (horizontally opposed/air cooled) engine mated to a three-bladed prop. The larger engine necessitated lengthening the engine cowl, while the landing gear was reinforced to accommodate the added weight of the heavy photographic equipment and the larger engine. The cabin section was reinforced to withstand loads of up to 1,000 pounds (the H-391B normally stressed to around 600 pounds), and the aft baggage area was strengthened to support the 451 pounds of photographic gear. The floor was modified to allow a 24-inch cutout for installation of optically true glass for camera use.

The cabin area aft of the cockpit seats was devoid of normal furnishings, save for a single seat for the photographer and bracing for equipment. An area approximately 6 feet long by 42 inches wide was reserved as a working area.

Although modifications on the H-392 were carried out to meet stress requirements of CAR Part 03, the aircraft operated under a restricted category CAA Pan 08 (industrial) certificate.

Due to its relatively potent supercharged engine, the Strato-Courier was capa-

H-392 Strato Courier. Bob Casebeer.

ble of operating under full load at over 30,000 feet. To underscore this capability, on October 18, 1957, Luis Struck (Mexican Servicio Aerotecnico) and Claudio Robles Ochoa (Mexican Civil Aeronautics Dept.) established a new international altitude record for aircraft weighing less than 3,740 pounds by taking the Strato-Courier up to 31,200 feet while flying over Mexico City.

As impressive as the numbers were for the Strato-Courier-an aircraft with a speed range from 25 to 200 MPH, capable of clearing a 50-foot obstacle within 300 feet, and able to fly for up to four hours-they were not enough to overcome the public resistance to the relatively stiff purchase price.

General Specifications

Model H-392 Strato-Courier

Powerplant: H-392 was powered by a Lycoming GSO-480-A1A6 supercharged six-cylinder, horizontally opposed, air cooled geared engine of 340 horsepower swinging a three-bladed Hartzell automatic constant speed 101" prop.

Price Range: $45,000

Length	30 ft.	Useful Load	1,980 lbs.
Span	39 ft.	Wing Loading	Unknown
Height	8 ft. 10 in.	Cruising Speed	182 MPH
Empty Weight	2,020 lbs.	Top Speed	194 MPH
GWT	4,000 lbs.	Minimum Speed (power on)	30 MPH

Minimum Speed	41 MPH	T.O. Distance to Clear 50' Obstacle	300 ft.
Initial Rate of Climb	2,000 FPM		
Service Ceiling	28,000 ft.	Landing Distance to Clear 50' Obstacle	225 ft.
Range	Unknown		

See Appendix 1 for further data specifications.

PROFILE : H-395

The model H-395 Super Courier was, for all practical purposes, the second major production version of the Helio line of C/STOL aircraft (preceding models H-391 and H-392 were one-time-only interim aircraft). Built between 1958 and 1964, a total of 138 H-395s were constructed (H-395 serials 502-639), making it the second most widely produced model of Helio built to date. The most widely built model of Helio was the H-295 (1200 and 1400 series), with 174 units built.

In brief, the H-395 Super Courier was essentially an H-391B airframe mated to a more potent 295-HP (instead of the H-391B's 260-HP) Lycoming GO-480-G1D6 engine. With the debut of this model, the Helio Aircraft Corporation touted its latest aircraft as offering: 1) greater horsepower, 2) even shorter takeoff, 3) improved ground handling, 4) faster cruise and 5) increased rate of climb.

A brief comparison of the performance statistics of the H-391B and the H-395 is as follows:

	H-391B	H-395
Horsepower	260	295
Takeoff*	542 ft.	475 ft.
Cruise	157 MPH	170 MPH
Rate of Climb	1,100 FPM	1,550 FPM

(*to clear a 50' tall obstacle)

H-395/L-28A Super Courier in Air Force paint scheme.

General Specifications

Model H-395 Super Courier

Powerplant: H-395 was powered by a Lycoming GO-480-G1D6 series six-cylinder, horizontally opposed, air cooled geared engine of 295 horsepower swinging a Hartzell 96" prop.

Price Range: $34,000

Dimensions & Performance:

Length	31 ft.	Top Speed	170 MPH
Span	39 ft.	Minimum Speed (power on)	28 MPH
Height	8 ft. 10 in.		
Wing Area	231 sq. ft.	Minimum Speed (power off)	41 MPH
Wing Chord	6 ft.		
Flap Area	38.1 sq. ft.	Initial Rate of Climb	1,350 FPM
Tailplane Span	13 ft. 4 in.	Initial Climb Angle	18 degrees
Dihedral	1 degree	Service Ceiling	22,500 ft.
Incidence	3 degrees	Range	600 Miles
Empty Weight	2,037 lbs.	T.O. Distance to Clear 50' Obstacle	475 ft.
GWT	3,000 lbs.		
Useful Load	1,100 lbs.	Landing Distance to Clear 50' Obstacle	355 ft.
Wing Loading	13 lbs./sq. ft.		
Cruising Speed	157 MPH		

See Appendix 1 for further data specifications.

PROFILE: H-395A

The model H-395A Courier was a very limited variant of the H-395. Built starting in 1959, a total of 9 H-395As were constructed (H-395A serials 049, 515, & 1002 through 1008), making it the sixth most widely produced model (tied with the model H-700) of Helio built to date.

In brief, the H-395A Courier is essentially a Model H-395 Super Courier airframe mated to a lower powered 260-HP Lycoming GO-435-C2B6 engine fueled with 80-octane aviation gas (instead of the H-395's 295-HP Lycoming GO-480-G1D6, fueled with 100/130 grade aviation fuel). The H-395A had a two-blade prop of 101-inch diameter instead of the Super Courier's 3-blade prop of a shorter 96-inch diameter.

The H-395A was envisioned as a lower cost alternative to its bigger brother, and with an engine designed to use a lower octane rated fuel, the H-395A offered advantages for use in remote areas.

A brief comparison of performance statistics between the H-395 and the H-395A is as follows:

	H-395	H-395A
Horsepower	295	260
Takeoff*	475 ft.	600 ft.
Cruise	170 MPH	160 MPH
Rate of Climb	1,350 FPM	1,250 FPM

(*to clear a 50' tall obstacle)

General Specifications

Model H-395A Super Courier

Powerplant: H-395A was powered by a Lycoming GO-435-C2B6 series six-cylinder, horizontally opposed, air cooled geared engine of 260 horsepower swinging a Hartzell 101" prop.

Price: $32,000

Dimensions & Performance:

Length	30 ft.	Top Speed	166 MPH
Span	39 ft.	Minimum Speed	30 MPH
Height	8 ft. 10 in.	(power on)	
Wing Area	231 sq. ft.	Minimum Speed	41 MPH
Wing Chord	6 ft.	(power off)	
Flap Area	38.1 sq. ft.	Initial Rate of Climb	1,250 FPM
Tailplane Span	13 ft. 4 in.	Initial Climb Angle	18 degrees
Dihedral	1 degree	Service Ceiling	20,050 ft.
Incidence	3 degrees	Range	850 miles
Empty Weight	1,965 lbs.	T.O. Dist. to Clear	600 ft.
GWT	3,000 lbs.	50' Obstacle	
Useful Load	1,035 lbs.	Landing Dist. to Clear	493 ft.
Wing Loading	unknown	50' Obstacle	
Cruising Speed	147 MPH		

See Appendix 1 for further data specifications.

PROFILE : H-250

The model H-250 Courier Mark II (also for a short time advertised as the H-250A Caballero) was developed concurrently with the H-295 Super Courier (the successor to the H-395) between 1963 and 1964. First flight occurred in May 1964, with FAA approval given in November 1964. A total of 41 H-250s were constructed (H-250 serials 2501 through 2541), making it the fourth most widely produced model of Helio built to date.

In brief, the H-250 Courier is essentially an economy model, featuring an H-395 Super Courier airframe which was lengthened by 6 inches and mated to the lower powered 250-HP Lycoming 0-540-A1A5 non-geared engine. It was originally directed

Helio H-250. Bob Casebeer.

at the "doctor & lawyer" market segment; however, like the H-395A, the H-250 lacked the stellar comparative performance of the H-295 and was overshadowed by its bigger brother. The H-250 had a shorter two-blade prop of 88-inch diameter instead of the Super Courier's 3-blade prop of 96-inch diameter. The H-250 model was the first Helio whose model designation reflected its engine's horsepower rating, with the subsequent H-295 reflecting a 295-HP rating.

The H-250 also offered an increased seating capacity (six seats) and an increased gross weight permitting an extra 500 lbs. of payload.

A brief comparison of performance statistics between the H-250 and the H-295 are as follows:

	H-250	H-295
Horsepower	250	295
Takeoff*	750 ft.	635 ft.
Cruise	133 MPH	150 MPH
Rate of Climb	830 FPM	1,150 FPM

(*to clear a 50' tall obstacle)

General Specifications

Model H-250 Courier Mk. II

Powerplant: H-250 was powered by a Lycoming 0-540-A1A5 series six-cylinder, horizontally opposed, air cooled non-geared engine of 250 horsepower swinging a Hartzell 88" prop.

Price: $35,900
Dimensions & Performance:

Length	31 ft. 6 in.	Top Speed	160 MPH
Span	39 ft.	Minimum Speed	31 MPH
Height	8 ft. 10 in.	(power on)	
Wing Area	231 sq. ft.	Minimum Speed	41 MPH
Wing Chord	6 ft.	(power off)	
Flap Area	38.1 sq. ft.	Initial Rate of Climb	830 FPM
Tailplane Span	13 ft. 4 in.	Initial Climb Angle	18 degrees
Dihedral	1 degree	Service Ceiling	15,200 ft.
Incidence	3 degrees	Range	644 Miles
Empty Weight	1,890 lbs.	Takeoff Dist. to	Approx. 750 ft.
GWT	3,400 lbs.	Clear 50' Obstacle	
Useful Load	1,510 lbs.	Landing Dist. to	520 ft.
Wing Loading	13 lbs./sq. ft.	Clear 50' Obstacle	
Cruising Speed	133 MPH		

See Appendix 1 for further data specifications.

PROFILE : H-295

The model H-295 Super Courier was developed as a replacement for the H-395. It was developed at about the same time as the lower-powered H-250 Courier Mark II. Construction was started in late 1964, first flight occurred on February 24, 1965, and FAA certification was received in April of the same year. The H-295 was built in two versions: first as the H-295-1200 Series (from 1965 until 1969), then as the H-295-1400 Series (from 1969 to end of production in 1974). A total of 174 H-295s were constructed (95 H-295-1200 Series, serials 1201 through 1295; 79 H-295-1400 Series, serials 1401 through 1479), making it the most widely produced model of Helio built to date.

The H-295-1200 Series Super Courier is essentially an H-395 Super Courier airframe and engine, but with a seating capacity of six (the H-395 seated five), and an increased gross weight permitting an extra 500 lbs. of payload.

The H-295-1400 Series, which debuted in 1969, was basically a cosmetic makeover of the aircraft in an attempt to make it more appealing to the civilian market. The appearance changes included a larger rectangular rear window replacing the unique "port-hole" window, newer interior decor (including new reclining seats), and an instrument panel redesigned to accommodate 3-inch gyro instruments and arranged in the now-standard "T" configuration. Perhaps the most noteworthy difference was the changeover to electrically operated flaps and trim instead of the old overhead hand cranks. The electric flap lever was located on the instrument panel, and the electric trim took the form of a toggle switch on the control wheel.

A brief comparison of performance statistics between the H-295 and the H-395 are as follows:

3. Geared for Success

Helio H-295 1400 Series with STC belly cargo pod.

	H-395	H-295
Horsepower	295	295
Takeoff*	475 ft.	635 ft.
Cruise	170 MPH	150 MPH
Rate of Climb	1,350 FPM	1,150 FPM

(*to clear a 50' tall obstacle)

General Specifications

Model H-295 Super Courier

Powerplant: H-295 series was powered by a Lycoming GO-480-G1D6 series six-cylinder, horizontally opposed, air cooled geared engine of 295 horsepower swinging a Hartzell 96" three-bladed prop.

Price Range: (1200 Series) $55,000–$65,000
(1400 Series) $60,000–$70,000

Dimensions & Performance:

Length	31 ft.	Dihedral	1 degree
Span	39 ft.	Incidence	3 degrees
Height	8 ft. 10 in.	Empty Weight	2,080 lbs.
Wing Area	231 sq. ft.	GWT	3,400 lbs.
Wing Chord	6 ft.	Useful Load	1,320 lbs.
Flap Area	38.1 sq. ft.	Wing Loading	13 lbs./sq. ft.
Tailplane Span	13 ft. 4 in.	Cruising Speed	150 MPH

Top Speed	167 MPH	Range	615 Miles
Minimum Speed (power on)	30 MPH	Takeoff Run	335 ft.
		Landing Run	270 ft.
Minimum Speed (power off)	41 MPH	Takeoff Dist. to Clear 50' Obstacle	Approx. 635 ft.
Initial Rate of Climb	1,150 FPM	Landing Dist. to Clear 50' Obstacle	515 ft.
Initial Climb Angle	18 degrees		
Service Ceiling	20,500 ft.		

See Appendix 1 for further data specifications.

Helio H-295 instrument panel.

Helio H-295 cabin doors detail.

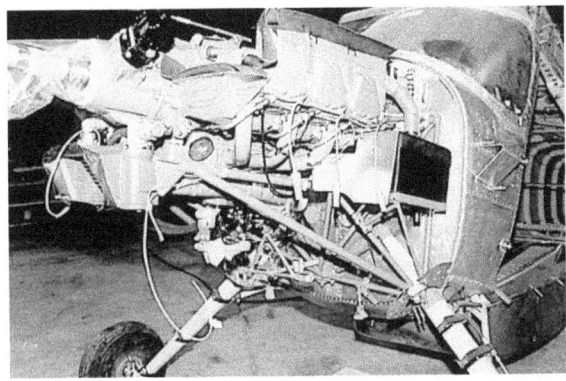

Left: Helio H-295 engine mount. *Above:* Helio H-295 Lycoming engine. National Air and Space Museum, Smithsonian Institute (SI NEG NO. 96-10522).

PROFILE : HT-295

The model HT-295 Tri-gear Super Courier was developed to satisfy a lingering market need for those who desired the superior ground handling/visibility characteristics afforded by the tricycle gear, although at the expense of foregoing some of the excellent rough-field capabilities of the original tail-dragger model. The specific impetus for the Tri-gear model, according to Bob Casebeer (former vice president of manufacturing operations), was a request from the Mexican government. Many conventionally geared Helios were used in Mexico to carry workers into remote areas to build schools. During a visit to perform overhaul work at the Helio plant in Pittsburg, Kansas, Mexican operators expressed an interest in fitting a tricycle-gear undercarriage to overcome the challenge of landing on mountainsides with quartering down-winds. It was noted that in this situation the tail wheel would get away from the pilot. Casebeer recommended that the Helio H-295 could be jacked up and fitted with a Cessna 185 main gear and a Cessna 310 nose gear. In this way, the aircraft would be high enough to clear the tail on takeoff while affording enough negative angle of attack when the aircraft was landed so as to hold to the ground and not bounce.

Certification was received in December 1973, with production commencing shortly thereafter. A total of 19 HT-295s were constructed (S/Ns 1701-1719), making it the fifth largest model produced by Helio. In addition to the official HT-295 production run, a number of military surplus (former U-10s) planes were converted to tricycle gear configuration (per STC SA138SW) for use by the Civil Air Patrol (approximately 19 more aircraft).

Performance was similar to the conventionally geared H-295. The modifications necessary to accommodate the tri-gear undercarriage were alterations to the engine mount in order to install the nose gear and reconfiguration of the tubular steel framework in the cabin to adjust to the loads imposed by the spring steel main gear.

A noteworthy sign of the times was the fact that, concurrent with the development of the HT-295, Helio Aircraft Company received a resoundingly favorable endorsement from public safety advocate Ralph Nader. Nader, who issued a "stinging indictment"[18] of the crash safety standards (or, more accurately, the lack of them)

Helio HT-295 Tri-gear Super Courier.

in most general aviation aircraft, also petitioned the FAA to suspend certification of any new general aviation aircraft until manufacturers incorporated additional crash safety measures. Two of "Nader's Raiders," James T. Bruce and John B. Draper (both Princeton engineering graduates), issued the paper "Crash Safety in General Aviation Aircraft," in which the Helio Courier is cited as being a good example of an airplane which shows that performance and crash safety design are completely compatible.[19]

	HT-295	H-295
Horsepower	295	295
Takeoff (50' Ob.)	635 ft.	635 ft.
Cruise	150 MPH	150 MPH
Rate of Climb	1,150 FPM	1,150 FPM

General Specifications

Model HT-295 Tri-gear Super Courier

Powerplant: HT-295 series was powered by a Lycoming GO-480-G1D6 series six-cylinder, horizontally opposed, air cooled geared engine of 295 horsepower swinging a Hartzell 96" three-bladed prop.

Price Range: $75,000

Dimensions & Performance:

Length	31 ft.	Wing Chord	6 ft.
Span	39 ft.	Flap Area	38.1 sq. ft.
Height	14 ft. 10 in.	Tailplane Span	13 ft. 4 in.
Wing Area	231 sq. ft.	Dihedral	1 degree

Incidence	3 degrees	Initial Rate of Climb	1,150 FPM
Empty Weight	2,010 lbs.	Initial Climb Angle	18 degrees
GWT	3,400 lbs.	Service Ceiling	20,500 ft.
Useful Load	1,390 lbs.	Range	615 Miles
Wing Loading	13 lbs./sq. ft.	Takeoff Run	335 ft.
Cruising Speed	150 MPH	Landing Run	270 ft.
Top Speed	167 MPH	Takeoff Dist. to Clear 50' Obstacle	Approx. 635 ft.
Minimum Speed (power on)	30 MPH	Landing Dist. to Clear 50' Obstacle	515 ft.
Minimum Speed (power off)	41 MPH		

See Appendix 1 for further data specifications.

4. Litterbugs and Black Ops
Military Versions
of the Helio Courier

Models YL-24, L-28A, U-10A, U-10B, U-10D and U-5A

The Helio Courier was the first STOL aircraft used by the CIA when they bought twelve to fifteen of them for use in Laos in 1957, and the plane immediately became the Agency's favorite workhorse. On one hand, it was a perfectly conventional small airplane that could fly 185 MPH and yet land on an unprepared strip comfortably in 120 feet. It was an aeronautical breakthrough and could fly unusually slowly if needed and land on the roughest of strips. All airstrips in Laos were classified as "Helio" or "Others." The plane could land on any strip that did not have boulders on it and had an enormous range of landing possibilities. Landing is a very fixed procedure for most aircraft, but the Helio Courier could land while turning, which meant it could use curved or "boomerang" shaped strips on the top of mountain ridges. — Christopher Robbins, *Air America*

Some of the U-10A planes are attached to the John F. Kennedy Center for Military Assistance. These are painted in civilian colors because they are used in clandestine missions.... The Helio U-10 is the best and safest plane I've ever flown. — Jay Sparks, civilian attaché, Fort Bragg, N.C.

If the Helio Courier was destined to become an imaginative, yet somewhat obscure, sensation in the civilian marketplace, its use by the military and the CIA may give it a more visible and enduring place in history.

As it became increasingly apparent that the Helio was too pricey an aircraft for widespread civilian marketing, its C/STOL (Controlled/Short TakeOff & Landing) features, plus its ability to withstand abuse and afford an added margin of safety, would make it an attractive candidate for military and para-military operations.

Indeed, as early as 1952, the Helio Courier was procured for military (Army) evaluations under the designation YL-24. The evaluation involved a single aircraft (52-2540), which was an evolution of the Helioplane-Four and was re-designated the model H-391. While the Army was impressed with the existing capabilities and potential of the YL-24, the budget for fixed-wing aircraft at the time was tight. Unfortunately for the Helio, this was a time when the trend was to allot higher budgets for

Helio YL-24.

the emerging class of rotary-wing aircraft. However, with its superior speed and potential payload, the YL-24 served notice that a unique alternative to the helicopter was available.

The military would continue to monitor the development of the Helio Courier for several years. In October 1956, it was announced that the Army would award the University of Wichita (Kansas) a $43,000 contract (Contract Number DA 44-177-TC-369) to evaluate the Helio Courier's STOL performance. The contract was awarded at a time when the Army was revising its long standing procedure of using the United States Air Force and Navy testing facilities/middlemen for evaluating aircraft and instead having reputable universities perform the evaluations for "off-the-shelf" aircraft. Effective October 1, 1956, Army research and development was transferred to the Office of Transportation Research and Development Command (TRADCOM), located at Fort Eustis, Virginia.

Evaluation of the Helio Courier by the University of Wichita's Department of Engineering Research was documented in a series of progress reports beginning in June 1956 and culminating in a 121-page final report dated February 1957. Titled *Evaluation of the Performance, Stability and Control of the Helio Courier Airplane*, by A. J. Craig, the report (impossible to duplicate in its entirety here) is well worth reading due to its wealth of exacting data.

A single Helio Courier model H-391B (N4203B) was leased from Helio's Pittsburg, Kansas, facility in August 1956 for the duration of testing. Hangar space was located at the former Seibel Helicopter facility at the old Ken Mar Air Park in Wichita, Kansas.

The flight tests were performed in accordance with AGARD (Advisory Group for Aerospace Research & Development) flight test manuals volumes I and II. A mirror-image photo-panel camera was installed to record all instrumentation readings during critical periods of testing. A Fairchild Flight Analyzer camera was utilized on the ground to record flight paths as a function of time. An electronic coupling between the on-board photo-panel camera and the Fairchild Flight Analyzer camera (by way of a model airplane transmitter/receiver) allowed a systematic correlation of data. The normal assortment of flight test equipment-booms, force dynamometers, gauges, meters and air-flow tuft cameras-was installed, while some consultation and advice was provided by research departments of the Cessna Aircraft Company and Rawdon Aircraft Company of Wichita.

Conclusions of the evaluation, as presented in the final report, were summarized in the following nine points[1]:

1. Assuming the criterion of 500-ft. total distance to a 50-ft. barrier for takeoff and landing, the test aircraft did not meet the STOL requirements.
2. In order to achieve the performance for which it was designed, the aircraft must utilize power in landing maneuvers. Power-off, its performance is not superior to aircraft of comparable wing loadings, but which do not possess full span slats or slotted flaps over a major portion of the span.
3. Steady-state helix angle values were found to be approximately 0.20, varying only from 0.21 to 0.19 for V = 50 MPH to V = 100 MPH. This is about twice the required roll performance for fighter-type aircraft.
4. Time delays of 0.25 to 0.5 seconds in roll acceleration in approach maneuvers resulted in the pilot stating that the aircraft possessed insufficient lateral control.
5. Slats produced an increment in CLmax of only 0.07 at a flap deflection of 40 degrees. Boundary layer surveys reveal that energy was not returned to lower layers of flow with slat extension, which accounts for the low increment in CLmax.
6. Cockpit forward visibility is inadequate in the approach configuration.
7. The forward location of the main gear, the high angle of attack in ground attitude, and the non-steerable tailwheel make taxiing in crosswinds particularly difficult.
8. At the high CL values which may be obtained only in a power-on approach, the net drag is insufficient to produce steep approach angles; consequently, the air distance constitutes the major portion of the total distance in barrier landings.
9. That portion of the takeoff flight path from the break-ground point to the point where steady-state climb is reached (commonly called the transition period) occupies an excessive portion of the air distance.

At first glance, the conclusions of the University of Wichita report might suggest that the Helio's future as an STOL machine worthy of military consideration was questionable at best. However, with the passage of time (plus the increased horsepower of the first Helio to be bought in significant numbers, the model 395) the Helio Courier would evolve to a point where its STOL capabilities would be considered outstanding. While at the time the report might have been a source of concern at Helio headquarters, its findings not only provided suggestions for improvement but also served to underscore some of the unique flight procedures required to extract the utmost performance from the Helio.

In reviewing the failure during evaluation to meet the STOL standard of being able to takeoff and land within 500 ft. over a 50-ft. barrier, its should be noted that the aircraft's best takeoff distance was 563 feet (with tail raised), while its best landing distance (with power) was 524 feet. The fact that the Helio was, and still is, a machine that places very high demands on even high-time in-type pilots to extract the utmost performance could explain the STOL requirement failure in this case. Indeed, the report noted that "design theoretical performance is not that which may be achieved in practice. If the pilot is required to monitor all parameters, i.e., attitude about all three axes, air-speed, flight path, and to sense deviations and make corrections; he will not utilize all the capabilities of the vehicle."[2]

Aside from the perceived peculiarities concerning lateral control (excessive roll velocity at high speeds/excessive time-lag in approach configuration), marginally adequate pitch attitude control and difficult forward visibility, the Helio was praised for its excellent directional stability.

4. Litterbugs and Black Ops

Interestingly, many of the observations contained in the report describe the techniques best used to fly the Helio. Moreover, although the test model (H-391B) had a 260-HP engine, the Helio Couriers that eventually were procured in large numbers by the Air Force and Army (models H-395 and H-295) all used the higher rated 295-HP engines to improve upon and meet the STOL takeoff and landing standard.

As stated in the report, and practiced in the field, the best STOL landings required the Helio to perform a high powered approach at a nearly constant pitch attitude with no flare, maintaining a 3-point attitude until it was planted with brakes locked.

For STOL takeoffs, while raising the tail lengthens the ground run, it reduces the total distance to a 50-ft. barrier (as documented in the report) by 75 ft. over not raising the tail.

Finally, the report notes that "An outstanding feature of the Courier is its ability to operate at low velocities without dangerous loss of control. The aircraft cannot be stalled; consequently skidding turns and abrupt pitch changes may be accomplished at Vmin without resulting in an uncontrollable loss in altitude."[3]

Following the University of Wichita evaluation, the Army awaited further refinements to the Helio Courier. With the development of the new H-395 in 1958, the Helio Aircraft Company finally had a contender to decisively meet the military's criteria for a specialized STOL aircraft. In what was to become one of the legendary demonstrations of the new Helio's capabilities, company officials showcased the aircraft's superior STOL qualities by landing a Helio Courier (N4160D) on the Pentagon's helicopter pad. Representatives of various military branches as well as other government agencies were able to witness first-hand this remarkable aircraft.

As the Army continued to deliberate on the acquisition of the latest version of the Helio Courier, the United States Air Force decided to move forward with a more in-depth program geared towards eventual mass orders.

Helio H-395A (N4160D) at the Pentagon with Helio company officials.

In 1958, the Air Force took delivery of three H-395s (aircraft serials 58-7026, 58-7027 & 58-7028) which were designated as military (liaison) models L-28A-HE and served as pre-production evaluation aircraft. At this time, the L-28A-HE's primary operational role was envisioned to be accessing and supplying isolated missile sites.

The L-28A-HEs received high marks by the Air Force, and follow-on orders were placed to expand the military fleet.

A news release in 1962 heralded the order for more L-28A-HEs, which by this time were re-designated as the military model U-10A (6 more U-10As were ordered, serials 62-3603 through 3608). The official Air Force press release states: "The L-28 STOL aircraft is one of the most versatile in the Air Force inventory. It combines unusual short takeoff and landing performance with rugged construction and operational dependability. In addition to its short field capability, the L-28 can cruise at relatively high speeds with good fuel economy. Safety is an outstanding feature of this aircraft. Since it is possible to land the L-28 in extremely small spaces, the number of suitable forced landing fields is greatly increased. This, coupled with a power-off rate of descent less than that of a parachute, also contributes to crew safety. With the acceptance of the L-28A-HE by the Air Force, the Army followed suit with its own block of Helio orders."[4]

Helio L-28A.

With orders from the Air Force for the U-10As in hand, it was not long before the Army requested its own fleet of U-10As (20 U-10As, serials 63-13166 through 13185). Following an informal evaluation in July 1962 of the Cessna 185 and the Helio H-395, the United States Army Aviation Board (Fort Rucker, Alabama) announced that "The Helio L-28A could be used as a utility airplane for special missions where takeoff and landing performance demand primary consideration and payload, range and endurance are secondary considerations."[5]

In the field, the Army U-10As fulfilled the role mentioned above. A release from the U.S. Army Special Warfare Center stated:

> The U-10 Helio Courier was purchased specifically for Special Missions, both counterinsurgency and unconventional warfare.... We do not pretend that the U-10 may compete with the helicopter in its appointed field. Obviously, when a need exists to hover motionless in mid-air, or to ascend or descend vertically, the helicopter is required. On the other hand, there is often a need for endurance, speed and range not attainable with the helicopter. Another point often overlooked is that, horsepower for horsepower, the airplane has a greater load-carrying capability than the helicopter.

Also, very importantly, the U-10 is more rugged and much more easy to maintain; consequently, it is more economical. These considerations are of paramount importance on Special Forces missions in regions remote from military logistical support systems.

Another factor considered worthy of mention is that the U-10, as configured by the United States Army, is sufficiently instrumented, carries sufficient fuel, and is a good stable platform for flights during inclement weather conditions.

Combination of the characteristics of this aircraft has provided an exceptional short radius of turn, a feature which has practical application to both civic and military actions of Special Warfare. Incredible as it may sound to pilots taught never to make steep climbing turns at low speed and low altitude, the pilot of the U-10 can pull the stick back as far as it will come immediately after the wheels leave the ground, apply as steep a bank as he desires, and spiral upward like a hawk riding a thermal.

The U-10 has been proven as a valued asset in worldwide Special Forces missions. By now introducing the aircraft into Aviation Companies of Special Forces Groups together with helicopters and CV-2 Caribou, the Group Commander has acquired special and essential tools organic to his organization and for his special purposes. He has gained a mobility advantage and a flexibility which has been desperately needed for a long time.[6]

Follow-on orders were placed for improved versions of the U-10 aircraft with the differences noted below:

U-10A— Military version of the civilian model H-395 Super Courier. Powered by a 260-HP Lycoming GO-435-C2B6 engine. Seating for five.

U-10B— Military version of the civilian model H-295 Super Courier. Powered by a 295-HP Lycoming GO-480-G1D6 engine. Seating for six; 120-gallon long range fuel capacity and paratroop doors.

U-10C—*Never Produced.* Was noted to have been a version of the U-10B with a 360-HP IGSO-540-B1A engine.

U-10D— Based on U-10B, except AUW increased to 3,600 pounds.

Totals of military models, used by Air Force, Army and Air National Guard are listed in the chart on page 92.

In order to fulfill the special requirements of the Army and Air Force, a series of equipment options were drafted for the U-10s. The following items were installed as noted in certain serial blocks of aircraft:

Para-Drop Doors— A 2-piece special door that was removable as an upper and a lower section, and kept in the aircraft. This door facilitated loading and unloading of cargo on the ground and in the air. (Available on U-10A, B & D)

Litter— A Stokes-type litter for transporting wounded personnel could be installed when aft seats were removed. (Available on U-10A).

Airborne Loudspeaker— Installed in the para-drop doors of some U-10Bs was a loudspeaker that allowed the broadcast of recorded or live messages through a microphone to persons on the ground. The system included the following components:
- Transistorized portable tape recorder
- B 24 1,000-watt loudspeaker-four audio amplifiers
- Microphone

U-10 Aircraft Deliveries

U-10A (29 Aircraft Total)

Serials 58-7026 thru 7028 (Formerly L-28A-HE)	Air Force	3 Aircraft
Serials 62-3603 thru 3608	Air Force	6 Aircraft
Serials 63-13166 thru 13185	Army	20 Aircraft

U-10B (58 Aircraft Total)

Serials 62-5907 thru 5920	Air Force	14 Aircraft
Serials 63-8091 thru 8098	Air Force	8 Aircraft
Serials 63-8099 thru 8110	Air Force	12 Aircraft
Serials 63-13090 thru 13113	Air National Guard	24 Aircraft

U-10D (44 Aircraft Total)

Serials 66-14332 thru 14345	Air Force	14 Aircraft
Serials 66-14346 thru 14369	Air Force	24 Aircraft
Serials 66-14370 thru 14375	Air Force	6 Aircraft

Total military U-10 variants officially delivered from the Helio factory: **131 Aircraft***

* Note: Grand total does not include an undetermined number of U-10s alleged to have been built without authorization.

Helio U-10 aircraft deliveries.

Typically, the standard procedure for maximum broadcast effect was to fly a ¾-mile-radius turn between 3,000 and 5,000 ft. utilizing an un-coordinated turn in order to properly aim the speaker at the on-ground target point. Installation of the airborne loudspeaker was restricted to certain serials of U-10Bs.

Camera— Vertical and oblique cameras could be installed in a modified para-drop door. The oblique camera could afford 60 degrees of coverage. A sight mount for the oblique camera was provided to the pilot, while a camera control box could be operated by either the pilot or another person on board acting as camera operator. Camera installation was restricted to certain serials of U-10Ds.

Fuselage Auxiliary Fuel Tank— A 25-gallon fuel bladder was available for use in certain U-10Bs. It was suspended aft of the crew compartment.

Dual Brakes— A dual braking system was made available for certain serials of U-10A & U-10B aircraft.

Armament— All U-10A, B & D models could be modified to mount four MA-4A/B drop shackle bomb racks (2 per wing at external stores stations) to carry MA-2A/A tube launchers for loading with 2.75" air-to-air/air-to-ground folding fin aircraft rockets (FFAR). Typical use was for white phosphorous (WP) target marking rockets. An ordnance delivery button was located on the pilot's control wheel, while an armament control panel was located on the top right of the instrument panel. The armament control panel consisted of a master arm switch, circuit breaker,

Inspection of loudspeaker system on Helio U-10.

four drop switches and four fire select switches. Additionally, an emergency salvo button was located on the instrument panel.

Because of the era in which the U-10 was utilized by the Air Force and Army, it's not surprising that the Vietnam War and related conflicts in Southeast Asia were its primary area of use. An interesting and little-known exception was the use of Helio U-10s by the U.S. Army to police large tracts of territory in Alaska to enforce an anti-drug-smuggling campaign. The Helios were used to counter the flow of drugs (most notably heroin) coming from the Soviet Union and Red China via the 50-mile-wide Bering Strait.

Introduced into the Southeast Asia conflict late in December 1962, the Helio was one of the first of a series of aircraft to partake in a covert program code-named "Farmgate." The program involved reinforcing a detachment of United States Air Force air commandos (1st Air Commando Squadron) that provided support for Republic of Vietnam ground units, escort of helicopters, reconnaissance, training, supply duties for remote U.S. Special Forces outposts, and psychological warfare.

Other duties included escort assistance to the "Mule Train" program (Tactical Transport) and the "Ranch Hand" (defoliation) campaign. Although the USAF aircraft inventory at this early stage consisted primarily of C-123s, T-28Bs, and B-26Bs, the U-10s mainly operated out of support sections along with C-47s.

Top: U-10D in bright polished livery, notable for its long-range capability. Bob Casebeer. *Bottom:* Helio U-10A during spring 1964, with wing and fuselage bands denoting its participation in the Operation Desert Strike war games. Dave Menard Collection (photograph by W. T. Smith).

As the conflict extended to include even larger expanses of territory, the U-10s were later employed (1964 and onwards) to re-supply Lima Sites in Laos. The Lima Sites were a primitive, temporary network of airstrips carved out of the countryside in Laos in which covert operations and helicopter rescue staging bases were located. TACAN (Tactical Air Navigation) long-range navigational facilities were also located at these sites. Helios were a vital part of not only protecting U.S. physical assets in Laos, but also coordinating with, and lending support to, the Royal Laotian Army as well as the Meo tribesmen trained by the CIA.

As used in its psychological warfare role, the U-10 gained the nickname the

4. Litterbugs and Black Ops

"Litterbug." Propaganda leaflets could be discharged through a chute in the aft right-hand door.

A news release item from the Directorate of Information, Headquarters Seventh Air Force, Tan Son Nhut Air Base, Republic of Vietnam, describes a typical "Litterbug" PSYWAR operation:

> Bien Hoa (7AF)-Coming in at 3,000 feet in his U-10 Courier, the Air Force pilot spots his target in the Mekong Delta region of Vietnam and readies his ammunition: a tape recording featuring "The Yellow Rose of Texas."
>
> This is the way Major Don W. Musgrove, 36, Brownwood, Texas, begins a psychological warfare mission to rally the Viet Cong to the side of the South Vietnamese government.
>
> Musgrove is a member of Flight B, 5th Air Commando Squadron at Bien Hoa Air Base. Flying C-47 Skytrains and U-10s, the 5th ACS is exclusively devoted to psychological warfare. Last year the 5th ACS, and its sister squadron the 9th ACS, were credited with convincing more than 24,000 Viet Cong to return to the side of the South Vietnamese government.
>
> "Of course, 'The Yellow Rose of Texas' is just a personal touch I add to my flights," commented Musgrove."Most of the tapes are recorded in Vietnamese and urge the VC to rally. We also drop 'Chieu Hoi,' or safe conduct passes on the enemy to present to friendly forces when they defect."
>
> Musgrove has flown more than 600 combat missions in his unarmed U-10 since his arrival at Bien Hoa.
>
> "I never know what my mission will be over," said Musgrove, "until I land at one of the Army or Australian camps near here. Their intelligence and rallying Chieu Hoi's tell them where the enemy is. After that it's up to me. I get the necessary tapes and leaflets and head for the target. I guess one might call me a professional litterbug," he added.[7]

Helio U-10B and C-47 over South-East Asia. United States Air Force Museum, Wright-Patterson AFB.

Top: Helio U-10B in typical South-East Asia camouflage paint scheme. United States Air Force, Wright-Patterson AFB. *Bottom:* Helio U-10B "Litterbug" (also known to troops as the "BS Bomber") distributing leaflets over South-East Asia. United States Air Force Museum, Wright-Patterson AFB.

If the propaganda leaflets that rained down upon the locals were of questionable long-term value, the musical strains of "The Yellow Rose of Texas" might at least have added a certain entertainment value to what was, upon reflection, a very controversial venture in foreign policy.

Use of the U-10s for psychological warfare was so extensive that records were being set on a routine basis. An October 17, 1966, article in *Aviation Week & Space Technology* credits the 5th Air Commando Squadron's Detachment 1 with setting several records when the unit dropped its 100-millionth leaflet and broadcast 1,000 hours of tape recordings in 3,000 flight hours (using U-10Bs).

In addition to its use abroad by the United States Air Force and Army, U-10s were stationed in the continental United States with several Air National Guard units. It was found that the U-10 was well suited to supplement the existing C-119s and HU-

Safe conduct pass typical of leaflets distributed from Helio Courier U-10s. United States Air Force Museum, Wright-Patterson AFB.

16s for Air Commando/Special Operations squadrons. Beginning in 1963, the U-10 was formally added to the 129th CA ANG (California) operating from 1963 to 1966 and then from 1967 to 1975; 130th WV ANG (West Virginia) operating from 1964 to 1974; 135th MD ANG (Maryland) operating from 1963 to 1965 and then from 1967 to 1971; and 143 RI ANG (Rhode Island) operating from 1963 to 1965 and then from 1967 to 1975. As the intensity of the South East Asian conflict increased, a significant number of Air National Guard U-10s were transferred to active duty in Vietnam for a few years. During this interim period, the Air National Guard units made use of U-6A DeHavilland Beaver light transport aircraft. Eventually, these U-10s were returned to their stateside Air National Guard units to continue service.

With Helio production facilities going full bore to meet military production

Helio U-10B float plane. United States Air Force Museum, Wright-Patterson AFB.

schedules, and with the military branches in 1965 having to press into active service all stateside reserve U-10s, the Helio Aircraft Corporation was perhaps at its zenith as a company facing pent-up demand for its product. An advertisement appearing during those heady days-in the March 12, 1962, issue of *Aviation Week and Space Technology*-fairly exulted in the company's rosy predicament of not being able to build them fast enough: Helio offered premium prices to buy back older models to refurbish, overhaul, and sell to a public that at the moment had to take a back seat to government orders. While the company basked in the glory of firm sales, the collective opinion at Helio's headquarters may have been that they had finally secured the Helio Courier's STOL market in sales to the military. But it would not be very long before forces not fully discerned at the time would make this situation disintegrate into a relative nightmare that would dog the company practically into extinction.

Aside from the relatively mundane "official" duties (utility/liaison) associated with the U.S. Air Force and Army U-10s, any discussion of this aircraft inevitably leads to its alleged use by the CIA and its air proprietaries for covert/"Black Operations." Without a doubt, it was the combination of this clandestine use of the Helio Courier and the aircraft's unique flight characteristics that has been responsible for creating most of the myths and legends surrounding the Helio.

As might be expected, use of the Helio Courier by the CIA appears to have been accomplished by way of discreet and unassuming channels. Some aircraft were suspected of having been commandeered from the U.S. military services, while many others were obtained through the agency's air proprietary companies. These "front" companies seem to have been either wholly owned or partially funded by the CIA, or were simply relied upon to provide "occasional favors" to the agency.

The "front companies" further functioned either in an "operating company" mode (in which case the company pursued the CIA's business under the guise of a private company) or as a "non-operating company" (in which case the company was

"Wanted — Used Helios" advertisement appearing in early 1962 aviation trade journals.

on standby under-cover status to prepare to do business). Reportedly, it was the "non-operating companies" that were relied upon to purchase Helio Couriers for use by the CIA. In his definitive history of the CIA's air arm, *Air America*, Christopher Robbins lists "Air Ventures, Atlantic General Enterprises, Inc., Aviation Investors, Inc., Consultair Associates, and King-Hurley Research Group"[8] as among the few companies that operated as "non-operating" CIA proprietary companies that were set up specifically to purchase Helio Couriers for use by the CIA.

Allegedly, the Helio Couriers that were purchased by these front companies eventually found their way to the CIA's major worldwide air operations. Most notably, it was the Pacific Corporation (incorporated in Delaware) that served as a holding company for its more famous Far Eastern subordinate CIA airlines: Air America, Inc., Air Asia Company, Ltd., and Civil Air Transport, Ltd. Of these companies, it was Air America (the largest airline in the world at that time) that is the one clandestine CIA airline that is most associated with the Helio, while other CIA airlines, such as Southern Air Transport (in the Caribbean), are less renowned.

The Helio Courier would prove ideal for the para-military covert missions envisioned by the CIA. Small, rugged, and with deceptive performance in a relatively unassuming package, the Helio/U-10 could be used for close-in air support for many types of guerrilla operations that involved accessing the most remote and primitive base camps imaginable, while at the same time dealing with the extreme threats of hostile enemy forces and perilous weather conditions.

Any use of the Helio Courier by the CIA was by no means limited to one particular theater of operation. Because of its unique capabilities, the Helio Courier seemed to lend itself to many missions worldwide where STOL/speed and range requirements were of prime importance. One such mission was related by the oft-quoted Fletcher Prouty (U.S.A.F), describing how the CIA "used a special Helio Courier L-28 STOL aircraft to land on a small road near Havana to infiltrate a team trained to attempt to assassinate Fidel Castro. We went to great lengths to support this operation, and the plane returned safely. The pilot informed us that he had left the assassin team exactly as planned. Later we learned that Castro's forces had rounded up the team."[9]

Perhaps the epicenter of activity involving the CIA Helio Courier/U-10s was the rugged mountainous jungle territory of Laos. Robbins, in his study of the CIA's air arm, states that "the plane immediately became the Agency's favorite workhorse.... [It] could fly unusually slowly if needed and land on the roughest of strips. All airstrips in Laos were classified as "Helio" or "Others.""[10]

It was during the secret war in Laos that Air America seemed to expand its aircraft inventory to very large proportions. Aside from the usual complement of agency aircraft such as DeHavilland Beavers, Otters, Caribou, C-46, DC-3/C-47, Beech/Volpar 18s, L-19s and an assortment of helicopters, the Helio Courier was highly instrumental in the success of the CIA's operations in areas where physical conditions were extremely difficult. A mission that could be accomplished by Helio Courier roughly within 20–30 minutes might have taken 8 days on foot.

On record, the CIA officially started operations in Laos during 1959. The key goal was to establish a regional intelligence-gathering network against the communist Pathet Lao by way of the allied help of the local Meo tribesmen. During the

Southeast Asia conflict, Laos was (on paper at least) a neutral state, having been ruled since the Geneva Agreement of 1954 by a coalition government headed by Premier Prince Souvanna Phouma and his communist counterpart Prince Souphanouvong.

Initial operations focused primarily in the Plain of Jars, with much CIA support based out of Long Tieng and Vientiane. However, as the Meo mercenaries were indigenous to the mountains and shunned the lowlands because of the ever-present threats of local flooding and mosquitoes, air operations tended to favor an aircraft capable of handling the vagaries of mountain flying and short strips. The Helio Courier with its STOL prowess could handle these easily. The fact that a portion of the Ho Chi Minh Trail meandered through Laos increased the value of control of the territory for both sides.

Flight operations in Laos were considered extremely hazardous duty: aircraft such as the Helio Courier were basically unarmed, had to make slow approaches to tight landing strips with hardly any perimeter guarding, and once there had to make do with extremely poor facilities in the field. Compounding the odds was the high number of missions flown per day; 12-hour days (8–10 hours in-flight) with multiple takeoffs and landings were typical.

Perhaps the deadliest factor that a pilot had to contend with was the weather. With very few exceptions, the physical geography and its attendant atmospheric conditions (some natural, and others induced by the locals) would test the wits of the most seasoned Helio pilot. Five months of the rain-laden monsoon season, followed by seven months of scorching summer, played havoc with high-turn-around flight schedules. Flights among the mountain ridges had their own natural challenges: (a euphemism for flying into a mountainside); "rock-filled clouds"; blind canyons that forced pilots to spiral upward like a hawk; quirky air currents/gusts/drafts and thermals; and fog and dust clouds rising from the jungle. In addition to these natural challenges, there was the occasional man-made threat of huge clouds of smoke resulting from the "slash and burn" agricultural practices of the local Meo tribesmen as they tended to their primary cash crop: poppies. On top of all this, there was the hazard of being shot at.

Adding to this list of challenges was the fact that much of the territory was defined either poorly or not at all on existing maps, topped off with the reality that ground control was frequently either inefficient or lacking altogether. Landing strips could prove perilous, as they were at times water-logged and/or strewn with hidden obstacles, making access a questionable venture. Routine support missions that involved ammunition re-supply ("hard rice"), food ("soft rice"), outpost relief (insertions/medical retrievals), fuel and other duties could easily be compromised by uncertain ground conditions.

As described in Robbins' work, anxious allies on the ground could sometimes add to an already difficult task by making ground conditions even more challenging: "Villagers eager to have Air America land with supplies under any conditions complicate things further. One pilot observed the windsock at a village strip hanging straight down, but when he landed found the wind dangerously strong. 'We know plane not land when sock flies,' an amiable native explained, 'so we put rocks in sock.'"[11]

Special "black" Helio Courier (actually very dark blue). Dave Menard/Paul E. Paulsen Collection.

In addition to re-supply and other routine support duties, the Helio Courier was used in an extensive campaign to facilitate an on-going recruitment program among the local villages. This program was intended to bolster the agency's already existing secret army in Laos. CIA agents, along with Meo officers, flew in a combination of helicopters and Helio Couriers from mountain to mountain in a "leapfrog" style to persuade potential recruits to join their effort in exchange for money, guns, clothing, medicine and food. In return, the recruits were relied upon for information, demolition of enemy bridges and supply dumps, and other activities disruptive to the Pathet Lao involving sniper work and harassment. Robbins states that "hundreds of trained Meo guerrillas were flown by Air America helicopters and Helio Couriers in a lightning advance from mountaintop to mountaintop. As soon as a village was captured and the Pathet Lao defenders eliminated, its inhabitants were put to work building a landing strip, further expanding Air America's communications."[12]

In an added attempt to break down the Pathet Lao infrastructure, the agency also employed the Helio Courier in its "litterbug" role to allegedly air-drop millions of dollars of forged Pathet Lao money in an attempt to wreck their economy.

Perhaps the one issue that remains most controversial is the alleged use of the Helio Courier by the CIA and its operatives to aid the Meo tribesmen in the transport of opium, the end product of the Meos' poppy plants.

In keeping with Air America's unofficial motto, "Anything, Anywhere, Anytime" (You Call, We Haul), there remain persistent rumors that the agency may have turned a "blind eye" to local economics. It was legal in Laos to grow, sell, smoke and transport opium. Indeed, the Meo operated in an area that was known as the "Golden Triangle" (roughly situated between the Shan hills of northeast Burma, the mountain ridges of northern Thailand, and the Meo highlands of northern Laos), famed as the world's largest source of opium, morphine and heroin. Allegations have been made that occasional shipments of these products were carried to market by way of CIA aircraft, with connections being made with Mafia/underworld distributors in order to help bankroll the agency's operations in Laos. Although, as even Christopher Robbins in his lengthy history of the agency's air operations noted, there was no hard evidence to support the argument, it has been accepted as plausible. One of the pilots with whom Robbins discussed this probability summed up the general feeling at the time with: "A box is a box, and if it contains grenades, baby food, or black, gooey opium, that was the customer's business ... AA (Air America) was pragmatic. They flew killers, but they flew doctors too...."[13]

The CIA recognized the Meo not only as a source for military information and manpower, but also as what they had historically been: opium farmers. It could naturally be assumed that the agency might have felt it logical to capitalize on this situation. With references being made to Air America as "Air Opium" by correspondents at the time, it can be considered a plausible scenario during a difficult time.

During much of the agency's operations, the Helio Couriers were operated as "sanitized" aircraft, with a variety of guises as far as registration and tail-codes were concerned. Some sported foreign registration, as well as non-attributable markings (for example, the markings on the photo of the Helio Courier with the registration sourced to a target drone aircraft). The idea was to disguise the aircraft used in covert operations, so that the agency could plausibly deny that it was one of theirs. Sometimes several aircraft might be sent up at the same time, with identical registration, to cover their involvement. Since some of the missions in which the Helio Courier was used were highly sensitive, involving the insertion and/or retrieval of agents into North Vietnam, Laos, Cambodia and even China, it was imperative that a reasonable measure of "plausible deniability" should exist.

As an extreme measure to ensure its ability to maintain "plausible deniability," the CIA was alleged to have manufactured (without the consent of the Helio Aircraft Company), its own copies of the Helio Courier. There is little doubt that the agency had the capacity to assemble its own aircraft at its facilities at Udorn, and at its giant Air Asia overhaul depot at Tainan on Formosa. An aircraft without any identification/serial numbers on airframe, engine and instruments was a very appealing idea if the owner wished to avoid any trace of accountability. The ultimate goal was to create an aircraft for covert mission work that, on paper at least, never existed. In this way, even the stateside manufacturer-in this case, Helio Aircraft Company- would certify that the aircraft in question had never been manufactured by them. Because of the lack of serial numbers on the knock-off aircraft, special crews were to have been assembled to keep track of, and maintain, the aircraft.

While it is difficult to determine the exact number, if any, of unauthorized "knock-off" Helio Couriers alleged to have been built by the CIA, it has been surmised that about thirty aircraft may have been constructed. A former officer at Helio Aircraft stated that the company began to become concerned when the agency's "front companies" started to order increasingly large numbers of "hard-to-manufacture" parts (wing spare carry-through and main landing gear structures) as spares, much more than anyone could possibly go through during "normal rates of attrition." It

Helio U-5A Twin Courier — One of the rarest Helios, as used in overseas covert actions. Dave Menard/Steve Miller Collection.

was suspected that the agency might somehow be using these hard-to-manufacture parts to construct new or rebuilt Helio Couriers, on which the agency performed the assembly and sheet metal work on its own.

The agency also was allegedly interested in obtaining "worldwide selling operations" for the Helio Aircraft Company in 1962 as another form of extending its covert influence. It was further alleged that CIA chief George Doole warned Helio Aircraft Company officials that if it did not cooperate, "it would never sell another plane in Asia."[14]

Ultimately, a 100-million-dollar lawsuit was filed against the CIA on behalf of the parent company of Helio Aircraft Company (the General Aircraft Corporation) in late 1977 in the district courts of Washington, D.C., Alexandria, Virginia, and the U.S. Court of Claims in Washington, D.C.

The claim states: "The facts alleged will demonstrate that the Agency, its proprietaries and individuals acted willfully and knowingly to misuse the company's name, misrepresent the company and otherwise appropriate the company's assets and good will to their own benefit for purposes of carrying on acts illegal under U.S. and foreign laws and gathering revenues for the individual profit of those involved and to avoid the laws of the U.S."[15]

The lawsuit further submits that "it now appears that agents of the CIA obtained by forgery, misrepresentation, and other devices, credentials indicating they were sales employees of Helio, knowing well that such was not the case." In a nutshell, Robbins asserts that "Helio was to become the victim of a vendetta carried out by George Doole. GAC's trade secrets had been illegally stolen from them to enable Air Asia to produce Helios."[16]

As might have been expected, because the Helio Aircraft Company had come to rely so heavily upon the U.S. government as the major customer for its products, the political fallout from the strained legal climate began to seriously threaten future sales in this once lucrative market.

While these particularly nasty legal allegations seemed to send the future of Helio Aircraft into the economic equivalent of a flat spin, the aircraft themselves performed with great distinction. In addition to the relatively common workhorse Helio Courier, Helio also built a twin-engined version known as the "Helio Twin," with the military designation U-5A-HE (see next chapter for description). This aircraft was built in very small quantities (total of 7 aircraft, with spare parts enough for approximately 10 more aircraft), and reportedly served the CIA in Indochina.

5. Above and Beyond
Turbo-Charged Helios and Concept Aircraft

Models H-370, H-500, H-580, H-1320 (U-5X), H-1650T & H1201, HST-550 (U-10X), and HST-600, HST-550A, AU-24A-HE, H-634 and GAC-100

"The Helio Stallion is a wondrous beast-a sprung-legged, prognathous, polished-aluminum monster with most of the helicopter attributes and none of its flapping, flailing problems. It can lift a ton and an eighth-or 11 people-and it can fly so slowly that it's literally impossible to stall it power-on; yet it's also quick enough, at 226 MPH, to be the fastest fixed-gear airplane ever put into production."— Stephan Wilkinson, *Flying*, April 1971

"Helio's superpowered "Stallion" has little use for an airport. The turboprop Stallion, an over-grown, over-powering version of Helio's reciprocating-powered Courier, just doesn't need conventional airports. Any old cow pasture, sandbar, short section of dirt road, or wide spot between the boulders that's over 320 feet long and smooth enough for a dune buggy is target-for-today with a Stallion.... Talk about STOL characteristics! This back-country work-horse can fly at 42 MPH, take off in 320 feet, and land in 250."— Don Downie, *AOPA Pilot*, April 1973

"The Helio is a big, high-powered airplane. The thing has a wingspan of 41-¾ feet, an area of 242 square feet, a length of 39 feet, 7 inches and is 9 feet, 3 inches high, tail down. The pilot's eyeballs are a good eight feet off the ground. Empty weight on the military bird is 3230 pounds, and certificated gross is 5800. It has full-span Handley Page automatic leading edge slats and Fowler flaps so big they make any Cessna's look dinky. The turbine swings a three-blade reversible paddle prop with a diameter of 8 feet, 5 inches."— Gene Smith, *Air Classics*

Rounding out the military aircraft built by Helio was one that, while built in relatively small quantity compared to the U-10 series, was no less significant at the time in regards to the planned future evolution of the company's STOL aircraft line. Perhaps even more significant is the claim that the Stallion was the world's first utility aircraft designed from scratch for turbine power.

Envisioned as the successor to the H-295, the HST-550A Stallion (the HST standing for Helio Stallion) and its military version, the AU-24A-HE (the AU designation standing for Attack Utility), featured the benefits of turboprop power: increased reliability and power while taking up less space and weight, plus an increased payload and increased overall utility.

While the Stallion line of turboprops was intended to ultimately supercede the H-295, its development certainly did not happen overnight. In fact, the Stallion design emerged amidst a series of separate aircraft development programs all aimed at increasing the overall utility so ably demonstrated by the H-295 aircraft. Many of these separate programs were in a parallel development cycle, with certain airframe features being shared among experimental models.

As stated by Robert B. Kimnach, then president of Helio Aircraft, in the company's 1967 annual report:

> Up to the present, the company has had only one model: a single engine, piston-powered, six-passenger STOL (Short Takeoff and Landing) airplane known as the Helio Courier. By the fourth quarter of this year, three new models are scheduled for production.
>
> We trust that all stockholders, new and old, recognize realistically why the increasing of Helio's line four-fold in one year's time will, during the first three-quarters of 1968, necessitate a planned suspension of production and deliveries for the re-tooling. From the fourth quarter on, we expect to show you a gratifying growth in sales.
>
> The original Helio Courier model, while still a good earning asset, has already fulfilled its objective. We believe it has earned a reputation as "The World's Safest Airplane." It has established Helio as a recognized leader in the new STOL sector of aviation, and has won competitively the bulk of single-engine utility airplane procurements by the U.S. Air Force and Army since 1960 (with total U.S. military deliveries of 131 units). Approximately twice that quantity have been delivered to civilian users.... During the past few years, however, while the Helio Courier model has been building up public acceptance of the STOL concept in general and of Helio's role in particular, market trends have shifted away from single-engine aircraft in this size and price class. The executive market for higher-priced six-place aircraft has shifted preponderantly to twin-engine equipment. The principal continuing users of single-engine utility aircraft-that is, the U.S. military services-have announced their intention to procure only larger and more powerful turbo-prop equipment.
>
> Thus, while the Courier model does continue to enjoy a civilian demand, it serves only a minor segment of the total general aviation market.
>
> Helio is therefore now scheduling production of a substantially expanded product-line consisting of four models:
>
> 1. A re-styled version of the original single-engine, piston-powered Helio Courier will offer improved appearance, quietness, and comfort. With such continuing year-to-year improvements, this model is expected to retain a worthwhile commercial and foreign market. [Author's note: This model was the H-295 1400 Series which debuted in 1969 and superseded the H-295 1200 Series.]
> 2. A substantially re-designed version of the six-place twin-engine Courier which was developed in a military configuration for U.S. government uses several years ago is now being prepared for production in a more attractive civilian tricycle configuration with retractable nose wheel. It cruises close to 200 MPH and still retains Helio's famous ultra-short-field capabilities together with all the original Courier's special safety characteristics. It is designed principally to serve corporate, executive and air-taxi markets. [Author's note: This model was the H-580 Twin Courier, which was to be a derivative of the H-500.]
> 3. The Turbo-Stallion, an enlarged ten-place version of the previous single-engine

Courier type airframe, has been completed and FAA certificated with a 600 horsepower turboprop engine. Its role is primarily to serve those rapidly growing military markets already opened by the military U-10 version of the original Courier model. Production of this model was initiated during January 1968 and military deliveries can start in June if any emergency military requirements should develop-however, we anticipate little probability of military procurements for this category of aircraft prior to the latter part of 1968. [Author's note: This model was the HST-550/A Stallion.]

4. The twin-turbine version of the Stallion has been designed using the identical airframe with only a change in the nose-section to re-power it with two 317 horsepower Allison turbo-prop engines. This twin-engine version is principally to serve corporate, executive and air-commuter needs. The Stallion Twin may hopefully also open up some new military markets, but no explicitly defined military requirement yet exists.[1] [Author's note: This model was the H-634 Twin Stallion.]

It is worthwhile to note that Kimnach's forecast occurred at a time (1968) when the company felt compelled to resuscitate its by-now-dwindling military orders, and to make an earnest attempt to address the needs of the civilian market.

No doubt, the possibility of rehabilitating sales seemed totally within reach for Helio management. Within months of the issuance of the 1968 annual report, Helio Aircraft Corporation would become a division of General Aircraft Corporation (April 28, 1969), and the December 1974 halt to all production and the lawsuits that were to be lodged by GAC against the CIA in 1977 were several years down the road. If anything, the scale of Helio's commitment to diversify, expand and capture larger segments of the world market (aside from the H-580, HST-550/A and H-634 programs) could be profoundly demonstrated by the GAC-100 program, a four-engined turboprop transport with seating for up to 40 passengers that should have been on par with the likes of the DeHavilland Dash-7.

The reality was that most of these new models would wind up as "paper airplanes," or at best a few prototypes, piles of unassembled parts, and extremely limited production aircraft (save for the H-295 1400 series). The vision of a broad range of exciting new models, built by world-wide, risk-sharing operations, would slowly fade, as Helio once again reverted to its fixation upon military orders as a means to remain financially solvent. Finally, the program that appeared to hold the most promise for the continued survival of Helio, the HST-550A/AU-24A-HE Stallion, and the one that relied upon significant military orders for success, ground to a halt. This was due, according to Helio management, to the ever-changing attitude of a U.S. government that seemed at various times to either bless or conspire against the fortunes of Helio.

Helio's frustration at once again becoming overly dependant upon the vagaries of continued military sales was summed up by Lynn L. Bollinger in an excerpt from the June 15, 1974, *Special Action Report to Stockholders by the Founding Chairman*: "the heavy hand of government, like that of the powerful moron, Lennie, in *Of Mice and Men*, is unwittingly crushing the small creature it only intended to pet!"[2]

Though Helio was reorganized many times following the termination of the Stallion program, it was never able to consistently maintain a large enough consumer base (civil or military) for its line of C/STOL aircraft. Under a whole series of confusing name changes and differing forms of leadership, operations at Helio continued on in either a spare-parts or a sub-contract-manufacturing mode, with manufacture of only two very short-lived "new" aircraft models (H-700 and H-800) during the early 1980s.

It was with the end of the Stallion program, an aircraft that performed very well in spite of the political fates that seemed to doom it, that the "heart" went out of the company, and from which Helio would never fully recover.

With this in mind, it is the pivotal HST-550A/AU-24A-HE Stallion that we will focus upon in the following text, with all other supporting or derivative aircraft treated in accordance. Moreover, aside from the generically similar series of aircraft models that came to be known as the H-391B, H-395 and H-295, it was the Stallion that was, despite its relatively paltry production numbers, to be the only "other" Helio model that seems to lodge in the collective memory of most aviation enthusiasts.

Perhaps the earliest ancestry of the Stallion turboprop can be traced to the development in 1958 of the H-500 Helio Twin aircraft. This assertion can be corroborated by an interview with Bob Devine, former Helio vice president and chief of engineering. Devine states that "from the Helio H-500 sprung the real start of the turbines."[3] Although the H-500 was built within a limited production program (7 production aircraft delivered and parts for 10 additional aircraft produced), with wooden tooling used for fuselage parts, it was primarily the design of the aft fuselage and tail section that was translated-with minor changes-directly into the Stallion design. Devine states that, in this sense, the Stallion was very much a "derivative" of the H-500 aircraft.

Much overlooked, the H-500 was termed by Devine, as well as by noted Helio demonstration pilot Larry Montgomery, one of the absolute best handling twins ever produced. Devine noted that "a lot of attention was paid to single engine stability and control. As Otto Koppen was fond of saying, 'a twin engine aircraft isn't worth a damn unless it can fly on one engine.'"[4] Distinctive to the aircraft were two 250-HP Lycoming 0-540-A2B engines located above and forward of the wing to reduce the chance for ingestion of debris when operated from rough fields. A bulbous, perspex type of nose afforded superior viewing for the pilot and co-pilot during takeoff, cruise and landing.

Cloaked in mystery, the H-500 (military version known as the U-5A) was produced according to specifications requested by a "certain U.S. government agency" for overseas covert assignments. All 7 U-5A aircraft were delivered to the United States Air Force for its discretionary use. The last known report on the whereabouts of the U-5As had them as abandoned somewhere in Red China.

Although they were relatively insignificant to the development of the Stallion, it is worth mentioning the existence of two model programs that were actively pursued at the time of the development of the Stallion, but which in the end resulted in mere "paper airplanes."

The H-580 Helio Twin was to be an improved version of the H-500, incorporating essentially the same basic airframe as the H-500, but sporting tricycle gear (with nose gear retractable), a more aerodynamically refined nose, and two 290-HP Lycoming IO-540-G1A5 engines. Work began in 1966, with all components built but never assembled. The project was cancelled, and parts were junked by 1970.

The Helio Courier Ultra C/STOL Aircraft

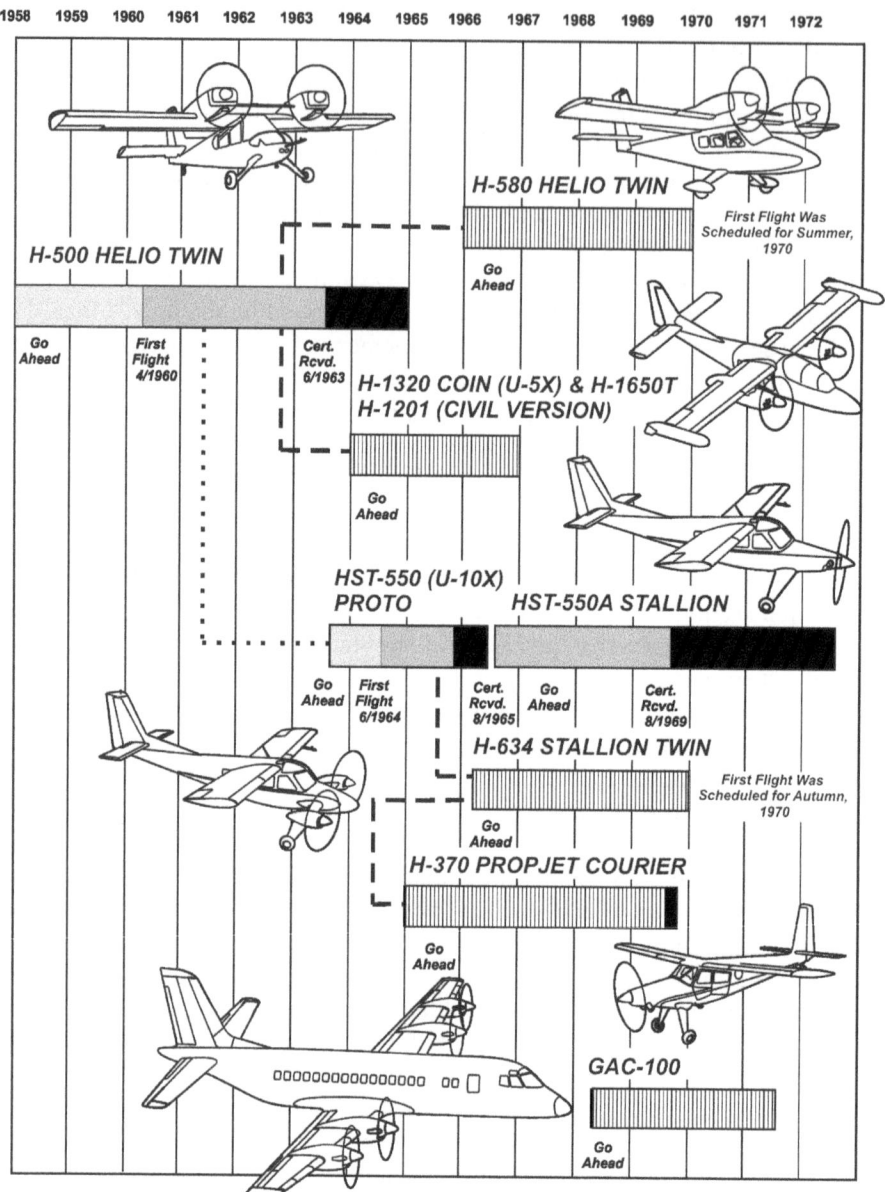

Development timeline leading to Helio Stallion program.

The **H-1320 (U-5X)** and its civilian counterpart, the Model 1201, was originally envisioned as a form of highly modified U-5A/H-500, making use of components from the U-5A and U-10 aircraft designs. Later, with the Stallion program gaining momentum over the H-500/U-5A program, the aircraft was promoted as sharing commonality of parts solely with the Stallion. The military model H-1320 was to be a COIN (*COunter INsurgency*) aircraft available in at least three forms: (1) H-1320 AR (Armed Reconnaissance); (2) H-1320 T (Transport); and (3) H-1320 XX. The civilian version, the Model H-1201, was to be capable of carrying up to 19 people. Both military and civil versions remained conceptual designs, with no parts manufactured.

The Stallion program sprung to life in July 1963, with an aft fuselage/tail section derived from the H-500/U-5A/H-580 design and up-scaled to proportions that would allow it to be used in the near future for a series of other models (H-1320/H-1201) through modularity of major airframe components. A turboprop powerplant had been undergoing testing within standard Courier airframes since 1964, with the Model H-370 being the latest. Although longitudinal instability problems beset the Courier test bed, the Stallion airframe would prove to be an ideal combination for turbo power.

Helio Aircraft Profiles

The remainder of chapter five consists of a series of profiles that detail the differences between the various main models and conceptual variants of mostly turbocharged Helios built between 1963 and 1972. The models profiled consist of the following aircraft: Models H-370, H-500, H-580, H-1320 (U-5X), H-1650T & H1201, HST-550 (U-10X), & HST-600, HST-550A, AU-24A-HE, H-634 and GAC-100.

PROFILE: H-370

The model H-370 Propjet Courier was an initial attempt by Helio to harness the advantages of a turboprop powerplant. Preliminary work started in 1964, but it would not be until the July 1969 Reading (Pennsylvania) airshow that the aircraft would be officially debuted.

Flight test work was carried out at Helio's Bedford, Massachusetts, facility. A standard Courier airframe was mated to an Allison 250-B15 turboprop engine rated at 317 SHP. The benefits that were anticipated included superior takeoff, climb and cruise characteristics, while the engine/prop combination as fitted with beta control allowed for shorter landings as well as steeper approach angles.

Useful load was increased due to the lighter empty weight of the aircraft when outfitted with the less-weighty turboprop.

As logical as this program appeared to be, it was fraught from the outset with developmental gremlins that would ultimately persuade Helio to abandon the idea of fitting a standard Helio Courier air-frame with a turboprop. Instead, they eventually developed an on-purpose designed airframe (Stallion planned derivative model H-634 Twin Stallion with 2 Allison 250-B15 turboprop engines) to make best use of the turboprop power.

A traditional Helio oversized prop was installed (to reduce tip speed/noise), but not without subsequent difficulties. The oversized prop exhibited a tendency to overpower the engine governor, in which case the engine would over-speed. It was noted that this scenario led to at least two in-flight shutdowns in the first 12 hours of flight

Helio H-370 Propjet. Bob Casebeer.

testing. Repositioning of the propeller counterweights appears to have resolved the problem.

Compounding the normal challenges involved in developing a new aircraft/powerplant combination was an on-going struggle to resolve an airframe instability issue (specifically, longitudinal instability). Ultimately, the H-370 project was abandoned in favor of pursuing the on-purpose designed HST-500/HST-550A Stallion project.

As best as can be determined, only one H-370 aircraft was built (N6309V), with no production follow-on aircraft.

General Specifications

Model H-370 Propjet Courier

Powerplant: H-370 was powered by an Allison 250-B15 turbine engine of 317 shaft horsepower.

Dimensions & Performance: Note: Airframe specifications derived from standard H-250 Courier. Performance data for the Model H-370 not currently available at this time.

Length	31 ft. 6 in.	Empty Weight	NA
Span	39 ft.	GWT	NA
Height	8 ft. 10 in.	Useful Load	NA
Wing Area	231 sq. ft.	Wing Loading	NA
Wing Chord	6 ft.	Cruising Speed	NA
Flap Area	38.1 sq. ft.	Top Speed	NA
Tailplane Span	13 ft. 4 in.	Minimum Speed (power on)	NA
Dihedral	1 degree	Minimum Speed (power off)	NA
Incidence	3 degrees	Initial Rate of Climb	NA

Initial Climb Angle	NA	T.O. Dist. over 50' Obstacle	NA
Service Ceiling	NA	Landing Dist. over 50' Obstacle	NA
Range	NA		

PROFILE: H-500

Aside from the relatively obscure and difficult-to-track service history of the H-500s (U-5As) as allegedly used by the CIA, the main claim to fame of the Twin Courier was its notable single-engine operating capability, as well as the translation of its empennage/tail configuration into the design of the HST-550/HST-550A Stallion.

Conceived to add multi-engine reliability to the Helio line of C/STOL aircraft, the H-500 was capable of speeds of up to 200 MPH (212 MPH "redline speed" CAS [Calibrated Air Speed]), while affording increased range and payload.

The H-500 Twin Courier was flown for the first time in 1960, with FAA certification (Type Certificate A2EA, Normal Category) granted on June 11, 1963. Power was supplied by two 250-HP Lycoming 0-540-A2B six-cylinder air cooled engines. A turbo-charged version, known as the H-500B "Chasqui," was powered by two 290-HP Lycoming IO-540-C2C engines, yielding a roughly 30,000-foot ceiling.

Both the H-500 and the H-500B were available with crosswind landing gear, as well as with provision for floats (at the time, the H-500 was touted as the only twin available capable of STOL operations). For emergency evacuation the U-5A could also be outfitted with two litters.

With limited production restricted to seven fly-away aircraft, components for the H-500 series were manufactured from temporary tooling at Helio's Bedford, Massachusetts, and Pittsburg, Kansas, facilities. Final assembly was carried out at the Hanscom Field, Massachusetts, facility. Long-term production arrangements were being set up late in 1964 through a venture then known as Helio Aircraft del Peru.

The H-500 utilized the same effective boundary layer control systems (automatic slats, interceptors and slotted flaps) shared by all the other previous Helio models. In addition to these devices, a slotted auxiliary airfoil (NACA 4418 airfoil/10" chord) was installed above the wings' leading edge and interconnected inboard between the two engine nacelles. This airfoil was intended to provide limited boundary layer control over the wing center section during slow-speed, high-attitude-angle operation and was considered necessary for engine-out STOL operation.

With a premium emphasis on single-engine operation, the H-500 was fully capable of maintaining a single-engine control speed of 51 MPH. Typical performance includes the assertion that the H-500 was "impossible to stall." With power off, and control wheel pulled full aft, the twin descended at an 1800 ft./minute rate, while capability was maintained to bank left and right. To underscore the superior single-engine operating capabilities, one pilot report stated: "Neither will the Helioplane (H-500) stall with one engine out at about 44 MPH the airplane will run out of rudder. The pilot can turn into the dead engine, and by just dropping the nose the airplane will straighten out."[5]

Additional single-engine operating routine involved the following comments: "Feathering is fast, being accomplished in about four to eight seconds. At 2,000 ft.,

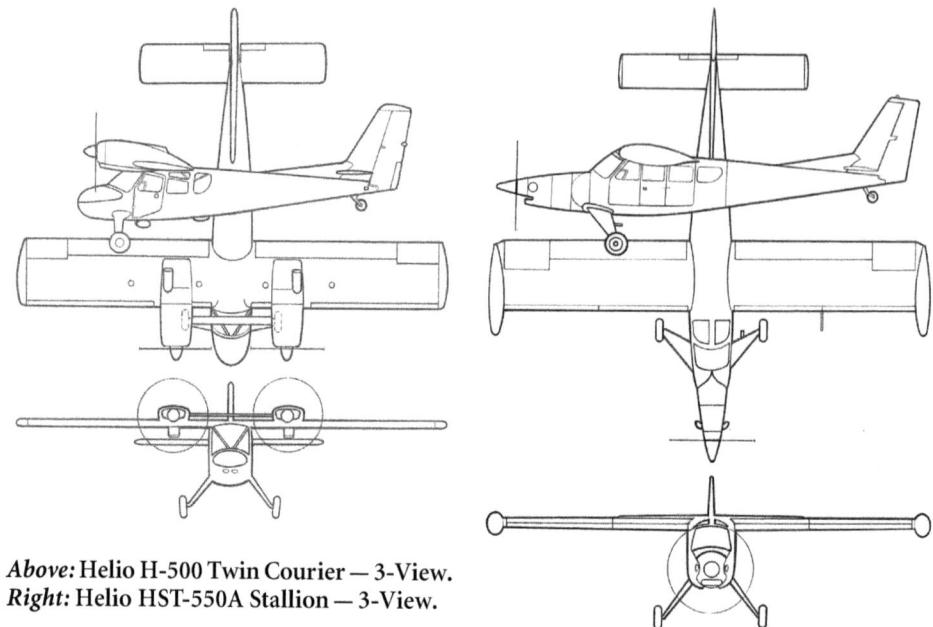

Above: Helio H-500 Twin Courier — 3-View.
Right: Helio HST-550A Stallion — 3-View.

the right propeller lever was moved back past the safety detent. With the left engine producing 60 percent power (23 in. and 2300 rpm) the airplane indicated 115 MPH. There were no control problems in turning into the dead engine; little rudder application was necessary before trimming. Best single-engine configuration is max power, 86 MPH IAS, and flaps set to 10 degrees."[6]

As a safety issue, pilot visibility in the H-500 was excellent. With the two engines above and forward of the wing, along with the see-through nose, the pilot was afforded with exemplary fields of vision. The placement of the engines also significantly reduced the chances for the ingestion of debris and prop damage when operating from unprepared strips.

Overall construction relied upon methods of fabrication similar to preceding Helios, with the fuselage cabin section using sheet-metal-covered tubular steel and the tail-cone area being of an all-metal, semi-monocoque structure. Empennage structure utilized a conventional rib-and-spar metal construction. Unique to the H-500 was the use of magnesium as a weight-saving element in its application to the build-up of the rudder and horizontal tail skins as located aft of the main spar on each of these surfaces.

Cabin doors were staggered (left front and right rear) to lend structural integrity to the overall design. In standard configuration, it was permissible to seat up to six. A cargo door was located on the left side, aft of the pilot door; approximately 60 cubic feet of cargo space was allotted.

Landing gear is typical tail-dragger, although (as is the norm with Helios) it is set well forward in order to facilitate hard braking without risking a nose-over. The tail wheel is of a steerable type, with provision of up to 75 degrees either side of neutral.

Instruments, with the exception of the tip tank fuel quantity gauges and flap

5. Above and Beyond

Helio H-500 Twin Courier illustration.

indicator, are located directly in front of the pilot. In a departure from prior Helio models, the power controls, along with the fuel valve selectors, are located in a central quadrant in the overhead. Fuel storage entails four 30-gallon cells. Fuel storage can be supplemented by two 52-gallon tip tanks or a 37-gallon flexible nose cell. Each engine is fed by its own independent fuel system, with the only interconnection provided by a pressure cross-feed line.

As impressive as the H-500 was, especially as demonstrated before selected members of the aviation media by Helio chief pilot Louis Droste, it would remain a rather enigmatic footnote in the development of the higher-profile model HST-550/HST-550A Stallion.

General Specifications

Model H-500 (U-5A-HE)
Twin Courier

Powerplant: H-500 series was powered by two Lycoming 0-540-A2B series six-cylinder, horizontally opposed, air cooled engines of 250 horsepower each, swinging a Hartzell 84" two-bladed prop (controllable-full feathering). (Optional Riley turbo-superchargers available with Lycoming IO-540-C2C engines-H-500B.)

Price: Standard H-500 $112,000
Price: (With turbo-superchargers) $121,000
Dimensions & Performance:

Length	31 ft. 10 in.	Tailplane Span	18 ft.
Span	41 ft.	Dihedral	1 degree
Height	8 ft. 10 in.	Incidence	3 degrees
Wing Area	242 sq. ft.	Empty Weight	2,010 lbs.
Wing Chord	6 ft.	GWT	3,065 lbs.
Flap Area	41 sq. ft.	Useful Load	1,055 lbs.

116   The Helio Courier Ultra C/STOL Aircraft

Wing Loading	23.66 lbs./sq. ft.	Initial Rate of Climb	230 FPM
Cruising Speed	170 MPH	(1 engine out)	
Top Speed	187 MPH	Initial Climb Angle	UNKNOWN
Minimum Speed (power on)	34.5 MPH	Service Ceiling	22,000 ft.
		Range	810 Miles
Minimum Speed (power off)	48 MPH	Range (with tip tanks)	1,458 Miles
		T.O. Distance over 50' Obstacle	665 ft.
Minimum Speed (1 engine out)	51 MPH	Landing Distance over 50' Obstacle	530 ft.
Initial Rate of Climb	1,830 FPM		

See Appendix 1 for further data specifications.

PROFILE: H-580

Conceived as a refinement of the H-500, the Helio H-580 Twin Courier was intended as a light personal and corporate STOL monoplane, and was to feature the ground-handling benefits of tricycle gear (with a retractable nose gear), a more aerodynamically and aesthetically re-contoured nose, and improved cabin styling/definition.

Initial work on the H-580 began in 1966, with the construction of a prototype commencing during 1969. It was planned that the first flight would occur in the summer of 1970, with certification to FAR Part 23 rules to follow. As envisioned by Helio, production of the center fuselage would be subcontracted out to a business entity named ALAR in Portugal, with licensed production assembly planned to occur in Peru. Ultimately, a limited number of parts were manufactured for the prototype, but they were never assembled, and the project was subsequently cancelled shortly after 1970. It was during this period that the HST-550/HST-550A Stallion program was receiving top priority, and all other programs were put on hold.

Helio H-580 Twin Courier concept illustration.

Powered by two Lycoming IO-540-G1A5 engines, the H-580 was to have provided comfortable transport for up to 6 (three rows of 2 seats). Touted as "the world's first twin-engine airplane to offer truly safe low-speed maneuvering capability-even with one engine out-plus a 190 MPH cruising (performance cruise) speed,"[7] the H-580 would never reach production.

General Specifications

Model H-580
Twin Courier

Powerplant: H-580 series was powered by two Lycoming IO-540-G1A5 series six-cylinder, horizontally opposed, air cooled engines of 290 horsepower each, swinging a Hartzell 88" two-bladed prop (controllable-full feathering).
Price: Standard H-580 $85,000
Dimensions & Performance:

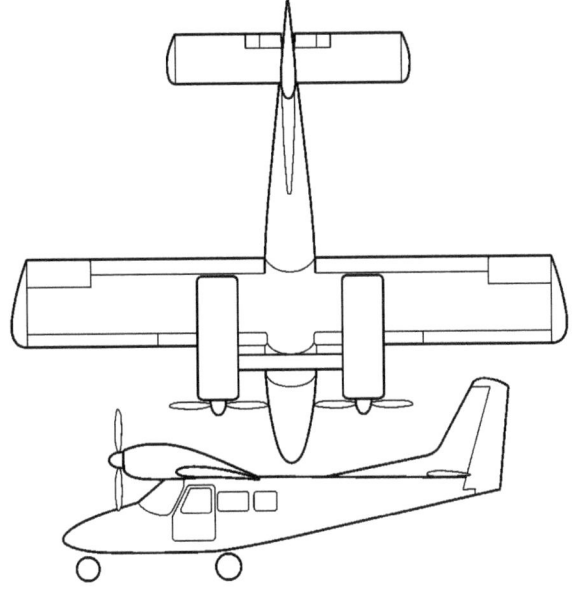

Helio H-580 Twin Courier — 2-View.

Length	33 ft. 6 in.	Minimum Speed (power on)	33 MPH
Span	41 ft.		
Height	12 ft. 4¾ in.	Minimum Speed (power off)	UNKNOWN
Wing Area	242 sq. ft.		
Wing Chord	6 ft.	Initial Rate of Climb	1,720 FPM
Flap Area	41 sq. ft.	Initial Climb Angle	UNKNOWN
Tailplane Span	18 ft.	Service Ceiling	20,000 ft.
Dihedral	1 degree	Service Ceiling (1 engine out)	6,500 ft.
Incidence	3 degrees		
Empty Weight	3,463 lbs.	Range	785 Miles
GWT	5,100 lbs.	Range (with tip tanks)	1,180 Miles
Useful Load	1,637 lbs.	T.O. Distance over 50' Obstacle	780 ft.
Wing Loading	21.1 lbs./sq. ft.		
Cruising Speed	165 MPH	Landing Distance over 50' Obstacle	ft.
Top Speed	196 MPH		

PROFILE: H-1320
PROFILE: H-1201

The Helio models H-1320 and H-1201 were interrelated, in that the H-1320 (also known early on as the U-5X) was the military armed reconnaissance/counter-insurgency aircraft on which the civilian adaptation (model H-1201) was to be based. Both aircraft, conceived around 1964, were strictly "paper airplanes" that never flew, but from a historical standpoint they deserve mention.

As previously noted, both the H-1320 and H-1201 were to have been an extension of the H-500 (U-5A) airframe, with parts derived from U-5A and U-10 aircraft.

With power provided by two 660-SHP Garrett AiResearch T76-G-6/8 turboprops, the design was to have incorporated standard Helio boundary layer control systems as well as the welded steel-tube-truss fuselage frame as proven in prior Helios. A unique feature was to have been removable fiberglass skin panels (which could be replaced with plastic sandwich armor panels for application on the fuselage and engine nacelles) to facilitate maintenance.

The H-1320 wing was derived from the H-500, but was shortened 8 feet, strengthened and re-stressed. Tail surfaces and stabilator were also derived from the U-5A, but with the stabilator being shortened 3 feet. All aerodynamic surfaces were reportedly strengthened and re-stressed. Landing gear was of a tricycle type, but with the main gear being wing-mounted in order to withstand the rigors of one-wheel landings at high sink rates.

Designed to carry 8 paratroops, the H-1320 also featured tandem ejection seats for pilot and observer.

Use of existing U-5A and U-10 parts in the manufacture of the H-1320 was anticipated in order to expedite development of the aircraft in order to meet mili-

Helio H-1201 civilian concept version illustration of the military H-1320.

tary deadlines. Kaman Aircraft Corporation had agreed to build up to 60 of the Helio H-1320s in order to hasten deliveries.

For close air support missions, the military stores were to have included 4 Mk. 82 bombs, 4 Mk. 60 7.62-mm machine guns, and other racks. Lynn Bollinger noted "that due to the superior structural integrity of the welded truss fuselage, there was virtually no limit to the number of armament attachment points that could be provided."[8]

Four military variants of the H-1320 were envisioned, those being for Armed Reconnaissance, Close Support, Ferry, and Transport. Also envisioned was a "Super COIN Transport " version of the H-1320, known as the H-1650T.

The civilian version of the H-1320, known as the H-1201, was to be essentially a refinement of the military transport variant H-1320T (Transport). The H-1201 Twin Stallion was advertised as being capable of carrying up to 19 persons, with a gross weight of 9,300 lbs., as well as a useful load of 4,570 lbs.

Perhaps noteworthy, at least as far as the evolution of Helio models is concerned, was the proposed mounting of the engines in an under-slung manner beneath the wing, totally retractable landing gear, and provision for wing-mounted cargo pods.

General Specifications

(Performance specifications pertain to the Model H-1320T variant.)

Model H-1320
Twin Stallion

Powerplant: H-1320 series was to have been powered by two Garrett AiResearch T76-G-6/8 series turboprop engines of 660 SHP each.

Price: H-1320 $100,000 (based upon 500 aircraft military production run)

Dimensions & Performance:

Length	36 ft. 4 in.	Initial Rate of Climb	5,400 FPM
Span	33 ft.	Service Ceiling	30,300 ft.
Height	12 ft. 6 in.	Range	385 Miles
Empty Weight	4,760 lbs.	Range (for ferry	1,245 Miles
GWT	9,300 lbs.	operations)	
Wing Loading	40.4 lbs./sq. ft.	T.O. Distance over	830 ft.
Cruising Speed	240 MPH	50' Obstacle	
Top Speed	329 MPH	Landing Distance over	453 ft.
Stall Speed (power on)	44 MPH	50' Obstacle	

Three of the four military variants of the Helio H-1320 are illustrated on the following pages.

PROFILE: HST-550

The model designation HST-550 (Helio Stallion-550 shaft horsepower) applied to a series of 10-place, prototype turboprop aircraft that ultimately served as development articles for the full production version, known as the HST-550A Stallion.

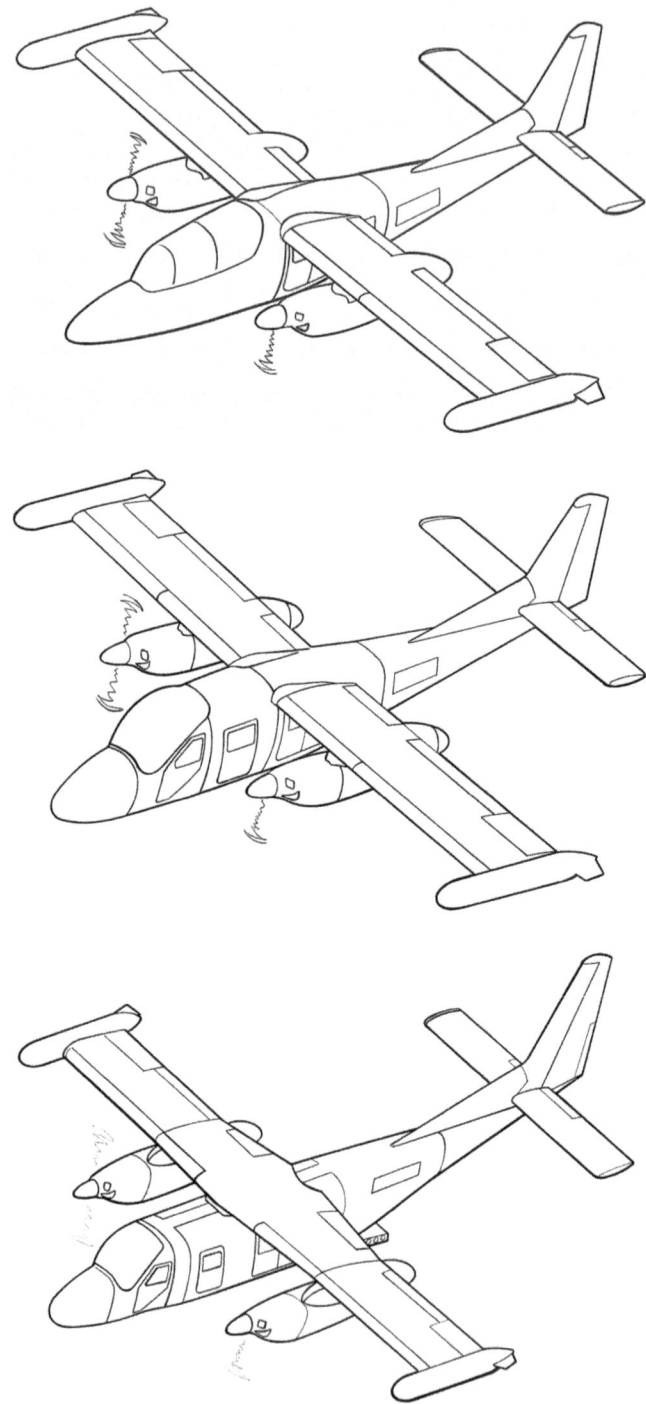

Top: Helio H-1320AR (Armed Reconnaissance) COIN military concept aircraft. ***Middle:*** Helio H-1320T (Transport) COIN military concept aircraft. ***Bottom:*** Helio H-1650T COIN supertransport concept aircraft. All three sketches: Bob Casebeer.

5. Above and Beyond

Helio HST-550 prototype aircraft. Paul E. Davis.

The Stallion program was conceived as an answer to the U.S. military's needs for an improved version of the basic Helio Courier that would maintain its superior C/STOL handling abilities while significantly increasing its useful loads. (Note: the HST-550's useful load was roughly 1,000 lbs. over that of the H-295, while later improved versions of the Stallion would offer up to 1,500 lbs. more useful load.)

Targeted at existing utility aircraft such as the Pilatus Turbo-Porter and the DeHavilland Turbo-Beaver, the Stallion offered similar load-carrying capabilities with superior performance (speed and handling). It should be pointed out that while both the Pilatus and DeHavilland products were both very fine utility aircraft, both aircraft were also airframe limited due to the fact that their overall design was a conversion from original piston engine power to turboprop power.

With initial design beginning in July 1963, the HST-550 was a departure from the H-295 Super Courier airframe in that the Stallion's fuselage was 9 feet 7 inches longer than the H-295, with the aft end being adapted from the H-500 Twin. The H-295 wing was scaled up (2 feet longer in span for the basic wing, and 2 feet 9 inches longer for the wing as fitted with tip tanks), and the airframe was strengthened from scratch to withstand the power/loadings imposed by what was originally a 550-SHP Pratt and Whitney PT6A-6 turboprop engine.

Also considered during development were two other powerplants: a Garrett TPE 331-2-1 turboprop (600 SHP) variant known as the HST-600, and a Lycoming-powered 295-HP GO-480-G1F6-engined variant.

Construction of the first HST-550 prototype aircraft began in November 1963, with the first flight recorded as having occurred on June 5, 1964.

Application for the type certificate was dated October 8, 1963, with approval for type certificate A4EA (Normal Category) granted on August 26, 1965, in accordance with CAR Part 3 regulations.

A total of 3 HST-550s were produced, with the original prototype HST-550

Helio HST-550, September 25, 1969, at Dulles International Airport. Central Arkansas Library System/Aerospace Branch and the Arkansas Aviation Historical Society.

(N550AA) and the second prototype (N10038) being used for most of the testing and publicity work.

It would be the second prototype machine (N10038) that would be further modified and re-engined to serve as the first production Stallion (N10038 being changed to N9550A as the first HST-550A production machine).

General Specifications

Model HST-550 STALLION

Powerplant: The initial HST-550 was powered by a Pratt and Whitney PT6A-6 turbine engine of 550 SHP. Mated to the engine was a Hartzell 3-blade prop featuring reversible pitch and constant speed. Prop diameter was 101 inches.

Projected Price: HST-550 $110,000 (1966)

Dimensions & Performance:

Length	39 ft. 7 in.	Wing Aspect Ratio	6.93
Span	41 ft. 9 in.	(w/out tanks)	
Height	9 ft. 3 in.	Flap Area	40.32 sq. ft.
Wing Area	248 sq. ft.	Tailplane Span	18 ft.
Wing Chord	6 ft.	Dihedral	1 degree

Incidence	3 degrees	Service Ceiling	26,500 ft.
Empty Weight	2,777 lbs.	Range	555 Miles
GWT	5,100 lbs.	Range (with tip tanks)	1,200 Miles
Useful Load	2,323 lbs.	Fuel capacity (std.)	120 Gal.
Wing Loading	20.56 lbs./sq. ft.	Fuel Capacity (w/tip tanks)	224 Gal.
Cruising Speed	160 MPH	T.O. Run	415 ft.
Top Speed	204 MPH	Landing Run (w/reverse thrust)	250 ft.
Minimum Speed (power on)	38 MPH	T.O. Distance over 50' Obstacle	790 ft.
Minimum Speed (power off)	52 MPH	Landing Distance over 50' Obstacle	504 ft.
Initial Rate of Climb	1,600 FPM		

PROFILE HST-550A

The model designation HST-550A applies to full production versions of the Helio Stallion, for which the HST-550 aircraft served as pre-production development models.

Construction of the first production aircraft started in April 1966, in which a Pratt and Whitney PT6A-27 turboprop of 680 SHP was installed, replacing the PT6A-6 (550 SHP) of the HST-550 development aircraft. Tied directly to the evolution of the HST-550A Stallion was its military version, dubbed the AU-24A (*Attack Utility*) aircraft. While only one civilian version of the HST-550A Stallion was built and delivered, it was the AU-24A-HEs that comprised the bulk of production, with some 15 aircraft (Helio serials 02 through 16, military serials 72-1319 through 72-1333) being delivered for service trials and field deployment.

Helio HST-550A production Stallion aircraft. Paul E. Davis.

FAA certification was received on August 1, 1969, but not without the expenditure of an extraordinary amount of time and effort on the part of Helio to satisfy the FAA's persistent concern as to how to certify this latest C/STOL aircraft that would not stall in a conventional manner.

In spite of the fact that, prior to the application for certification of the HST-550A, several hundred Helio Couriers had been successfully delivered and had provided safe, satisfactory performance in the field, the Stallion, with its increased horsepower, continued to vex the "you must stall" FAA organization.

To expand on this quandary, it is worthwhile to quote from the June 15, 1974, *Special Action Report to Stockholders by the Founding Chairman* (Lynn Bollinger).

During the Stallion's first certification test flights, however, the FAA pilot rediscovered the obvious fact that the gradient of changing control pressures the pilot feels is different when a non-stallable airplane is flying at speeds below those at which a conventional airplane would stall and plunge hazardously out of control. (At speeds above the stalling point of a conventional, the non-stallable STOL aircraft still responds the same as the conventional stallable type.)

After first suggesting that the new safety features be removed to make the airplane comply with the old regulations, the FAA review board finally recognized and conceded that the difference actually produces a marked increase in safety. Following further protracted internal discussion as to whether the approval should be consummated by the Washington or Regional office, FAA issued a waiver. That prolonged certification process on the original Stallion prototype cost the company an added 9 months delay and over $750,000.

With the Stallion's competitive market entry and budget already badly hurt, the company carefully refrained from making otherwise desirable engineering refinements. We accordingly kept the subsequent production model identical in all elements affecting aerodynamics. Astonishingly, when it was ready for final airworthiness certification, another FAA test pilot reported the same control force variation that had previously been approved as now being "different and unsatisfactory."

After months of uncertainty, the company finally offered to prove that the aerodynamics and control forces on both Stallion versions were identical. The company offered to pay for an expensive but irrefutable pressure-instrumented series of tests. FAA personnel then advised that regardless of any such findings, the new pilot's purely subjective opinion would not be reversed. Without possibility of review by independent authorities, plausible rationalizations to support their position were easy for them to build up and maintain.

The final compromise on the stalemate required the company's adding to the Stallion's control system an expensive electronic "black box" control-force-augmenting device (stick-pusher). In our judgment and in that of the Air Force who quickly removed the gadget-it was considered unnecessary at best. That compromise, however, we can live with. More serious has been the competitive market loss of an additional year and the forced dissipation of another approximate $1.5 million of capital (over and above the added previous loss on the prototype). This has put the company in a very difficult position.[9]

Counter to Helio's mindset and cost ledger, a stick-pusher system (officially known as SFAS, *Stick Force Augmentation System*) was supplied in which increasing amounts of forward pressure was added as the angle of attack on the wing was increased. Specifically, at airspeeds below approximately 60 knots IAS, the servo force (SFAS) gradually increases, with decreasing airspeed, from zero pounds to a maximum of 50 lbs. at approximately 42 knots IAS. When airspeed is increased, the process is reversed. The only outward evidence of this system was a probe-mounted vane installed on the left-hand leading edge of the wing; the vane, acting as an angle-of-attack sensor, triggered the SFAS action.

Also installed as a means to generate improved "feel" by way of providing resistance to rapid control movements was a Houdaille viscous damper. Finally, an electric trim button with "slower deployment speed" was installed to handle elevator and aileron settings.

The frustrated sentiments at Helio were perhaps best summed up in an excerpt from a flight test review article appearing in the May 1971 issue of *Flying* magazine: The author of the article, Stephan Wilkinson, noted that anxiety at the Helio Aircraft Company was so high due to the lengthy process to get the Stallion certified that Helio would've added a swimming pool and two tennis courts to the aircraft, if that was what the FAA deemed necessary. Wilkinson also points to the unfortunate timing of events-just as the aircraft was certified, the market for highly specialized and pricey ($140,000) single-engine turboprops had dissipated.[10]

Helio SFAS vane. Paul E. Davis.

Despite all of the lengthy wranglings and subsequent gadgetry that were a part of the Helio/ FAA political fallout over the Stallion's ability or inability to stall, it is worthwhile to recall an account of the aircraft's flying capabilities (with regard to stall) from one of the true masters of the Helio Stallion. Former Stallion demo pilot Larry Montgomery recounts that the Stallion possessed so much performance in a power-on stall that it simply defied the "normal airplane" descriptive wording according to then-published FAA wording on stalls: "with a wing that is virtually stall-less, the nose can get to a very awkward attitude if the pilot puts it there purposely ... even with the nose pointed practically straight up, all that is needed to correct the situation is a slight reduction in power, and the nose comes forward and down-not violent, or a "whip," as is the case with so many 'naked wing' airplanes."[11]

With certification finally received, amidst a depressed civilian market the Stallion would continue towards its true principal market as envisioned by its creators: the military.

Based on its outward appearance, the Stallion has been regarded through time as fitting in somewhere between beauty and the beast. Certainly when compared against its primary military rival, the rather angular and less than aerodynamic looking Fairchild Pilatus Porter (AU-23A), the description offered by former Helio Technical Representative (Cambodia) Paul Davis is noteworthy: "the Fairchild Pilatus Porter is the box that the Stallion came in."[12] The fact that the Helio Stallion could top out at 217 MPH versus the Porter's 175 MPH gives a certain amount of credence to Davis's descriptive analysis.

Also serving as physical hallmarks for the Stallion were the unusually swept-back cantilevered main landing gear struts and relatively large vertical tail. The main gear is set at a 41-degree angle in order to locate the oleo shock struts inside the engine compartment for ease of access/maintenance (instead of constructing separate attachment points under the cabin floor). The fact that the relatively large vertical tail surface was mated to a rather long and slender aft fuselage was mandatory in a design sense in order to absorb the turboprop's power on takeoff.

Installation of the Pratt and Whitney PT6A-27 engine is similar to that of the HST-550's PT6A-6; however, the exhaust stacks on the -27 were reconfigured—extended and further streamlined in order to reduce the chance of exhaust fumes entering the cabin.

Helio HST-550A left-hand access doors. Central Arkansas Library System/Aerospace Branch and the Arkansas Aviation Historical Society.

Construction of the airframe is similar to preceding Helio models, in that the cockpit is reinforced with 2¾-inch and 1¾-inch outside diameter chrome-molybdenum steel tubing for a safety type cage with aluminum semi-monocoque structure serving the remaining fuselage.

Wing design also uses the typical NACA 23012 airfoil as found on prior Helios, with an all-aluminum single spar structure. The wing also incorporates Dacron-covered Frise-type balanced ailerons interconnected to the "interceptor" lateral control roll augmentor systems as found on prior Helios. Fully automatic Handley Page leading edge slats occupy the entire span of the leading edge of the wing.

The tail consists of a one-piece all-movable stabilator type of design in which trim and anti-balance tabs are combined, while a separate flap trim interconnect tab has been integrated.

Access to the cabin is provided by jettisonable doors on the pilot and co-pilot sides. A fairly large double door, located aft of the pilot and without central pillar, can be used to facilitate loading and unloading of cargo. The forward section of this double door is hinged on the forward edge, while the aft section of the door slides aft. When both doors are open, it provides up to 62 inches of opening to load or unload. The Stallion can accommodate as standard seating a pilot, co-pilot, and eight passengers as seated in three rows.

The non-retractable landing gear could be outfitted with crosswind landing gear, while the tail wheel was steerable. Also available was a type of wheel ski. Although compact in appearance, the narrow (9'8") main gear track could prove a challenge for novice pilots on landings.

A typical flight test of the HST-550A was described in an article in the April 1973 issue of *AOPA Pilot* magazine. Entitled "Pilot Flight Check: Hello's Stallion," by Don Downie, the article covered the phases of static/taxi, takeoff/climb, cruise/in-flight and approach/landing.

> It's only when you climb aboard that you realize the Stallion is a BIG airplane: 41 feet across the wings, and 39 feet 7 inches long. With the tail-wheel on the ground, your eye-level is almost 8½ feet above the turf. Over-the-nose visibility is excellent, since the narrow cowling is canted five degrees nose-low so that the thrust line of the propeller will be more nearly in level flight during takeoff.
>
> Takeoff procedure calls for full power, according to Montgomery, who has checked out more than 300 pilots in various versions of the Helio in the past 17 years. Full throttle is 98 percent of turbine speed (up to 101.5 percent for short periods of time), and to stay within engine operating limits it is governed on a hot day by the maximum ITT (inter-turbine temperature) of 725 degrees C or, on a cooler day, by 53 lbs. on the torque meter. Propeller redline is at 2,200 rpm forward and 2,090 rpm in reverse ("beta").
>
> At full power, there's so much slipstream that the two inboard slats may pop open before the aircraft has begun to move. The Helio has two independent, air-loaded leading-edge slats on each wing. It isn't unusual to see the slats on the inside wing pop open in a tight turn, while those on the faster-moving wing on the outside of the turn remain closed. In flight, but not during run-up on the ground, the inner slats tend to open last, due to the influence of the big 101-inch propeller. If there's a malfunction or sticking flap, Montgomery suggested, "add about 10 MPH to the airspeed and proceed as usual. Should severe icing freeze the slats shut (and this has happened), the wing is flown with some additional airspeed and provides about the same performance as a conventional wing under similar conditions."
>
> Short-field takeoff calls for 30 degrees of flap (flaps comprise 72 percent of the trailing-edge span of the wing), brakes locked, power to maximum limits, release brakes, allow the tail to come up slightly (three to four seconds at light weight and six to seven seconds at full gross), and haul back on the stick as the air-speed hits 40 MPH.
>
> It takes just one takeoff to realize why the Stallion has such a large dorsal fin (37 square feet). With its long fuselage and high rudder, the Stallion still takes FULL (and I mean FULL) right rudder for takeoff. On a couple of takeoffs, I had to tap a little right brake to keep the nose up front, but the takeoff roll is so short that there's really very little time to get too far out of line. A tailwheel lock is also available as an option, but Montgomery said he prefers not to use it.
>
> The long-fuselage, dorsal fin, and high rudder combination can be a pain in the neck on crosswind landings, but it's essential to absorb the power on takeoff. The crosswind landing gear can be a great assist under these conditions, once a pilot has mastered its care and feeling.
>
> Deck angle on climb is somewhere between 25 and 30 degrees, but it feels as though you're lying on your back. Flaps up at 60 MPH, and the trim changes automatically to compensate. Best rate of climb is 100 MPH, and all flaps should be up before reaching 95 MPH.
>
> One of the important performance features of the Stallion is its broad speed range. It will stay in the air under full control at 42 MPH, yet cruise at 206 and top out at 216 MPH at 10,000 feet.

N9550A was equipped with a dual throttle quadrant-actually a power lever quadrant-with single prop and fuel controls in the center of the cockpit. The second power lever is mounted on the left of the instrument panel, a location welcomed by pilots accustomed to flying a stick with the right hand and making power changes with the left.

Stick forces are high during flareout for landing because of an SFAS (stick force augmentation system) or "stick pusher." The FAA flight manual explains: "At airspeeds below approximately 60 knots IAS, the servo force (SFAS) gradually increases, with decreasing airspeed, from zero pounds to a maximum value of 50 pounds at approximately 42 knots IAS.... When airspeed is increased, the process is reversed ... In the event the stick-force augmentation system is inoperative ... a very-light-to-neutral stick force results at approximately 50 knots IAS. At lower speeds with high power settings, stick-force reversal may reach or exceed 40 pounds."

...Because of the SFAS system, you may find increasing stick pressures while practicing stalls in the air and during landing flareout. It's a minor annoyance, but something that five hours of practice in this workhorse would cure. Since the propeller-thrust line is pointed five degrees nose-low, you can use considerable nose-up trim to take some of the pressure off SFAS and still not be trimmed so nose-high that a go-around would present a pitch-up problem. Actually, during one of our C/STOL approaches, I wasn't lined up the way I wanted to be, so I made a go-around with full power. It took surprisingly little forward stick pressure to take care of the power.

The Stallion uses military-type trim tab, a small button on top of the stick that handles both elevator and aileron trim. Rudder trim and a manual backup elevator (stabilator) trim are mounted on the cabin roof at the aft of the windshield.

Simple, 25-inch-long spoilers-Helio calls them "interceptors"-extend up to about 2½ inches to cut lift and increase drag only when the aileron is in the up (wing down) position. This spoiler action is most effective at slow STOL speeds when the slats are open. At high speeds, only small movement of the ailerons is needed, and the spoilers remain buried inside the wing. The spoiler/aileron combination is a vital part of Helio's excellent slow-speed control.

We shot a series of "touch and goes"—perhaps better referred to as they are in Canada, "circuits and bumps"—at Atkinson Airport. Except for the "beef" imposed by the SFAS system, everything was completely normal.

Since the Helios are tail-draggers, previous experience in Stearmans and AT-6 types is desirable. For those of us who go back that far in aviation, Montgomery explained: "The ground-looping tendencies of the Stallion are not as probable as in either the Stearman or the AT-6. The Stallion, however, has Goodyear's crosswind gear that smoothes out many of these potential problems."

The crosswind gear is a fine piece of machinery when you get used to it. Particularly when you're taxiing in a strong crosswind, it's great sport to kick the gear out to its 20-degree deflection and taxi with 110 percent forward visibility and the nose far to the upwind side. I did have a problem on one landing, however, where the crosswind gear helped trap me. My approach had been normal, but a slight crosswind drifted us to the left of centerline. After flare and touchdown, the ship wanted to continue drifting to the left with the crosswind gear unlocked. I applied right brake and promptly activated the gear. This kicked the nose off to the right, but we were still drifting toward the left side of the strip-and the runway lights.

"Get on both brakes and reverse the prop," Montgomery snapped. This was the only time in over two hours in the air that he spoke quickly. I stood on the brakes and came back into reverse pitch with the power lever. After sliding to a stop in too-close proximity to the edge of the runway, I suggested locking out the crosswind gear to eliminate one of the variables that a new pilot encounters in the big C/STOL turboprop.

Key to C/STOL landings is a planned approach. The air-loaded slats come out at about 60 MPH (somewhat higher with heavier loads) and double the effective lift. Fowler-type flaps extend both down and aft to increase the effective wing area, just as they do in today's jet transports. The electric flaps take about seven seconds to reach a full 40 degrees. There's a slight nose pitch-up as the flaps extend, but the flap interconnect system does about two-thirds of the trim work.

Montgomery's graduation obstacle course is a 280-foot patch of turf between Runway 10 and the south taxiway, adjoining the big tetrahedron at the Atkinson Airport (Pittsburg, Kansas). I finally tried it for size and almost got the job done. The approach was satisfactory, and I could feel and hear the slats pop out. I wrestled with the SFAS stick pusher and finally planted the tailwheel on the edge of the runway just short of my spot. Tail-wheel-first landings are not unusual in the C/STOL, but its a "no-no" in the backcountry if you undershoot your spot, since you might leave your tail feathers on a stump or in a ditch.

As we rolled onto the grass, I applied hard braking and noted no tendency for the tail to come up, despite our light loading. Then came full reverse on the power lever. The PT6A-27 let out a muffled roar as the blades switched angle, and a shower of cut grass came up off the turf. We stopped and would have backed up if I had not cut the power by pushing forward on the power lever into idle range. We almost stayed within Montgomery's 280-foot target. With another hour of landing practice, I believe I could have stayed in the ballpark three landings out of four.

Even in the flat country of Kansas, the Stallion is an impressive airplane, but in the backcountry for which it was really designed, it's undoubtedly even more impressive.

The C/STOL characteristics of the Stallion are far removed from flight characteristics of the "naked wing" aircraft. One could write flight evaluations or study brochures for weeks without having a feel for what this big workhorse will do. You really have to see it at work, then fly it yourself, to become a card-carrying convert to C/STOL.[13]

Because of its significance to STOL operations, it is perhaps worthwhile to expand on the takeoff/landing procedures described above.

Once the engine has been started (simply by spinning the compressor until it attains a speed of at least 12 percent of maximum rpm), set the fuel lever to "ground idle," at which point ignition will occur. The generator is kicked in once the compressor is turning roughly 60 percent (to avoid compressor stall). Aside from monitoring the T. I. T. (temperature inlet temperature) and torque pressure gauges, this is about it. Pre-takeoff checklist items are relatively minimal.

While the technical aspects of takeoff in the Stallion are aptly described in Downie's article, the overall sensation is also well captured in an article written by Stephan Wilkinson in the April 1971 issue of *Flying* magazine. Wilkinson notes that the Stallion displays no extreme launch upon takeoff. Rather, "it simply levitates, as though winched smoothly upward on a mystic skyhook." Forward motion is maintained at about 70 or 80 MPH, with a significant gain in altitude.[14]

However, it is the landing procedure that deserves more detailed commentary in order to understand and appreciate the full potential of a C/STOL landing. Perhaps the key to planting the Stallion on the ground within the shortest distance is the judicious use of the power control lever and its special propeller pitch settings, with particular emphasis on the "Beta" setting. The power control lever has a type of lift trigger attached to it that allows selection of various propeller pitch settings. The selections include coarse, cruise, fine, extreme-fine, Beta, deep–Beta and finally

Helio HST-550A production Stallion aircraft. Paul E. Davis.

reverse pitch. While the course through extreme-fine pitch settings may be familiar, the Beta modes demand attention. In the Beta selection, the propeller is in flat pitch, and is actually working as an air brake, due to its flat plate area. In the deep-Beta selection, the propeller offers a certain amount of reverse thrust to the aircraft. The use of deep-Beta and reverse pitch settings requires a high degree of expertise in their application, as the consequences of applying them incorrectly (or inadvertently) can be serious. As recalled by Helio Vice-President Bob Casebeer: "we were on our way to demo the aircraft (Stallion) as a trainer when over Lemar, Missouri, the aircraft went inadvertently into reverse pitch at a 50-foot altitude. It about virtually destroyed the aircraft and threatened the program. It took us about 2,000 hours over the weekend to rebuild the entire aircraft to keep the program alive."[15]

However, use of Beta, deep–Beta and reverse settings is critical to get the best out of the aircraft. In order to facilitate this, the Stallion uses a very steep final approach with full flap deployment and the engine/prop set to flat pitch. In the event that the aircraft is too high, altitude can be adjusted by resetting into Beta and dropping the nose. If the aircraft is coming in short, pilots can adjust the power setting forward.

To get the aircraft down in a hurry, Stephan Wilkinson (in his test flight of the Stallion) observed that it is best to dispense with the traditional concept of leveling and flaring the aircraft. Wilkinson recommends: "Get that horse in a level altitude and reasonably close to the ground-a foot or two up-and jerk that fool into Beta. Guaranteed: It will stop flying now." Once the aircraft has contacted the ground, pull back into the reverse setting for a full stop.[16]

While the Stallion would continue to "wow" the aviation press in its various reviews, it would have next to no impact on the civilian market. The only civilian sale was for the first production Stallion, which went to Texas Instruments Corporation. Ultimately, it would be as its military variant, the AU-24A-HE, that the Stallion would play a role in aviation history.

5. Above and Beyond

General Specifications
Model HST-550A STALLION

Powerplant: The HST-550A was powered by a Pratt and Whitney PT6A-27 turbine engine of 680 SHP. Mated to the engine was a Hartzell 3-blade prop featuring reversible pitch and constant speed. Prop diameter was 101 inches.

Price: HST-550A (BASIC) $138,900 (1971)
HST-550A (IFR) $146,145 (1971)

Dimensions & Performance:

Length	39 ft. 7 in.	Top Speed	217 MPH
Span	41 ft. 9 in.	Minimum Speed (power on)	42 MPH
Height	9 ft. 3 in.		
Wing Area	242 sq. ft.	Minimum Speed (power off)	52 MPH
Wing Chord	6 ft.		
Wing Aspect Ratio (w/out tanks)	6.93	Initial Rate of Climb	2,200 FPM
		Service Ceiling	28,000 ft.
Flap Area	40.32 sq. ft.	Range	445 miles
Tailplane Span	18 ft.	Fuel Capacity (standard)	120 gal.
Dihedral	1 degree	T.O. Run	320 ft.
Incidence	3 degrees	Landing Run (w/reverse thrust)	250 ft.
Empty Weight	2,860 lbs.		
GWT	5,100 lbs.	T.O. Distance over 50' Obstacle	660 ft.
Payload	2,240 lbs.		
Wing Loading	21.1 lbs./sq. ft.	Landing Distance over 50' Obstacle	750 ft.
Cruising Speed	160 MPH		

Note: The Stallion was later (1978) certified for a GWT increase from 5,100 lbs. to 5,800 lbs. (empty weight: 3,000 lbs., useful load 2,800 lbs.).

See Appendix 1 for further data specifications.

PROFILE: AU-24A

The model AU24A-HE (Attack Utility model 24A-HElio) was the highly modified military variant of the production HST-550A Stallion. Because the Stallion program was targeted primarily toward the military, and because AU24A-HE aircraft comprised the bulk of Stallion aircraft production, it is worth spending time chronicling the short but intriguing history of this unique aircraft.

Built to expand upon the legendary C/STOL attributes of the military Helio Courier (U-10), the AU-24A-HE received several modifications that placed it above the civilian Stallion as far as performance specifications are concerned.

The main differences that set the AU-24A apart from the civilian Stallion were as follows:

- The AU-24A possessed an increased maximum takeoff weight of 6,300 lbs. (as compared to the 5,100 lbs. gross weight figure for the civilian variant).

Helio AU-24A-HE (S/N 21327). United States Air Force Museum, Wright-Patterson AFB.

- Five munitions hardpoint pylons (type MA4A bomb racks) were installed (two on each wing, and one located along the fuselage centerline). Outboard pylon stations could handle 350 lbs., while inboard pylon stations could handle up to 500 lbs. The lone centerline pylon could handle a capacity of upwards of 600 lbs. Possible munitions included single bombs (500-lbs. bomb on centerline mount), cluster bombs (CBU-14A/A), rockets, napalm, flares and machine-gun pods. Total munitions capacity was 2,240 lbs.
- A General Electric Model M-197 20-mm (M50 series) three-barreled machine cannon (similar to the much vaunted M61A1 Vulcan Gatling Gun) was installed on a pintle mount to fire through the left hand cargo door opening. A 400-1500 shots per minute cyclic rate of fire could be attained with this weapon.
- Armament control system.
- Gunsight for the M-197 machine cannon.
- Installation of military communications systems (VHF, UHF, FM and HF hardware).

While there were just over 300 differences between the civilian and military variants of the Stallion, the items mentioned above were of standout significance.

In order to meet the higher structural loads imposed by the higher gross weight limits (6,300 lbs. for the AU-24A versus 5,100 lbs. for the civilian Stallion), as well as to accommodate the stress that resulted from firing the M-197 machine cannon, Helio contracted with Kaman Aerospace of Connecticut to reinforce the airframe on the prototype aircraft. The reinforcement and re-stressing of the prototype was accomplished, along with actual live-fire gun tests to ensure structural integrity.

While the AU-24A was capable of inflicting substantial damage to enemy ground targets with its diverse variety of pylon-mounted weapons, it was its gun system that would serve as its primary means of offense.

The United States Air Force was so enthusiastic about the devastating effectiveness of its Douglas AC-47 "Spooky" gunships (three 7.62-mm MXU 470A miniguns firing up to 6,000 shots per minute) and Lockheed AC-130A Hercules "Spectre" gunships (four 20-mm M61 cannons and four 7.62-mm miniguns, with-in some cases- an additional two 40-mm M-1 Bofors cannon or even an additional 105-mm howitzer) that a program was envisioned to produce what was loosely termed "mini-gunships," with the Helio AU-24A as one of the prime contenders. Although this mini-gunship campaign was never officially carried out, it did lead to an emphasis upon the development of the Helio's M-197 gun system. (Note: the Fairchild A-10 indirectly evolved from this early gunship concept.)

From its inception, the AU-24A was not necessarily without its peers as a utility aircraft capable of fulfilling the mission requirements of a STOL aircraft to be used for COIN (counter-insurgency), ground attack, reconnaissance and special operations.

Indeed, the Fairchild Pilatus Turbo Porter and the DeHavilland Turbo Beaver vied

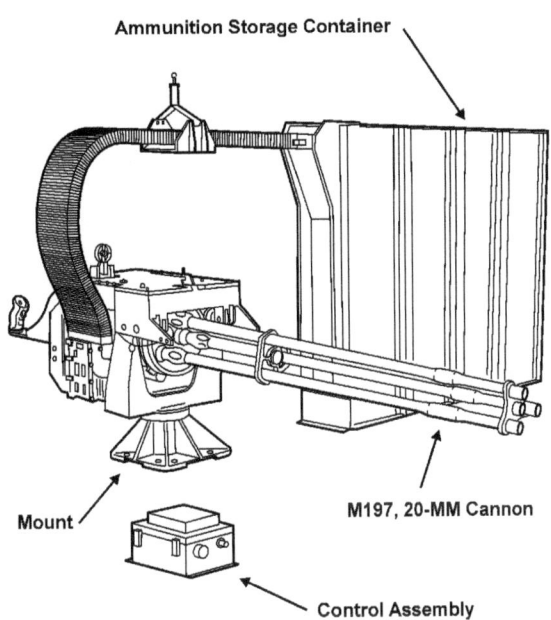

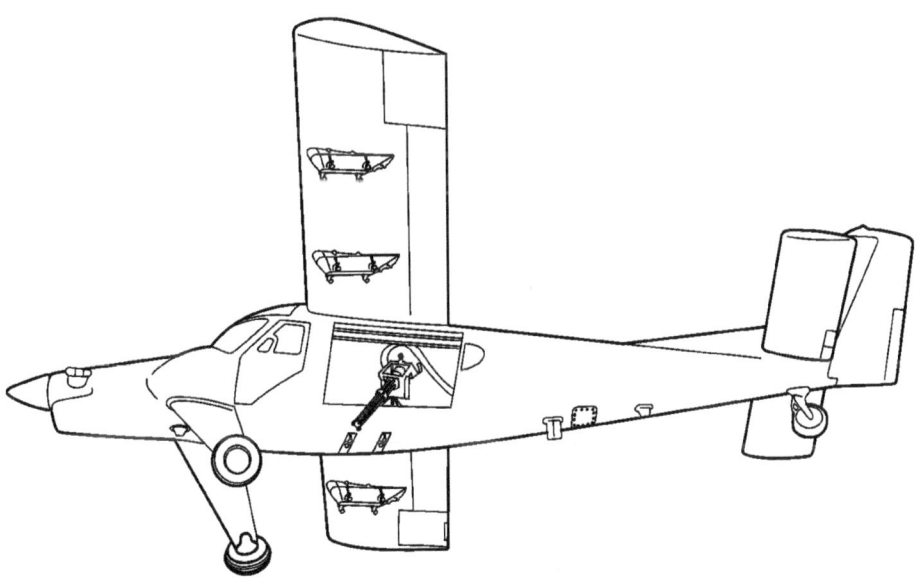

Top: M-197 20-mm minigun system. *Bottom:* Helio AU-24A-HE hard point locations (centerline and wing provisions for bombs and other munitions). Both sketches, Paul E. Davis.

Pilatus Porter AU-23A gunship — the Helio Stallion's counterpart in Southeast Asia. United States Air Force Museum, Wright-Patterson AFB.

equally to attract defense budget dollars. Of these two competitors, it was the Fairchild Pilatus Porter (AU-23A "Peacemaker") that offered the stiffest challenge.

Of foreign design, the Pilatus Porter was originally conceived as the model PC-6, featuring a six-cylinder Lycoming GSO-480-B1A6 supercharged engine (340 HP) and built by Pilatus Flugzeugwerke A.G., of Strans, Switzerland. The prototype first flew in 1959, and garnered acclaim for its impressive work in the field, most notably for rescue work (particularly on glaciers) as well as airlift service for alpine tourists and expeditions.

In the early 1960s, the increasing demand for more power led to the offering of a powerplant option in the way of a 530-SHP Turbomeca Astazou II turbine, in which the aircraft was known as the PC-6/A Turbo-Porter.

With the demonstration of this re-engined aircraft, Fairchild Aircraft Company of Hagerstown, Maryland, set out to obtain manufacturing and support licensing agreements from Pilatus. This was accomplished on December 16, 1964, with Fairchild carrying out plans to manufacture 100 Porters despite the lack of any firm orders stateside for the aircraft. (Initially, Turbo Porters were manufactured for Fairchild by Pilatus. It was not until mid to late 1966 that Fairchild built its own Porters.)

On-going concerns over maintenance/reliability issues with the original engine/prop combination led to the testing of a 550-SHP Pratt & Whitney PT6A-6 (Turbo Porter model PC-6/B) and a 575-SHP Garrett TPE 331-1 engine (Turbo Porter PC-6/C). Ultimately, it was the 650-SHP Garrett installation (TPE 331-1-101F) that was given the go-ahead, and which was used in the AU-23A Peacemaker. Combined with the Beta control for its prop, the Turbo Porter offered outstanding performance.

Fairchild anticipated the need for a counter-insurgency utility-type aircraft for the military, and pursued a self-funded development program in which 7.62-mm miniguns and wing-mounted rocket pods were integrated into a prototype aircraft.

Following a successful demonstration to the military, the United States Air Force expressed interest in the Porter for "night perimeter defense," and the United States

Navy foresaw it as an ideal candidate for Mekong Delta "river patrol operations" (Riverine).

It was the Navy's interest in the Turbo Porter STOL aircraft that seemed to add fuel and a sense of urgency to Helio's attempt to push the military Stallion variant towards acceptance.

So impressed was the Navy with the Turbo Porter STOL aircraft that plans were put into effect in 1968 to award a sole-source contract for 14 aircraft (without competitive bids from other manufacturers) for the Fairchild Turbo Porter (Navy designation: OV-12A).

Pilatus Porter in steep climb-out. United States Air Force Museum, Wright-Patterson AFB.

It didn't take very long for Helio representatives to raise objections to this apparent breach of evaluation/procurement practice; an official complaint was lodged with the U.S. General Accounting Office, and protests were filed with members of the House and Senate armed services committees, as well as with Defense Secretary Clark M. Clifford.

The upshot of this affair was that competitive bids were re-opened, with North American Rockwell joining in with its OV-10A Bronco as an additional candidate. Ultimately, the Navy let the program quietly die, with "lack of funds" given as the main reason for canceling the project.

Although the Navy's Riverine project ended in a stalemate as far as the selection of a STOL gunship was concerned, it did underscore the basic market need for such a machine.

Perhaps the best and most fair attempt to discern a winner for supplying an armed STOL utility aircraft would come in the way of a program code-named Credible Chase. Credible Chase was the follow-on evaluation to an initial competition termed Pave Coin, in which the Helio and Fairchild entries were selected from some other competitors, including a strike version of the Beech Bonanza (itself being replaced in the competition by Beech with an imported version of the Italian-built Aeronautica Macchi AM-3C).

In July 1971, Helio Aircraft received a research contract from the U.S. government to fully test the Stallion. At this same period, Fairchild received the same research contract to enter its Turbo Porter.

The Credible Chase program was intended to determine the best aircraft model to effectively serve as an armed STOL utility aircraft for special operations in overseas military assistance programs (particularly, as a light strike aircraft for the South Vietnamese Air Force).

Foreseen as a revolutionary approach to strengthening the national defense of undeveloped, third-world countries, the provision of armed STOL aircraft was envisioned as a cost-effective alternative to helicopters. Both the Helio Stallion and the Fairchild Pilatus Turbo Porter were presented as a means to help implement a foreign policy of "nation building" by way of an aircraft that was simple and reliable to operate, was easy to maintain in the field, could access unimproved landing sites, could serve a multitude of roles (especially as a gun platform and troop transport), and would not bankrupt either the United States' or the third-world country's budget.

As described by Thomas Turner (then corporate vice president of marketing for Fairchild), the new STOL armed utility class of aircraft "deescalates the defense needs of a country."[17] Turner offered the following points for consideration when comparing the STOL machines against helicopters: "Given a 300 foot airstrip on even the worst of terrains this plane can do everything a helicopter can do and at a fraction of the cost.... For instance, while the Peacemaker can fly one hour for $20, the same hour of flight would cost upwards of $180 with a helicopter.... Ground maintenance is another major cost factor. Upkeep is minimal with the Peacemaker. Where a helicopter demands 12 to 18 hours of ground maintenance for every hour it is airborne, the Peacemaker asks for only one hour of maintenance."[18]

Turner concludes with the assertion that "We (the U.S.) have faked the rest of the world into going to the rotary powered helicopter merely because our military has chosen to do so."[19] Although issued from the competitor's camp, this rhetoric was echoed by the Helio headquarters in their quest to provide an alternative to helicopters for third-world countries.

The Credible Chase evaluation trials for such an aircraft lasted 13 weeks, starting in late October 1971 and ending in February or March 1972, and were conducted at Eglin Air Force Base in Florida.

As outlined during the October 1971 hearings before the House Subcommittee on the Department of Defense (chaired by Rep. George H. Mahon, D–Tex.), the $14.5-million-dollar program would help facilitate the orderly transition of defense of South Vietnam. General Otto Glasser (Deputy Chief of Research and Development) stated at the hearings that, as combat action winds down in Vietnam, the Republic of Vietnam Air Force (RVNAF) "will be faced with a shortage of tactical mobility and strike capability."[20] The planes would be turned over to the RVNAF once American forces were pulled out of Vietnam, with armed STOL gunships being stationed in hamlets throughout the countryside. It was further noted that airplanes were selected over helicopters mainly because they were cheaper to buy and to operate.

During the trials, both the Helios and the Turbo Porters gave a good accounting of themselves. Tests involving munitions, general flight tests (including night flying) and structural evaluations were performed, although one of the two Turbo Porters was lost (allegedly due to ultrasonic vibrations while in deep-Beta mode that caused structural failure, reportedly in the tail section of the aircraft).

As an end result of the trials, both aircraft companies received orders for their respective aircraft. Helio received an order for 15 AU-24A Stallions totaling $3.398 million (all AU-24As to be delivered to the Air Force by mid–1972). Fairchild received a similar contract for 15 AU-23A Peacemakers worth $3.8 million.

General Otto Glasser had suggested that the eventual winner of the military

STOL contract could look forward to follow-on production orders in the range of possibly 1,000 to 3,000 aircraft. This government contract would have been substantial in sheer scale of manufacturing size and resultant cash flow for just about any airframe manufacturer. So large was the potential contract that Helio had tentatively entered into an agreement with Boeing-Wichita to make use of a 300,000-square-foot facility for AU-24A assembly and delivery, while its Pittsburg facility would concentrate on AU-24A component manufacture.

Unfortunately for Helio, politics would once again play a significant role in thwarting the sale of AU-24As. The money was apparently allocated as a grant for the purchase of the mini-gunships; however, South Vietnamese Premier and RVNAF Air Marshal Nguyen Cao Ky reportedly directed that the money be used to purchase C-130 transport aircraft, rather than mini-gunships. (Note: Ky departed South Vietnam on April 29, 1975.)

With this turn of events, the 15 Helio AU-24As (and similar Fairchild AU-23A aircraft) were transferred to the Davis-Monthon Air Force Base in Tucson, Arizona, for temporary dry-weather storage until a reason to re-activate them made itself clear.

Fairchild/Pilatus Turbo Porter
AU-23A Peacemaker

Engine	Garrett (Geared) TPE 331-1-101F 650 SHP	Range	485 Miles
		T.O. Run	510 ft.
Top Speed	175 MPH	Landing Run (w/reverse thrust)	295 ft.
Gross Weight	6100 lbs.		
Useful Load	2545 lbs.	T.O. Distance over 50' Obstacle	610 ft.
Minimum Speed (power on)	65 MPH	Landing Distance over 50' Obstacle	550 ft.
Initial Rate of Climb	1,500 FPM		
Service Ceiling	22,800 ft.		

+ Fairly forgiving aircraft to fly.
+ Very stable landing gear (9'10" track).
+ Good STOL capabilities due to very large wing (nearly 50' span & 310 sq. ft. gross wing area), no leading edge slats, only slotted flaps.
+ Overall design is simple to manufacture and maintain compared to Stallion.

− Relatively slow top speed.
− Useful load not as good as Stallion.

Both aircraft (AU-23A and AU-24A) possessed roughly the same features found to be desirable for third-world support missions. The following comparison, although not definitive, yields a general overview of each plane's respective capabilities and favorable/unfavorable attributes.

The Helio AU-24As (and Fairchild AU-23As) remained at the Davis-Monthon Air Force Base "bone-yard" for roughly a year, until 1973, when an opportunity presented itself in which both aircraft would finally see significant, although low profile, field use.

Of the 15 AU-23A Peacemakers originally built, 13 were transferred from Davis-Monthon to Thailand (a neutral land during the Vietnam conflict) and one was retained by the United States Air Force; the fifteenth had crashed during Credible Chase evaluations at Eglin Air Force Base. Fairchild would later supply another 20 Peacemakers to the Royal Thai Air Force as late as the mid-1970s under the United States Air Force Foreign Military Sales Program.

Helio AU-24A Stallion

Engine	P&W PT6A-27 (free turbine) 680 SHP	Range	445 miles
		T.O. Run	320 ft.
Top Speed	217 MPH	Landing Run (w/reverse thrust)	250 ft.
Gross Weight	6,300 lbs.		
Useful Load	3,440 lbs.	T.O. Distance over 50' Obstacle	660 ft.
Minimum Speed (power on)	42 MPH	Landing Distance over 50' Obstacle	750 ft.
Initial Rate of Climb	2,200 FPM		
Service Ceiling	19,000 ft.		

+ Significantly (42 MPH) faster than Peacemaker.
+ More maneuverable than AU-23A.
+ Superior useful load over Peacemaker.

– Needs wider track for main gear to improve ground handling.
– Overall design is more complex than Peacemaker, requiring added labor for manufacture and maintenance.

The Helio AU-24As were sent from Davis-Monthon to Cambodia, for use by the Royal Khmer Air Force. Of the 15 AU-24As constructed (manufacturer's serial numbers 02 through 16, or military serials 72-1319 through 72-1333), 14 were transferred to Cambodia (Republic of Khmer), while one was retained for additional service trials by the United States Air Force.

With the departure on March 18, 1970, of Cambodia's Prince Norodom Sihanouk, his successor, General Lon Nol, established Cambodia as a republic and welcomed assistance from the United States to help root out Communist elements throughout the country. Provision of aircraft, training for aircrews, and ground support began shortly thereafter, as the U.S. sought to reinforce Lon Nol's government. Aircraft such as North American T-28B counter-insurgency fighters, Cessna T-41 trainers, Douglas C-47 transports, Fairchild C-123K transports, Cessna A-37B light attack jets and Bell Huey helicopters were supplemented by the Helio AU-24A Stallions by 1973.

In addition to the military aircraft that were channeled into Cambodia, airliners belonging to commercial American airlines were extensively chartered to aid in the influx of material in support of these operations.

Massive support for the Lon Nol government's Khmer Air Force (under the code

Helio AU-24A-HE gunship and Khmer crew. Paul E. Davis.

name Project Flycatcher) would formally continue until about June 1974, with varied assistance being provided until the actual fall of Pnom Penh in April 1975.

The AU-24A would be used generally as a ground support and utility transport aircraft to access Cambodia's border territories of Laos, Thailand and Vietnam. Offensively, the Stallion was usually employed at night as a gun/rocket platform to intercept sampan movements along the Mekong River.

Because of its high, strutless wing, the AU-24A offered a superior, unobstructed firing platform to sweep ground targets with its 20-mm electric machine cannon.

The aircraft could very slowly loiter in an area, circling in a tight pattern while raking an enemy position with a withering rain of fire.

As recounted by Helio's manufacturer's technical representative in Cambodia, Paul Davis, the AU-24A served with unique distinction during the campaign in Cambodia.

Serving with the MEDTC (Military Equipment Delivery Team-Cambodia), Davis was no stranger to this part of the world, having logged experience as Helio's manufacturer's technical representative in South Vietnam from 1970 through 1972.

With the introduction of the AU-24As to Cambodia, Davis was called back to duty in October 1973. An AU-24A had gone down in Cambodia in March 1973, when it was being flown over-gross and out of C.G. Davis oversaw and coordinated efforts to educate Khmer Air Force crews in order to insure that such an incident did not happen again.

An essential procedure that Davis drilled into the Khmers following this accident was the need to use up *all* of the 500 rounds of 20-mm machine-cannon ammu-

Helio AU-24A-HE gunship coming in for a landing. Paul E. Davis.

nition *before ever launching the rockets*. This was cited as the main contributing cause of the March crash. Apparently, since the ammunition for the M-197 gun is stored in the aft section of the fuselage, if the rockets are fired *before* getting rid of all ammunition, an unfavorable aft C.G. condition will prevail; the aircraft will tuck under and resist all attempts to recover. This condition, combined with a stabilator that was apparently not balanced correctly (along with Khmer pilots that were not fully trained), led in this specific case to the aircraft's going into the ground, killing all on board.

Ultimately, Davis was able to re-rig and test fly all of the remaining AU-24As in Cambodia to the point that he felt that they were totally safe to restore to active duty.

As Davis relates, "initially, a lot of our time was spent overcoming the hesitancy of the Khmer pilots to trust flying the plane. Along with educating them about the use of the guns and rockets, we had to convince the Khmer crews to fly lower than the 5,000 foot altitudes that they were comfortable with. In order to increase the effectiveness of the gun and rockets, they really needed to be flying down around 2,000 foot levels. I flew on one occasion about 50 feet off of the deck along the Mekong River as a demonstration. We also spent some time making sure that the aircraft was rigged just right as far as engine and flight controls are concerned. Eventually they got the hang of it."[21]

With apparent success, Davis was able to achieve an impressive record for the AU-24A fleet in Cambodia. Davis states: "We'd normally fly three or four missions a day, an average of 2.9 hours per mission. We had the highest utilization rate in Southeast Asia. Three days before we shut down the war, every AU-24 in Southeast Asia, except for one already shipped out in a box on a C-123, was available and flyable. The fleet racked up an estimated 19,000 hours total time in the two countries, much of it combat use."[22]

The AU-24As operated out of bases such as Phnom Penh, Pochentong, Ream, Kompong Chhnang and Battambang. Many of the flight hours were utilized for tactical operations such as gunship day/night sorties (e.g., sampan interdiction), troop and cargo transport as well as training sorties.

In addition to patrolling the Mekong River for enemy shipping, Davis notes that an additional tactical use was for convoy support, in which case 2 or 3 AU-24As would fly in a sortie, with at least one aircraft flying high cover while the other one came in for a rocket or gun run. During the day the gunships used mostly bombs, rockets and 20-mm; at night, flares and 20-mm.

Helio AU-24A-HE undergoing field maintenance in South-East Asia. Paul E. Davis.

All of these tactical sorties made use of a three-man crew, consisting of pilot, co-pilot and gunner. For gun runs, the optical sight that was provided with the aircraft (located next to and outboard of the pilot) was replaced with a simple yet effective grease-pencil cross-hair sighting mark on the pilot's windscreen. This would allow the pilot to control the gunfire (maximum of 500 rounds of belt-fed 20-mm), with the gun locked into a fixed position. On the other hand, having an on-purpose gunner operating the gun could allow for covering fire to the aft of the aircraft as it pulled away from a run.

In reflecting on the use of the AU-24A in Cambodia, Davis discusses with candor how the aircraft served not only as a tactical machine, but also as an indirect source of support for the family and community: "Many times the Khmers might fly just a 30 minute mission, and they'd drain the remaining fuel from the aircraft for their cars and homes. Much of the cartridge brass from our spent 20-mm guns was salvaged by local artisan metalworkers to smelt down and make brass artifacts for their livelihoods. And I can't tell you how often they would fly over-gross just hauling all kinds of stuff around.... Maslow's Law of Hierarchy — you feed your family first-fit well over there."[23]

With the fall of Lon Nol's government in 1975, the Helio AU-24As were generally left abandoned to the discretion of the controlling Communist Pol Pot regime. Davis would later prove to be highly instrumental in obtaining the export of three of these AU-24As, and in performing the conversion and re-certification of these ex-warbirds for civilian sale.

The short, but intense, field history of the AU-24A Stallion should be considered honorable, despite conditions such as gun systems that were pushed way beyond acceptable maintenance schedules (guns that normally are overhauled after 75,000 rounds were pushed on average to 110,000 rounds and higher as of February 1974), as well as the political vagaries of dealing with a culture that is used to being overrun by its neighbors. As Davis noted, "overall, the Khmers flew with distinction, and didn't quit till they ran out of gas."[24]

General Specifications

Model AU-24A-HE Stallion

Powerplant: The AU-24A-HE was powered by a Pratt and Whitney PT6A-27 turbine engine of 680 SHP. Mated to the engine was a Hartzell 3-blade prop featuring reversible pitch and constant speed. Prop diameter was 101 inches.

Price: AU-24A-HE $292,000 (1972)

Dimensions & Performance:

Length	39 ft. 7 in.	Minimum Speed (power on)	42 MPH
Span	41 ft. 0 in.		
Height	9 ft. 3 in.	Minimum Speed (power off)	52 MPH
Wing Area	242 sq. ft.		
Wing Chord	6 ft.	Initial Rate of Climb	1,350 FPM
Wing Aspect Ratio (w/out tanks)	6.93	Service Ceiling	19,000 ft.
		Range	445 miles
Flap Area	40.32 sq. ft.	Fuel capacity (std.)	120 gal.
Tailplane Span	18 ft.	T.O. Run	320 ft.
Dihedral	1 degree	Landing Run (w/reverse thrust)	250 ft.
Incidence	3 degrees		
Empty Weight	2,860 lbs.	T.O. Distance over 50' Obstacle	660 ft.
GWT	6,300 lbs.		
Useful Load	3,440 lbs.	Landing Distance over 50' Obstacle	750 ft.
Wing Loading	21.1 lbs./sq. ft.		
Cruising Speed	160 MPH	Weapons Load	2,240 lbs.
Top Speed	217 MPH		

PROFILE: H-634

The model H-634 Stallion Twin was an attempt by Helio to capitalize on the Stallion airframe by adding the reliability and extra utility of twin turbine engines (two Allison 250-B15 turboprop engines of 317 SHP each). With preliminary design starting in January 1966, the first flight of this 10-place workhorse was planned to occur in the fall of 1970. The aircraft was intended to address the corporate, air taxi and small commuter airline markets. However, the project would remain a concept only (with no prototype or pre-production aircraft built), as overall efforts leading into the early 1970s were focused towards bringing the basic HST-550A and AU-24A Stallion to acceptance by the FAA, and tooling up for anticipated large military orders. It is worth mentioning that the model H-370 Prop-Jet Courier (a highly modified H-295 Super Courier, with one Allison 250-B15 turboprop engine) was used to develop the engine mount, propeller and fuel control system that would have found its way into the H-634 Stallion Twin.

Development of the H-634 Stallion Twin was to have been initially financed in

Helio H-634 Stallion Twin concept aircraft illustration.

part by a $2.85 million stock issue (part of this money was also to have been allocated for simultaneous development of the 6-place, non-turbine model H-580 Twin Courier). At the time, the model H-580 Twin Courier (planned as the replacement for the model H-500) was envisioned as offering about half the performance of the H-634, while selling for about half the price of the H-634. Like the model 580, the production of the H-634 was to have involved manufacture of major airframe components by the Lisbon, Portugal, firm of ALAR. Final assembly was to have occurred in the United States, with an assist from contract work by Hayes International Corporation of Birmingham, Alabama.

Although the single-engine HST-550A Stallion was quite capable of handling air-taxi and corporate commuter work, Lynn Bollinger pointed out that many corporations have regulations that prohibit their key personnel from being transported in a single-engine aircraft (due to safety concerns about engine failure) regardless of how unique the safety and reliability of that aircraft might be. Bollinger noted that "many corporations have bought the STOL idea, but can't use STOL aircraft because of the single-engine limitations."[25]

Bollinger further noted that the H-634 Stallion Twin would excel in the small commuter market since the aircraft would be able to take air traffic control holds in the same airspace that is used by helicopters on approach to major airports. It was also pointed out that, as a commuter aircraft, the H-634 could better access congested hub airports by approaching beneath other traffic and by using shorter runways.

A military version of the H-634 was also being considered, in which four forward-firing mini-guns (one fixed-mounted in the nose, along with three other guns mounted below the belly of the aircraft) and provision for 2,500 lbs. of fuselage- and wing-mounted ordnance (four hardpoints per wing) could be utilized. The military model would have afforded an increased gross weight allowance of 6,100 lbs. (compared to 5,100 lbs. for the civilian variant). It was believed that the added reliability of twin engines, along with their accompanying dual fuel systems, would reduce loss rates due to small-arms fire in a combat environment. Single-engine-out handling characteristics (asymmetric thrust issues) should also have been favorable for this aircraft.

General Specifications

Model H-634 Stallion Twin

Powerplant: H-634 was powered by two Allison 250-B15 Turbine engines of 317 shaft horsepower each. Propellers were Hartzell, 3 bladed, fully feathering constant speed props of 8'0" diameter.

Price: (PROJECTED) H-634 $150,000

Dimensions & Performance:

Length	39 ft. 7 in.	Minimum Speed	35 MPH
Span	41 ft.	(power on)	
Height	8 ft. 8 in.	Initial Rate of Climb	1,900 ft./min.
Wing Area	242 sq. ft.	Service Ceiling	27,000 ft.
Wing Chord	6 ft.	Service Ceiling (1 engine)	5,000 ft.
Flap Area	40.32 sq. ft.	Range	495 miles
Tailplane Span	18 ft. 0 in.	Range (w/optional	945 miles
Dihedral	1 degree	tip tanks)	
Incidence	3 degrees	T.O. Run	335 ft.
Empty Weight	2,845 lbs.	Landing Run	345 ft.
GWT	5,100 lbs.	T.O. Distance over	660 ft.
Useful Load	2,255 lbs.	50' Obstacle	
Cruising Speed	180 MPH	Landing Distance over	655 ft.
Top Speed	210 MPH	50' Obstacle	

PROFILE : GAC-100

The model GAC-100 (General Aircraft Corporation, Model 100) Light STOL Transport project was perhaps the grandest STOL project (at least as far as projected scale was concerned) to have been considered by Helio. As previously mentioned, Helio Aircraft Company became a division of General Aircraft Corporation in April 1969, and the Transport Division of General Aircraft Corporation was assigned to the development of the GAC-100. Because the GAC-100 made extensive use of Helio advanced high-lift design concepts (some of which were under license from Helio) and was in fact the result of Lynn Bollinger's input, the GAC-100 warrants inclusion in the Helio line-up.

Conceived primarily as a 36- to 40-seat light STOL transport for third-level commuter and local airline markets, the GAC-100 would ultimately never get off the ground due to regulatory and financial roadblocks.

The project was formally announced at the Helio annual meeting in 1966, during which a long-range plan was presented for a light air transport STOL machine that would serve as a DC-3 replacement to cover light-density air line routes. It was mentioned that Helio would seek out an independent licensee for manufacture of the aircraft, with royalties being forwarded to Helio.

During 1968, it was announced that PAC (Pacific Airmotive Corporation, a subsidiary of Purex Corporation) would build the fuselage and tail components, while the Australian Government aircraft factory would build the wings and engine nacelles.

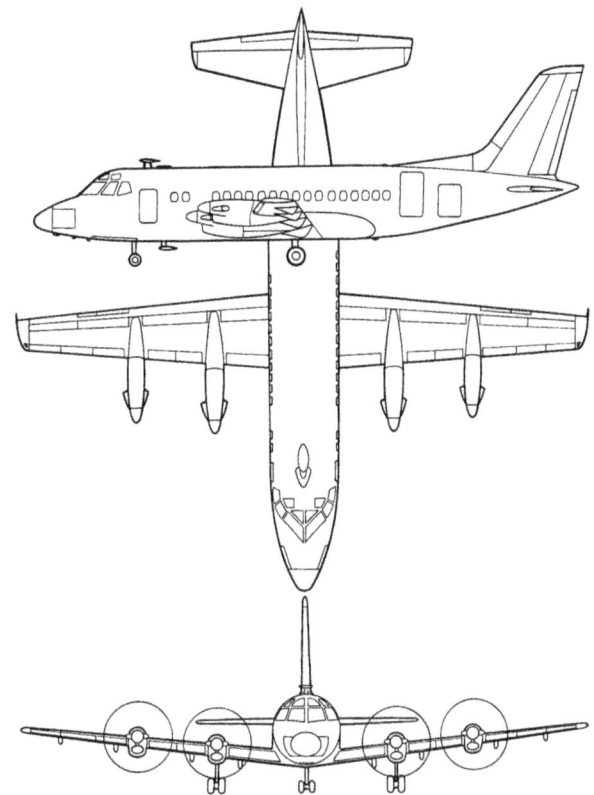

GAC-100 transport — 3-View. Bob Casebeer.

At the time, an initial batch of 100 fuselages/wings sets was contemplated. In 1969, a wholly owned Australian subsidiary of General Aircraft Corporation was being formed, called General Aircraft Corporation Pty, Ltd., to handle assembly. However, not long after the GAC-100 project was given the full program "go-ahead" (October 8, 1969), all these production arrangements were cancelled (late fourth quarter of 1969).

The extent to which a lack of financial commitment among the partners may have contributed to the derailing of the GAC-100 project is debatable. It *can* be said with absolute certainty that the project would have been doomed anyway (at that time) due to regulatory differences between Helio/GAC and the FAA.

At issue was the FAA definition of the maximum number of seats permitted in U.S. commuter category aircraft with respect to aircraft weight (CAB Part 298, Weight Load Limitation Investigation). Specifically, commuter airline transports at that time were restricted to approximately 18 passenger seats, with aircraft weight not to exceed 12,500 lbs. Since the GAC-100 had between 36 and 40 seats, and weighed in at 15,660 lbs., the GAC-100 was precluded from certification.

It was noted in a General Aircraft Corporation *Special Report to Stockholders* (July 20, 1972) that "Since early 1970, when the CAB announced that the weight limitation rule would be changed to some undetermined extent, the company [GAC] had suspended efforts to produce the GAC-100 and wrote off the $1,823,690 developmental investment in that model during 1971."[26]

In a business world where "timing is everything," the GAC-100 program was a bust. No aircraft were ever built. As of June 1969, all expenditure on the aircraft was halted, with business deals in Australia and lease agreements at the GAC research facility in El Segundo, California, terminated. Eventually, the FAA would revise its seat/weight formula for commuter aircraft; the new ruling would have covered the GAC-100 design. But it was too late for what could have been a worthwhile aircraft design. As late as April 1973, GAC was entertaining the possibility of a joint-venture manufacturing program in Canada ($3.5 million equity share), but this too came to naught. As proof of the validity of Helio's light STOL transport concept, a similar design was realized in the production of the DeHavilland Dash-7 commuter aircraft.

On paper, the GAC-100 would have used full-span Fowler-type double-slotted flaps, full-span segmented spoilers, full-span automatic leading edge slats, and no ailerons (an outboard spoiler mixer would serve for roll control). Basic structure of the aircraft was to be all metal, semi-monocoque with a double wing spar (covered with chemically milled wing skins). The tail was fairly conventional, being a cantilevered all-metal structure consisting of tail plane, elevators and rudder.

The cabin was to have been pressurized (AirResearch twin-pac system) with an aft-located galley and toilet. The interior was designed to allow quick conversion to a cargo configuration.

General Specifications

Model GAC-100 STOL Transport

Powerplant: GAC-100 was to have been powered by four Pratt & Whitney (UACL) PT6A-40 turboprop engines of 850 SHP each, as mated to three-bladed variable-pitch propellers of 9'0" diameter.

Price: (PROJECTED) $1,000,000 (1970).

Dimensions & Performance:

Length	70 ft. 0 in.	Useful Load	10,840 lbs.
Span	70 ft. 0 in.	Wing Loading	57.5 lbs./sq. ft.
Height	24 ft. 10 in.	Cruising Speed	293 MPH
Wing Area	461 sq. ft.	Top Speed	340 MPH
Wing Chord (at wing root)	9 ft. 7 in.	Minimum Speed (power on)	71 MPH
Wing Chord (at wing tip)	3 ft. 7 in.	Initial Rate of Climb	2,300 ft./min.
		Service Ceiling	UNKNOWN
Flap Area	50 sq. ft.	Range	656 miles
Tailplane Span	27 ft. 6 in.	T.O. Distance over 50' Obstacle	2,410 ft.
Dihedral	7 degrees		
Incidence	3 degrees	Landing Distance over 50' Obstacle	2,420 ft.
Empty Weight	15,660 lbs.		
GWT	26,500 lbs.	Landing Run	1,460 ft.

6. Twilight of the Courier
The Last Production Helio Courier Models and Concept Aircraft, 1983–1985

Models H-600, H-700, H-800, H-1100, H-2000 and H-21A

"If a Cessna Caravan mated with a Piper Cub, certainly their offspring would look like the Helio Courier. It would be less than accurate to describe the H-700 as pretty, but its appeal lies in its outrageous flight characteristics and practicality." — Ron Grable, *Plane & Pilot*, July 1993

"The Helio is a remarkable airplane with a max cruise of 153 MPH at 75 percent power and a stall speed nearly rivaling helicopters. It won its wings in some brutal conditions in Southeast Asia and in developing nations where the word airport means a dirt road. The company is marketing its airplanes not only to the military and bush users but to businessmen who normally might be forced into a helicopter. To this end the company has been progressing, causing more than a few 'happy faces' in Pittsburg, Kansas." — Phil Buttram, *Pilot News*, May 1984

"So far, most Helio orders are from bush operators with obvious needs for STOL performance. Oil-field operators, construction companies and others who need to operate away from airports are interested. A Helio can be purchased and flown for a fraction of the cost of a helicopter of equal capacity, and can operate from a very limited space." — J. Mac McClellan, *Flying*, March 1984

As suggested by the title of this chapter, the Helio models built or conceived between 1982 and 1985 were the last glimmer on the horizon of this historic C/STOL aircraft; as of the date of this publishing, no others have been seen.

As noted earlier, with the premature ending of the Stallion program, a depressed general aviation market and the stifling effects of the 1977 lawsuit against the government combined to create a malaise that forced Helio to all but shut down operations from 1975 until the early 1980s. The aircraft that was touted as being impossible to stall (at least not according to conventional definition) was mired in a marketing situation that was.

The 1974 cooperative arrangement with John Roberts, LTD., to handle sole distribution (Roberts had world-wide marketing rights to the Helio line since 1973) and eventual manufacture of Helios had fallen through. It was not until the November 8, 1976, acquisition of Helio by New York investor Allan Goldhush that Helio (at this time renamed Helio Aircraft LTD) was restructured, and sub-contract work was sought to "keep the doors open," while newer designs for an updated line of Helios could be considered.

In its darkest hours Helio had less than a dozen employees (and some sources record just two) handling sub-contract work for Boeing-Wichita during the mid–1970s. With Allan Goldhush overseeing the re-shaping of the company, Jim Cox was installed as general manager along with Clarence Brent as chief engineer.

At the time of the first flight (March 1983) of the newest Helio model (H-800, as flight tested by Gene Corsini), it had been nearly 8 long years since the company had produced any aircraft under the Helio banner.

As envisioned by Goldhush and Cox, the re-introduction of the Helio line of C/STOL aircraft was to be accomplished in two distinct phases. Each phase would involve the introduction of new models as shown below.

Phase 1 (1983 & on) would involve the production of the models H-700 and H-800.

H-700: The model H-700 was an updated version of the H-295 Super Courier, but powered by a 350-horsepower AVCO-Lycoming TIO-540-J2B turbocharged and fuel-injected, non-geared 6-cylinder engine. This aircraft was produced primarily to address the utility market that required an aircraft capable of flying out of high altitude airstrips.

H-800: The model H-800 was also an updated version of the much-vaunted H-295 Super Courier, and shared an airframe with the H-700, but was fitted with a 400-horsepower AVCO-Lycoming IO-720-A1B fuel-injected, non-geared 8-cylinder engine. (Note: Despite the model numbering sequence (H-700 vs. H-800), the model H-800 was available before the model H-700 due to engine availability.)

Principal differences between the H-700 and H-800 airframes (aside from engines) and their predecessor H-295 are as follows:

A new, reinforced wing carry-through assembly design was employed and was manufactured from stainless steel. The design was meant to correct a past weakness in Helio wing structural integrity (problems with cracks and corrosion) as addressed in FAA Airworthiness Directive number 82-16-08, Amendment 39-4427 (for specific serials of the older models H-250, H-295, HT-295, H-391, H-391B, H-395 and H-395A). This new design was approved and certificated to the latest FAR Part 23 regulations when both the H-700 and H-800 designs went into production.

A new, adjustable composite main-gear landing gear was integrated into both the models H-700 and H-800, primarily because the old oleo-pneumatic shocks were no longer available. In the haste to get production going again, it was decided to use a type of spring gear for the main gear. The main gear was designed of a polymer (glass fiber and resin matrix) composition to offer weight savings along with an overall strength that was theoretically stronger that steel. The design also afforded the pilot the ability to adjust the stiffness of the gear for landing with varying payload weights. The pilot could select a setting that yielded more flex for landing with lighter loads, or a stiffer setting for landing with heavier loads. Also seen as a side benefit was the fact that the lower profile gear would allow easier ingress/egress for the aircraft cockpit/cabin. Although valid in principle, the composite gear as supplied on H-700 and H-800 aircraft was found to be susceptible to delamination. That problem was subsequently addressed by FAA Airworthiness Directive 87-04-09 (Amendment 39-5533), that required the composite gear to be replaced within the next 100 hours TIS with an approved set of metallic legs (STC SA2171CE).

Provision for four types of landing gear without major modification to airframe was made available on the H-700 and H-800. Either tricycle gear, conventional gear, skis or pontoons could be readily installed, with a minimum of labor as compared to past Helio models. It is quite easy to see the airframe provision for this type of flexibility when looking at the underside contour of the aircraft, just aft of the trailing edge of the wing. There is a noticeable structural bulge that can serve as a mounting point for the aft legs of a tricycle gear installation, as well as for pontoon mountings.

A new, re-styled and re-contoured engine/ nose cowling was added to both the H-700 and H-800. The cowling, aside from offering a distinctively new and more aggressively chiseled appearance, allowed for the installation of additional landing lights, as well as providing for better airflow to the engines. Improved airflow was considered necessary due to the need to maintain a consistent fuel (not vapor) flow to the fuel-injected engines.

New, re-styled and re-contoured wing tips were added to both the H-700 and H-800. These glass-fiber wing tips were designed to help reduce the formation of vortices, thereby offering a certain amount of improved performance.

A new fuel management system was installed in both the H-700 and H-800 to offer improvements from both a safety and performance aspect. A single fuel gauge monitors the flow of fuel. One hundred and twenty gallons of fuel is held by four 30-gallon fuel-cell bladders, with the main cells located just outboard of the fuselage, and fed electrically from the outboard fuel cells. The two 30-gallon mains drain directly into a headtank (about 1.5 gallon capacity) to facilitate fuel flow during "unusual" attitudes.

Phase 2 (1986 & on) would involve the production of the models H-2000 and H-21.

H-2000 The model H-2000 Freightliner was envisioned as a freight-hauling variant of the HST-550A Stallion airframe. To have been powered by the same Pratt & Whitney PT6A-27 powerplant that was fitted to the Stallion, the H-2000 was intended to compete with the likes of the Cessna Caravan. The aircraft was never built, and the project only served as a suggestion as to the direction the company was headed before H-700 and H-800 production was totally shut down.

H-21 The model H-21A Rat'ler was to have been a revolutionary ag-plane C/STOL aircraft that made use of a large number of H-700/H-800 airframe components. Powered by the 400-horsepower AVCO-Lycoming IO-720-AlB engine that was used in the H-800, only two prototypes were reported to have been constructed before the company closed operations in 1984. Although not of much consolation to Helio, since no H-21A production aircraft were ever built, it is to Helio's credit that the aircraft was intended to address one of the most perilous activities in aviation: agricultural spraying operations, cursed with a high rate of stall/spin incidents. Championed as a "pilot saver," the H-21A most notably could have prevented accidents that frequently occur when the pilot, having just dusted a row of crops, pulls up and tries to turn around very quickly for the next pass, thereby risking stalling the lower/slower wing-usually with disastrous results. Unfortunately, the aircraft was conceived at a time when the company itself was locked into its own equivalent of an economically unrecoverable spin. Under-capitalized while trying to sell an extremely expensive aircraft amidst one of the worst recessions to hit the general aviation industry in years, Helio had no other alternative but to cease production for the foreseeable future.

Despite the model H-800's and H-700's late production start (and associated developmental problems), the aircraft appears to have been well received by the few owners that took delivery of the aircraft. However, the viewpoint held by many former Helio company officials, as well as a good number of owner/operators, is that the H-700s and H-800s pale somewhat in comparison to the much-coveted model H-295s.

To underscore this opinion, it may help to briefly examine the performance figures shown in the table below in which the H-295 is compared to the H-800 and H-700.

Although the H-700's performance statistics compare fairly well with the H-295's (roughly equal useful loads, with takeoff and landing numbers within the same ball park), it is the better slow-speed performance of the H-295 that is most noticeable. The lack of modern-day geared engines, along with shorter props (about 10" difference in prop diameters) meant that the modern day versions departed from one of the most important goals of Koppen/Bollinger: an aircraft with safe, slow speeds.

Bob Casebeer (former Helio vice president of manufacturing) recalls that, toward the very end of H-700/H-800 production, they had the Hartzell Propeller Company manufacture a new prop specifically for the types of C/STOL missions for which the planes were intended. The resulting new prop/engine combination amounted to a reported *25 percent gain in performance.*

In all, the evolution of the Helio Courier is perhaps best summarized by David Thurston in his 1995 book *Design for Safety*: "for operation in close areas, off small strips, or out of short ponds on floats, no airplane available compares with the Helio Courier.... During its lifetime the original excellent and useful Helio Courier had actually evolved into an expensive dinosaur. As a result, most of its outstanding operational functions could be performed equally well and at less cost by a helicopter; so the market slowly shrank to uneconomically low production levels and manufacturing was terminated."[1]

Performance Comparison

	H-295 (1965-1974)	H-800 (1982-1984)	H-700 (1984-1984)
Engine horsepower	295 HP	**400 HP**	350 HP
Propellor size	96"	**86"**	87"
Empty weight	**2,080 lbs**	2,527 lbs	2,479 lbs
Gross weight	3,400 lbs	3,800/4,000 lbs	3,800 lbs
Useful load	1,320 lbs	1,273 lbs	**1,321 lbs**
Wing loading	**13 lbs/sq ft**	16.4 lbs/sq ft	16.5 lbs/sq ft
Power loading	11.5 lbs/hp	**9.5 lbs/hp**	10.9 lbs/hp
Take-off run	335 ft	290 ft	**245 ft**
Landing run	270 ft	**228 ft**	240 ft
Take-off to 50 ft obstacle	635 ft	690 ft	**610 ft**
Landing over 50 ft obstacle	515 ft	730 ft	**493 ft**
Max structural cruise speed	**160 mph**	153 mph	153 mph
Minimum speed (power on)	**30 mph**	52 mph	51 mph
Service ceiling	20,500 ft	21,000 ft	**29,000 ft**

Note: Data in **bold-face** represents superior comparative performance.

Performance Comparison.

Helio Aircraft Profiles

The remainder of chapter six consists of a series of profiles that detail the differences between the various main models and conceptual variants of Helios built betwen 1982 and 1984. The models profiled consist of the following aircraft: H-700 (and H-600 Concept), H-800, H-2000 (and H-1100 Concept), H-21A (Prototype).

PROFILE: H-700
PROFILE: H-600

The model H-700 Helio Courier was an attempt by Helio to harness the advantages of a turbocharged, fuel injected powerplant to handle high-altitude airstrips. With preliminary work starting in 1981, type certification would be granted on January 24, 1984 (Normal Category) as related to the original 1A8 type certificate, and which also pertains to the other Couriers (H-391, H-391B, H-395, H-395A, H-250, H-295 and HT-295).

In all, only seven model H-700 Couriers were produced (serials H-8 and up),

Helio H-700 (photograph by Nathan Mackey).

with production being halted towards the end of 1984. The balance of production Helios being delivered at this time were the model H-800 Courier.

Basic airframe and wing geometry is essentially the same as used on the H-295 (Handley Page automatic leading-edge slats, slotted flaps, interceptors and stabilator for control); however, the engine, a turbo-charged and fuel-injected 350-horsepower AVCO-Lycoming TIO-540-J2B flat six was of a non-geared variety. Offsetting the overall relatively impressive performance of this engine installation was the high fuel consumption rate. It reportedly consumed roughly 40 gallons per hour (compared to roughly 12 gallons per hour for the model H-295's GO-480 with its Bendix pressure carburetor) as a result of the need to use fuel to help cool the engine. At the time of the model H-700's inception, consideration was also given to offering an additional model to be designated the H-600. This aircraft was to have the same airframe as the H-700 but was to have been powered by a 250-horsepower Lycoming 0-540.

Contemplated as a more affordable Courier, the H-600 was to have offered the same basic gross weight as the H-700, but with lesser overall performance (e.g., 15,200' service ceiling, maximum speed of 160 MPH). Ultimately the model H-600 was confined to the drawing board, with no actual aircraft produced.

The interior of the H-700 was updated with a cleaned-up trim package, as well as abrasion-resistant nylon covered seats. All seats were fitted, as is customary, with 15-G seat belts with shoulder harness as standard. Seating provision was for one pilot and five passengers, with the seats installed in rows of twos.

While the H-700's (and H-800's) unique airframe provided for up to four types of landing gear options (tricycle gear, conventional, skis or pontoons could be fitted to an undercarriage mounting that was integrated into the standard Courier's airframe), it was reported that most of the new-generation Couriers were outfitted with pontoons.

6. Twilight of the Courier

Highly modified Helio H-700 ("Too Loud, Too Bad") with Garret turboprop engine (photograph by Nathan Mackey).

General Specifications

Model H-700 Courier

Powerplant: The model H-700 Courier was powered by an AVCO-Lycoming TIO-540-J2B turbocharged and fuel-injected engine of 350 horsepower. Mated to the engine was a Hartzell 3-bladed constant-speed metal prop of 87" (7' 3") diameter.

Price: Model H-700 $151,600 (1984)

Dimensions & Performance:

Length	32 ft. 6 in.	Cruising Speed	160 MPH
Span	38 ft. 0 in.	Top Speed	167 MPH
Height	8 ft. 8 in.	Minimum Speed	51 MPH
Wing Area	231 sq. ft.	(power on)	
Wing Chord	6 ft.	Initial Rate of Climb	1,180 FPM
Wing Aspect Ratio	6.6	Service Ceiling	29,000 ft.
(w/out tanks)		Range	1,380 miles
Flap Area	40.32 sq. ft.	Fuel Capacity (std.)	120 gal.
Tailplane Span	15 ft.	T.O. Run	245 ft.
Dihedral	1 degree	Landing Run	240 ft.
Incidence	3 degrees	T.O. Distance over	610 ft.
Empty Weight	2,479 lbs.	50' Obstacle	
GWT	3,800 lbs.	Landing Distance over	493 ft.
Useful load	1,321 lbs.	50' Obstacle	
Wing Loading	14.72 lbs./sq. ft.		

PROFILE : H-800

The model H-800 Helio Courier was a sister ship to the turbocharged and fuel-injected model H-700 Courier, and was an attempt by Helio to reintroduce a mod-

Helio H-800.

ern version of the highly regarded model H-295. With preliminary work starting in 1981, the first flight of the model H-800 was recorded as having taken place on March 24, 1983. Type certification would be granted on July 19, 1983 (Normal Category, 4 PCSM), and on September 28, 1983 (Normal Category 6 PCLM) as related to the original 1A8 pertaining to the other Couriers (H-391, H-391B, H-395, H-395A, H-250, H-295 and HT-295).

In all, only nine model H-800 Couriers were produced (serials H-1 through H-7, with the balance following the introduction of the Model H-700 with serial H-8 and on). Most of the owner/operators taking delivery of the H-800/H-700 before production was halted towards the end of 1984 were described as being involved in bush operations, oil-field and construction-type businesses. It is interesting to note that the Model H-800 preceded the Model H-700 into production (in spite of the model numbering sequence) due to a lack of engine availability for the H-700. The first Model H-800 off the line was also in fact an aircraft with (EDO 3500) amphibious pontoons.

Basic airframe and wing geometry is essentially the same as used on the H-700 (Handley Page automatic leading-edge slats, slotted flaps, interceptors and stabilator for control); however, the engine, a fuel-injected 400-horsepower AVCO-Lycoming IO-720-A1B flat eight, was of a non-geared variety.

The interior of the H-800 was updated with a cleaned-up trim package, as well as abrasion-resistant nylon covered seats. All seats were fitted, as is customary, with 15-G seat belts with shoulder harness as standard. Seating provision was for one pilot and five passengers, with the seats installed in rows of twos.

While the H-800's (and H-700's) unique airframe provided for up to four types of landing gear options (tricycle gear, conventional, skis or pontoons could be fitted to an undercarriage mounting that was integrated into the standard Courier's airframe), it was reported that most of the new-generation Couriers were outfitted with pontoons. None of the model H-800s (nor H-700s) were ever delivered with tricycle-type landing gear.

At the first flight of the model H-800, Helio General Manager Jim Cox envisioned a production rate of about four aircraft a month, as produced by the 80 employees at the Helio plant in Pittsburg, Kansas. Cox stated that Helio had orders for about 20 aircraft at the time (March 26, 1983).

General Specifications

Model H-800 Courier

Powerplant: The model H-800 Courier was powered by an AVCO-Lycoming IO-720-A1B fuel-injected flat eight engine of 400 horsepower. Mated to the engine was a Hartzell 3-bladed constant-speed metal prop of 86" (7'2") diameter.

Price: H-800 $145,000 (1983)
$185,000 with floats (1983)

Dimensions & Performance:

Length	32 ft. 6 in.	Cruising Speed	152 MPH
Span	38 ft. 0 in.	Top Speed	153 MPH
Height	8 ft. 8 in.	Minimum Speed	52 MPH
Wing Area	231 sq. ft.	(power on)	
Wing Chord	6 ft.	Initial Rate of Climb	1,120 FPM
Wing Aspect Ratio	6.6	Service Ceiling	21,000 ft.
(w/out tanks)		Range	1,064 Miles
Flap Area	40.32 sq. ft.	Fuel Capacity (std.)	120 gal.
Tailplane Span	15 ft.	T.O. Run	290 ft.
Dihedral	1 degree	Landing Run	228 ft.
Incidence	3 degrees	(w/reverse thrust)	
Empty Weight	2,527 lbs.	T.O. Distance over	690 ft.
GWT	3,800 lbs.	50' Obstacle	
Useful Load	1,273 lbs.	Landing Distance over	730 ft.
Wing Loading	16.45 lbs./sq. ft.	50' Obstacle	

PROFILE : H-2000
PROFILE : H-1100

The model H-2000 Freightliner project was a concept to produce a utility freight and passenger turbo-prop transport (seating up to 16) like the Cessna Caravan. The concept would use as its basis a highly modified turbo-prop Stallion-type airframe. With preliminary work starting in the early 1980s, the aircraft was expected to see production within the year 1986.

The basic design would have incorporated the Pratt & Whitney PT6A-27 turboprop engine as used in the Stallion and Cessna Caravan, and would have retained the same basic C/STOL design elements (four Handley Page automatic leading-edge

Helio H-2000 Freightliner concept. Bob Casebeer.

slats, slotted flaps and interceptor "spoilers" as part of a cantilevered overhead wing) as other Helio aircraft.

Unique to the modern (early 1980s) line of Helio models, the Freightliner would have come standard (like the Cessna Caravan) with tricycle gear.

A four-foot by four-foot sliding cargo door on the aft left-hand side would have allowed access for loading/unloading shipping pallets and over-sized cargo.

The H-2000 was envisioned as being offered in two versions. The first (lighter) version was to have been certificated to a maximum gross weight of 5,000 pounds, permitting C/STOL operation on shorter airstrips (300' ground roll, 2,000 ft./min. rate of climb, 32,800 ft. service ceiling, with cruise at about 207 MPH). The second (heavier) version would have had a maximum gross weight of 6,090 pounds, allowing for a greater (500') ground roll.

The Freightliner was intended to address the needs of small commercial commuter airlines, cargo haulers and other industrial as well as military patrons. However, the H-2000 project would remain a concept only, with no prototype or production aircraft ever built.

Sharing space on the drawing table was a little-known model designated as the H-1100. Essentially an H-700/H-800 airframe mated to a Pratt & Whitney PT6A engine, the H-1100 never made it to prototype stage either.

General Specifications

Model H-2000 Freightliner

Powerplant: The model H-2000 was to have been powered by a Pratt and Whitney PT6A-27 turbine engine of 680 SHP. Mated to the engine was a Hartzell 3-bladed prop featuring reversible pitch and constant speed. Prop diameter was 101 inches.

Price: H-2000 $[UNKNOWN] (1984)

Dimensions & Performance:

Length	UNKNOWN	Wing Chord	UNKNOWN
Span	UNKNOWN	Wing Aspect Ratio	UNKNOWN
Height	UNKNOWN	Flap Area	UNKNOWN
Wing Area	UNKNOWN	Tailplane Span	UNKNOWN

Dihedral	UNKNOWN	Service Ceiling	32,800 ft.
Incidence	UNKNOWN	Range	737 miles
Empty Weight	UNKNOWN	Fuel Capacity (std.)	250 gal.
GWT	5,000 or 6,090 lbs.	T.O. Run	300 or 500 ft.
Useful Load	Quoted at 3,190 lbs.	Landing Run (w/reverse thrust)	300 or 500 ft.
Wing Loading	UNKNOWN		
Cruising Speed	207 MPH	T.O. Distance (50' Obstacle)	UNKNOWN
Top Speed	UNKNOWN		
Minimum Speed (power on)	62 MPH	Landing Distance (50' Obstacle)	UNKNOWN
Initial Rate of Climb	2,000 FPM		

General Specifications

Model H-1100

Powerplant: The model H-1100 was to have been powered by an unspecified version of the Pratt and Whitney PT6A turbine engine. Mated to the engine would have been a Hartzell 3-bladed prop featuring reversible pitch and constant speed. Prop diameter was noted as to have been 101 inches.

Price: H-1100 $[UNKNOWN] (1984)

Dimensions & Performance:

No accurate dimensions or performance data could be obtained for the H-1100 at the time of publication. However, it can be assumed that general dimensions should be about the same as those for the models H-700/H-800.

PROFILE : H-21A

The model H-21A RAT'LER Ag (agricultural) aircraft was an attempt by Helio to offer crop dusters an aircraft that would drastically reduce the number of stall/spin incidents that had long plagued the profession, while affording increased utility. With preliminary work starting in the early 1980s, it would not be until the near the final closing of Helio operations that the aircraft would debut in prototype form.

The H-21A was limited to two prototypes, with no production aircraft built. The first prototype was about one-fourth engineered when it was set aside as a result of a change in design philosophy that resulted in a second prototype. The aircraft itself (prototype number A1, with registration number N4405S) debuted at the Agricultural Aviation Convention in Las Vegas, Nevada, during December 1984, but it was mothballed shortly thereafter once Helio closed operations.

The prototypes and production aircraft were designed to make extensive use of existing H-700/H-800 components. To this extent, the H-21A design used the H-800's 400-horsepower AVCO-Lycoming IO-720-A1B fuel-injected powerplant, as well as the H-700/H-800's high-lift wing (although now of a low-wing installation) and tail. Typical of generic ag aircraft design, a new fuselage featuring a raised single seat cockpit was integrated into the basic Helio wing/engine mount design, with a 400-gallon dry chemical hopper located forward of the cockpit.

Helio conceived the H-21A as a brand new generation of ag aircraft, and the company felt it was as revolutionary as the Cessna AgWagon was compared to the Stearman biplanes that were modified to perform crop-dusting duties.

With its 400-horsepower engine, the aircraft was seen as having the speed that is desirable for spraying long fields, while its C/STOL abilities would be vital during the dangerous slow speed phase of flight when the pilot needs to perform tight turns for hard-to-access portions of the field.

Helio General Manager Jim Cox (a former Cessna ag aircraft salesman himself) noted that: "Hundreds of ag pilots have been killed over the past years in one maneuver alone. As the pilot finishes spraying a row, he tries to get up, turn around, and get back down ASAP. This puts him in high angles of attack and steep turns at low speeds, resulting in the lower wing stalling out thus putting the plane in a spin to the ground. The Helio Ag is designed to provide (1), fewer crashes by providing more lift for the slower wing situations by using the air-controlled slats which automatically deploy at about 55 MPH, (2), a more stable and dependable workhorse, and (3), increase the margin of safety and comfort for the pilot."[2]

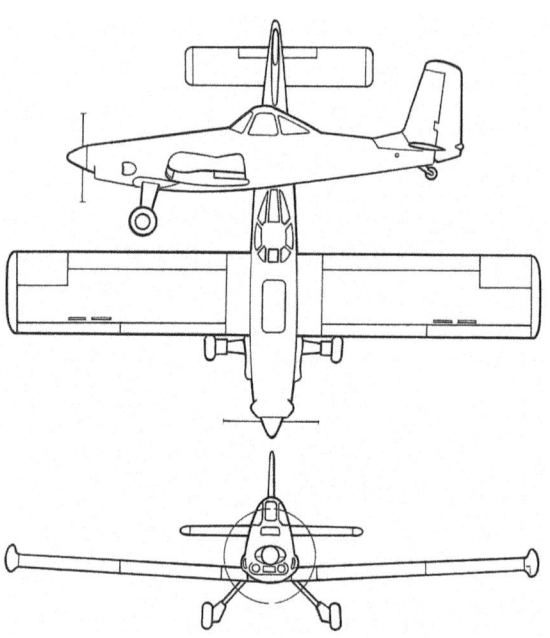

Helio H-21A "RAT'Ler"—3-View.

It was also pointed out that, with the H-21A's proven C/STOL abilities, it would now be possible to actually land the ag aircraft in a field (to underscore the rough-field capabilities of the H-21A, Cox said: "I mean a freshly tilled field"[3]) or on a dirt road to reload the chemical hopper on site, thereby making the job quicker and more profitable.

Cox was quoted in a March 1983 article in the *Pittsburg Morning Sun* as expecting to build roughly "300 H-21As a year."[4] Typical of these frustrating times for Helio, that vision of H-21A production died away about as quickly as it takes for the sun to set on a cold winter's day in Kansas.

Several unresolved engineering challenges (including a wing that was reportedly too close to the ground for spray booms to be fitted, due to the use of the short-legged composite landing gear) would accompany the prototype to its long-term storage at Pittsburg's Atkinson Airport.

Although the promise of the revolutionary H-21A would go unfulfilled, the concept is perhaps one of the most intriguing applications of C/STOL design in general aviation.

6. Twilight of the Courier

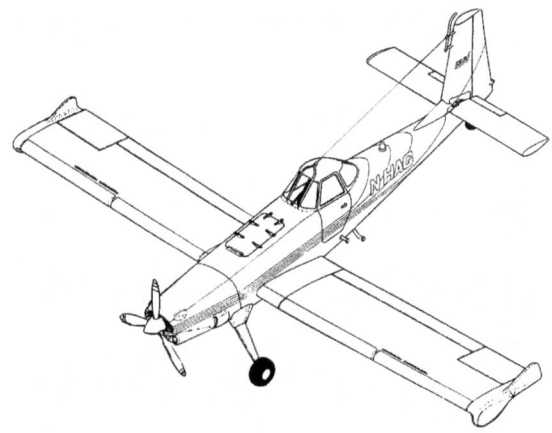

Helio H-21A "RAT'Ler." Bob Casebeer.

General Specifications

Model H-21A "Rat'ler"

Powerplant: The model H-21A was powered by a fuel-injected Lycoming IO-720-A1B flat-eight engine of 400 SHP. Mated to the engine was a constant-speed Hartzell 3-bladed prop (diameter 101 inches).

Price: H-21A (1st 50 A/C): $100,000 (1984) (after 50 A/C): $120,000

Dimensions & Performance:

Length	31 ft. 6 in.	Cruising Speed	152 MPH
Span	43 ft. 0 in.	Top Speed	UNKNOWN
Height	10 ft. 3 in.	Minimum Speed	UNKNOWN
Wing Area	UNKNOWN	(power on)	
Wing Chord	6 ft. 0 in.	Initial Rate of Climb	UNKNOWN
Wing Aspect Ratio	UNKNOWN	Service Ceiling	22,356 ft.
(w/out tanks)		Range	UNKNOWN
Flap Area	UNKNOWN	Fuel Capacity (std.)	120 gal.
Tailplane Span	9 ft. 0 in.	T.O. Run	220 ft.
Dihedral	UNKNOWN	Landing Run	165 ft.
Incidence	UNKNOWN	T.O. Distance	542 ft.
Empty Weight	2,400 lbs.	(50' Obstacle)	
GWT	4,850 lbs.	Landing Distance	689 ft.
Useful Load	2,450 lbs.	(50' Obstacle)	
Wing Loading	UNKNOWN		

7. Couriers of the World
JAARS Helio Operations

"It is one of the delightful paradoxes of this life that the aircraft which began its career in so sordid an enterprise is now chiefly employed in a much more wholesome business. Twenty-six of the aircraft-certainly the largest fleet of Helio Couriers operating in the world-are employed with JAARS, the Jungle Aviation and Radio Service, which is the logistical support arm of the Wycliffe Bible Translators organization. The Helio Courier is an unusual airplane and it seems to find its way into the most remote locations, doing unusual work. If you are flying people and supplies out of remote areas, you can get no better airplane than the Helio Courier. It is a truly outstanding workhorse."—John W. Conrad, *Air Progress*, July 1992

Without a doubt, no history of Helio could be considered complete without acknowledging, as well as briefly detailing, the part an organization known as JAARS, Inc. (formerly Jungle Aviation and Radio Service), has played in the use and continued development of the Helio Courier. Located outside the town of Waxhaw, North Carolina, JAARS is one of the longest-lived of several missionary-type outreach organizations that address the needs of those primarily located in third-world countries. Mission organizations have been highly instrumental in making use of aircraft to support their staffs in the field, as well as to facilitate evangelical ministries for stateside revivals and rallies. Other such groups include the Missionary Aviation Fellowship (MAF) and the Church of the God of Prophecy, an organization which used a fleet of airplanes-known as the "great white fleet" and amounting to some 70 aircraft-to spread the word of God as based upon the interpretation of scripture such as Ecclesiates 10:20 ("For a bird of the air shall carry the voice, and that which hath wings shall tell the matter).[1] While the latter two organizations used an assortment of Cessnas, Luscombes, DC-3s, Turbine Islanders, Pipers, Aeroncas, Stinsons and Taylorcrafts, it was— and still is— JAARS that relies heavily upon the Helio Courier to fulfill its aviation requirements.

While the use of the Helio Courier for outreach operations may have been just one of the many possible applications envisioned by its original designers, in the long term it seems to have turned out to be one of the most notable and enduring. To many observers, it is most satisfying to see the aircraft being used in a manner that makes the best and fullest use of its C/STOL utility and safety capabilities, while

William Cameron Townsend and HelioCourier. JAARS, Inc.

serving in a uniquely humanitarian role (though, in many cases the worldwide CIA missions and Special Forces operations that Helios were flown in over the years deserve credit as well).

The historical connection between the Helio Courier and the JAARS organization can be traced back to the founder of JAARS and Wycliffe Bible Translators: William Cameron Townsend, known to his acquaintances as "Uncle Cam." Townsend's goal was to translate the New Testament into every language on earth. The need for this undertaking was revealed to him when, at age 21, Townsend embarked upon a one-year journey to South America to sell Spanish Bibles. The necessity of translating the Bible into languages that were indigenous to the territory was made clear when Townsend discovered that most natives did not speak Spanish and could not read. As if to underscore his mission, a frustrated native posed to Townsend the question: "Why doesn't your God speak my language?" In response to this pointed question, Townsend made it his life's work to translate the Bible into every one of the world's languages, based upon the precept that "only a person's mother tongue truly speaks to the heart."

On the surface, this goal of translating the New Testament into every language that had been previously un-addressed is almost assuredly met with praise and admiration. However, it is a daunting task when one considers that in many instances the local inhabitants are less than receptive to foreigners (for example, one M.A.F. missionary and four others were murdered by the Auca tribe in Ecuador). Moreover, there is the challenge of overcoming conditions counter to establishing good will, such as blood feuds, infanticide, drunkenness, and general malaise sometimes caused by years of enslavement.

To date, nearly 600 languages now have translations of the New Testament with the help of Wycliffe translators; work continues in about 1300 language groups. Lending further insight to the magnitude of this mission is the fact that in many cases an alphabet must be established before any other work occurs. On average, it takes a two-person team 15 years to establish a basic grammar, construct a dictionary, and ultimately translate the New Testament into the new language.

In the most challenging situations, sometimes the local inhabitants may communicate only by whistling tonal words, or the language may be so complex that a single verb may consist of up to 12 syllables with as many as 100,000 possible forms. In such cases the time required to ultimately translate the New Testament is lengthened considerably.

According to the Ethnologue database, there are a total of 6,809 languages currently being spoken in the world; the New Testament has yet to be translated into at least 2,700 of them. There are over 5,000 Wycliffe Bible translators performing duties in over 50 countries throughout the world.

The formal establishment of an organization to address this challenge occurred in 1934, when Townsend returned to the United States to set up courses to instruct translators at what would become the Summer Institute of Linguistics (SIL).

Ultimately, in order to provide continuous support for translators in the field, Townsend would incorporate his activities into the Wycliffe Bible Translators, Inc. Named after John Wycliffe, a fourteenth-century heretic who was condemned for translating the Bible into the English language, the Wycliffe organization has evolved to the point that it is called the largest missionary outreach program of its type in the world.

Members of the missionary outreach program include translators, pilots, mechanics, and radio/communication experts as well as a host of medical, construction and other support personnel.

Members work for no pay, except that money required to finance day-to-day operations and training is solicited from churches throughout stateside communities. Administration of the funds is handled by the headquarters of Wycliffe Bible Translators in Orlando, Florida.

The origin of the JAARS aviation fleet and support operations can be traced to several of Cameron Townsend's early experiences.

One compelling story involves Townsend's hearing of a translator who (along with his family) was faced with the dangers of hiking for weeks through the Peruvian jungles. Townsend felt an aviation program (with aircraft capable of withstanding the rigors of jungle/mountain flying) could provide many benefits to the organization's staff and mission.

Significantly, after Townsend himself was involved in an aircraft accident in 1946, he resolved to develop the aviation capability that would provide benefit to many JAARS volunteers throughout the world.

In this accident, Townsend, his wife Elaine, their six-month-old baby, and a pilot were in a Piper Super Cruiser. The aircraft was apparently overloaded, and upon takeoff was unable to clear some trees. Townsend, his wife and the pilot were all injured; the baby was removed unharmed from the wreckage, although fuel was dripping onto the child until it was rescued. During the two hours required to extricate

7. Couriers of the World

Helio Courier in a typical third-world-country outreach work environment. JAARS, Inc.

Townsend from the remains of the aircraft, he began to plan for an aviation fleet that would require highly trained pilots capable of negotiating the perilous challenges of jungle flying. The fleet eventually would become an affiliate, non-profit organization serving the Wycliffe Bible Translators.

Initial response from the headquarters at Wycliffe to the proposal for an aviation fleet showed little enthusiasm. Townsend responded that "I'll not be responsible for sending young people out in the jungle any longer unless we have our own air arm."[2] Additionally, Townsend asserted: "It is impossible to do our job without planes-properly run and serviced. If you insist on your approach, you can just find someone else to take charge of our advance into the Amazon jungle. I shall not be responsible for the hardships you are forcing on these men and women who are giving their lives for Christ."[3]

By 1948, the administration at Wycliffe came around to granting permission to develop an aviation division with logistical support to serve Wycliffe translators in a timely manner. Betty Greene became the first pilot, with Larry Montgomery to be added later.

While Townsend's personal accident in the Piper may have been the final impetus for launching JAARS, conditions had long warranted the creation of the air arm for Wycliffe. Considering the impenetrable jungle terrain, with its mountain ranges, perilous rivers and dense vegetation (not to mention the swamps, floods, mosquitoes and steaming climate), common sense practically demanded it. The introduction of aircraft allowed an efficiency that would greatly reduce overall operations, with a direct impact on the time it would require to translate local languages.

Considering that one minute of flying time was equivalent to one hour of trekking, it was calculated that three months of flying would save roughly 25 years' worth of foot travel.

Initially, Townsend made use of an odd assortment of aircraft, including a Grumman Duck, a surplus PBY Catalina flying boat, DC-3s and other aircraft.

Loading "the canoe that flies" (as known by local inhabitants) for a trip deep into the jungle of Peru, South America. JAARS, Inc.

Although an improvement, the JAARS fleet of aircraft in its early days was a rather ragged lot, with parts being cannibalized on a routine basis and components held together by "screws and a prayer," to the point that in 1953 it was described in a report to the Moody Bible Institute as a "flying junkyard." Aircraft were obtained for next to nothing through the sympathetic giving of sponsors, or were obtained at rock-bottom costs and very creative terms of financing. In all cases, prayer was the foundation upon which JAARS was able to realize its fleet (e.g., Psalm 37: "Delight thyself also in the Lord; and he shall give thee the desires of thine heart").

Despite these conditions, spirit and comradery were high amongst the pilots of JAARS, with their own motto being: "We do our best, God does the rest."

As welcome as JAARS's early aircraft were, jungle flying demanded more-in particular, aircraft capable of accessing the most remote outposts with reasonable safety.

Conditions demanded that the pilot be extremely wary all of the time. Like any other competent pilot flying anywhere else in the world, the jungle pilot must constantly be scanning his instruments. However, the jungle pilot is also constantly scanning the terrain below for a spot where he or she could land the plane in the case of an emergency, as well as constantly checking and rechecking the plane's location in case of quickly developing bad weather. All-too-well-known to most jungle pilots is the old saying, "the jungle is sprinkled with the bleached bones of pilots, some of whom were on God's missions."[4]

Having to fly over terrain that is not accurately represented on the chart, or not charted at all, also serves to compound the challenges of flying, not to mention the demands of flying in thin air associated with flying over the ever present mountain

The Helio Courier "Spirit of Pontiac" being loaded aboard the USS *Kearsarge* (March 1961) in San Diego, California, on its way to a jungle outpost in the Philippines. JAARS, Inc. (U.S. Navy photograph).

ranges. Jungle pilots were particularly fond of flying along river routes that might afford the opportunity to land on a sandbar (or playa) in case of an in-flight emergency.

Within these constraints, the stage was set for the Helio Courier to be discovered and used by missionary jungle pilots. Like so many of Cameron Townsend's visions, the Helio seemed to materialize out of the blue in response to his prayers in order to teach primitive people throughout the world to learn to read, and to translate the Bible into their language while preserving their culture and leaving behind the word of God.

The Helio Courier attracted the attention of William Cameron Townsend while he was driving near Tulsa, Oklahoma, in 1955. Townsend spied this unusual aircraft flying above the highway and was immediately intrigued by the way it seemed to merely hang suspended in the sky. Upon following the aircraft to a local airport, Townsend was further amazed at the angle of climb the aircraft could achieve, as well as how quickly it could cover ground once airborne. Townsend realized that he had found the answer to his prayers for the ideal aircraft for missionary support work: "an aircraft that would not only cruise at very low speeds for jungle surveys, but would race across the sky on emergency flights, one that could land on small, muddy jungle fields and takeoff with maximum loads."[5]

Upon closer examination, the Helio's superior cabin structural integrity impressed Townsend as adding a significant safety factor to the perilous jungle flying routine. In actual field usage by JAARS, the aircraft has lived up to its expectations in terms of utility and safety, with no accidents involving fatalities despite having to negotiate extremely short airstrips carved into dense jungle terrain flanked on all sides by trees and mountains.

Inspired by the aircraft's potential for missionary support work, Townsend acquired the first Helio, a model H-391B (serial # 22), during the fall of 1955. It would be the first of many Helios to be operated by JAARS throughout the years. In fact, on average, the JAARS Helio fleet has numbered some 20 aircraft in recent years. The experience that JAARS has gained with flying, modifying and repairing the Helio has also made them perhaps the premier source (in the absence of an official Helio factory support system) for spare parts and service advice. While the Helio Courier models that have been utilized by JAARS constitute a large percentage of their fleet air arm, it should be pointed out that JAARS also uses other modern aircraft such as various models of Cessnas (particularly the model 206) as well as helicopters (primarily ex-military Hiller helicopters, the last of which was retired in 2004 and replaced by Bell/R44 models).

Helio over mountainous terrain. JAARS, Inc.

The stateside home base for the JAARS Helio fleet is located on 600 acres of land outside of Waxhaw, south of Charlotte, North Carolina. The site was donated to JAARS in 1960 by businessman Henderson Belk, and serves as a training, education, administration and logistical service center for worldwide missionary operations. For the Helio aficionado, it is a must-see priority; it also provides a beneficial insight into the other unique operations that are a part of the JAARS charter (i.e., a radio lab to build and repair equipment, printing operations, general training facilities to prepare overseas missionaries, and the "jungle jump-off" youth program, as well as other unique features including the superb Museum of the Alphabet and the Mexico Museum).

The JAARS Helio fleet has served with distinction while under the command of some of the world's most experienced and competent pilots. Pilots such as Larry Montgomery and Bob Griffin, along with many others, have flown the Helio Courier in far-off places such as Luzon and Mindanao of the Philippines, Papua New Guinea, Zaire, Liberia, Nepal, Indonesia, Peru, Colombia, Ecuador, Bolivia and other countries throughout the world.

Upon visiting the JAARS aviation complex in Waxhaw, North Carolina, the guest is impressed by the orderly and professional layout of the hangars and service areas. Access to the Townsend Field runway at the JAARS center is based upon the Fort Mill VOR and use of UNICOM. The typical assortment of Helio Courier models includes several former military U-10 versions that have been converted over for civilian use, as well as the very first Helio Courier, serial number one (referred to, and with script letters painted on its engine cowling certifying it, as "Ol' Number One").

JAARS "Gray Goose," H-395 (S/N 558).

The added fact that noted Helio pilot Larry Montgomery's Helio service and sales facility (Larmont Aviation in Spartanburg, South Carolina) is located a relatively short distance to the southwest of the JAARS facility can perhaps lend validity (in the absence of a current Helio factory) to this region's being considered the current epicenter for all things Helio.

As would be expected considering JAARS's experience in the field with Helios (along with the lack of a current Helio factory support system), JAARS has assumed a role of pioneering Helio improvements and modifications through a series of STCs (Supplementary Type Certificates).

Many of these improvements have been integrated into, and tested in, their own experimental prototype aircraft affectionately referred to as "the Gray Goose" (H-395, Serial Number 558). A former U-10B Helio Courier (military no. 62-5918) reconverted (2/15/85) to civilian specs, the Gray Goose (N87763) is finished in dull, grayish aluminum skins with the occasional evidence of light blue composite panels lending the only flash of color.

According to JAARS aviation engineer Terry Heffield, the following improvements have been addressed and evaluated, and have been (or may be at a future date) integrated into the fleet of JAARS-operated Helios.[6]

JAARS Helio Modifications:

1. Modified fiberglass fairing above windshield where wing intersects cabin. Removed fiberglass to allow better aerodynamics/less drag.*
2. Modified wrap-around fairing at base of windshield to improve aerodynamic flow and reduce drag.*
3. Modified fiberglass nose cowling to improve aerodynamic flow and reduce drag. Moved oil cooler to back instead of in the chin area (did not use).*

4. Modified tail to close off the area located above the stabilator for aerodynamic improvements.*
5. Modified tail-wheel boot for aerodynamic improvements. Changed from flexible Naugahyde material to aluminum to keep boot from acting like a mini-parachute.*
6. Modified tail wheel A-frame.
7. Incorporated several tail wheel shimmy-dampener modifications.
8. Modified ventral panel.
9. Reinforced stabilator with cadmium-plated steel ribs. Former installation was susceptible to cracking at the juncture of the fuselage and stabilator.
10. Added under-belly cargo pod, affording approximately twenty cubic feet of additional storage space. The pod could either be attached directly to the outer skin of the aircraft by way of conventional fasteners, or the belly fairing could be cut away, allowing for an additional six inches of height for even more storage space in the pod. Either way, the pod added only a reported 1-MPH drag penalty.
11. Added stronger seat tracks to cabin.
12. Improved structural integrity of shoulder harness installation by welding through aft carry-through spar, and installing Brownline fitting.
13. Reinforced flap tracks.
14. Modified tomahawk leading-edge slat support tubes.
15. Designed, tested and integrated three new cabin-type safety seats capable of withstanding higher degrees of impact (two S-type seat frames based upon a concept originally attributed to Piper Aircraft, and one crushable foam-type block seat for use in aft sections of the aircraft).
16. Modified fuel tanks to accept Cessna style fuel caps.
17. Changed main landing gear design by adding flange at bottom and gussets to allow use of either a "right-hand" or "left-hand" gear for installation in either location.
18. Provided option to bolt down right seat rudder pedals to avoid inadvertent operation by passenger.

 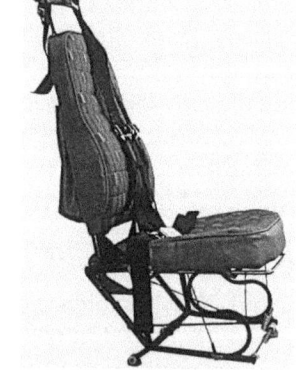

Left: Field maintenance and refueling before a trial flight in the Philippines. JAARS, Inc. *Right:* JAARS' energy-absorbing safety seat — a feature meant to enhance survivability in the event of rough landings.

JAARS' Helio "Ol' No. 1" at Waxhaw, North Carolina, facility.

19. Provided option to install special light/alarm warning system to alert pilot if flaps are not set at 20 degrees and full power to ensure proper climb-out on short strips. Also provides warning if prop control is not set to high RPM.
20. Option to install JASCO alternator instead of a generator.

*Note: The aerodynamic improvements as noted in items 1 through 6 (as flight tested on the "Gray Goose" experimental aircraft) accounted for a reported 7- to 8-knot improvement in operating speeds, which in field use would convert to precious fuel savings in remote parts of the world.

Also being considered at the time of publication of this book was the possible installation of a Zoche Aero-Diesel powerplant. The engine would be a 300-horsepower, direct-drive, 4 cylinders per row, highly charged, fuel-injected, air cooled, two-stroke radial operating at 2,500 RPM. The Zoche would add the benefits of offering lower weight (estimated at a 200-pound savings) than conventional powerplants, as well as providing 25 percent more fuel efficiency. The engine would run on either JP 4, JP 5, JP 8, Jet A jet fuel or diesel fuel number 2, with TBO (Time Between Overhaul) estimated at approximately 2,000 hours.

With a supercharger located in front, and a turbocharger situated in back, the Zoche would offer superior high altitude capability for mountain flying situations.

Because the Zoche is a two-stroke design, the low parts count should ensure drastically reduced maintenance: no gearbox, no valves or valve springs, no rocker arms, no pushrods, cams or other things to break or leak.

With the price of avgas in some parts of the world pushing $5.30 a gallon ($9.00 in Cameroon), it is estimated that with a Zoche equipped Helio (or other type of

2-stroke super-charged powerplant) savings on the order of $56.00 an hour could be realized.

Because the Zoche is a much lighter and physically compact design, the engine must be located farther forward on the Helio airframe (by an estimated 12-inch extension) for CG (Center of Gravity) considerations, thereby giving it an unusual long-nose look. While an engine mount for installation of the Zoche into the H-395 JAARS "Gray Goose" has been completed, delivery of the actual powerplant was still pending.

In a book that recounts some of the evolution and day-to-day life experiences of JAARS pilots (*Into the Glory* by Jamie Buckingham), the author recounts a conversation that he had with fellow JAARS pilot-mechanic George DeVoucalla. In it, DeVoucalla relates, "the word "Helio" comes from a Greek word meaning sun. And "Courier," in Latin, means one who runs with a message. Very literally, the Helio Courier was bringing light to those who dwell in darkness."[7]

While the JAARS Helio Courier fleet continues to evolve technically (and may even eventually include cost-saving turboprop power), the mission will continue as it has always been. The special capabilities of the Helio Courier will go on helping to bring the Word and light to others throughout the world.

8. Epilogue
Plans for Future Helio Production

The story of the development and production of the Helio line of aircraft has been a long and winding one. Many of the details, and even the basic philosophy, have been altered since the original concept. In spite of the many business obstacles that have challenged, and sometimes completely halted, production, the Helio Courier remains a truly incredible machine unique in the realm of great general aviation aircraft.

Despite the cessation of the latest full-scale production activities in early 1985 (primarily the models H-700 and H-800), the lure of this fantastic aircraft has not been overlooked. There are many who believe that there is still a valid business case for producing an aircraft with the performance and utility of the Helio Courier for today's worldwide market.

As of this book's publication, the latest development effort has taken place under the auspices of Helio Aircraft, LLC. Early development work included several Helio airframes (one an H-250, the other an H-800) which were modified to accept 360-HP and 400-HP Russian M-14 radial engines and served as experimental hybrid testbeds.

Latest production plans include to re-introduce the basic Helio Courier and Stallion airframes, along with new instrument panels, an updated interior, and engine and landing gear system improvements designed to optimize the performance and utility of the aircraft.

An excerpt from an article dating to the very beginning of the Helio Courier's development could sum up the Helio Courier's continuing place in history. A May 16, 1949, story appearing in the *Christian Science Monitor* noted that "the fact remains that the big companies were not much interested in doing this kind of job. All the big research money has been turned in exactly the opposite direction: Into planes which go faster and carry greater loads longer distances. There lies the jackpot. In all this struggle for high-speed performance, the little plane was almost forgotten. It remained for the professors who were looking in their allegedly academic way into the problems of the aircraft industry to see what was needed."[1]

The rationalized dream and technical visions of Dr. Otto Koppen and Dr. Lynn Bollinger, as supported by so many others throughout the years, continue to inspire and shape the world we live in. Their "little plane," which emerged so many years ago and evolved through decades of distinguished service, may never become as well known to the general public as some products from other major "airframers." Still, it will undoubtedly continue to serve, whether in remote jungles or in more high-profile special mission work, with truly spectacular ability. In doing so, it will continue to awe and amaze many future generations of pilots.

Appendix 1: Data Specification Sheets

Helio Model H-391 & H-391B
Data/Specification

Note: A plus (+) or a minus (-) sign preceding the weight of an item indicates that the net weight will change with the installation of that item.

Model H-391 (USAF YL-24), 4 PCL-SM (Normal Category, Approved August 5,1953)

Model H-391B, 4 PCL-SM (Normal Category, Approved June 29, 1954)

NOTE: This Data/Specification is intended for general historical reference only, and is not intended for actual aircraft use. Anyone needing access to specific Aircraft Type Data Sheets should query the latest revision level offered by the FAA.

Note: The model H-391B is essentially the same as the model H-391 except for engine, propeller, semi-monocoque fuselage, minor fuel system changes, minor control system changes and other miscellaneous changes.

Engine	(H-391)	Lycoming GO-435-C2
	(H-391B)	Lycoming GO-435-C2B, GO-435-C2B2 and GO-435-C2B2-6
Fuel	(H-391)	91/98 minimum grade aviation gasoline
	(H-391B)	80/87 minimum grade aviation gasoline with standard ejector exhaust system.

Engine Limits   Takeoff   3,400 RPM (260 HP)
                All other operations 3,000 RPM (240 HP)

Propeller   (H-391)   Hartzell controllable prop HC12X20-8C, blades 9333C-0. Diameter: not over 93", not under 91". Pitch settings at 30" Sta: low 14 degree 15', high 29 degree 15"

Prop governor, Hartzell B-1 or B-3

Prop spinner and mount, Hartzell D-164

(H-391B)   Hartzell controllable propeller hub HC82X20-1A or HC82X20-1B, blades 10133D. Diameter: not over 101", not under 95". Pitch settings at 30" Sta: low 13 degree, high 31 degree S/N 001 through 081, except 075, as delivered by manufacturer.

Prop governor, Hartzell B-1 or B-3

Prop spinner, Hartzell C-888 dome with C-807-2 bulkhead

H-391 and H-391B Data/Specification (Sheet 1). FAA, Wichita ACO.

Appendix 1: Data Specification Sheets   175

NOTE: This Data/Specification is intended for general historical reference only, and is not intended for actual aircraft use. Anyone needing access to specific Aircraft Type Data Sheets should query the latest revision level offered by the FAA.

Airspeed Limits

LAND PLANE

Maneuvering (2,800 lb.)	94 mph (82 knots) CAS
Maneuvering (3,000 lb.)	98 mph (85 knots) CAS
Max. structural cruising	150 mph (134 knots) CAS
Never exceed	189 mph (164 knots) CAS
Flaps extended	80 mph (69 knots) CAS

FLOAT PLANE - with Edo Model 249-2870 floats (H-391B only).

Maneuvering	94 mph (82 knots) CAS
Min. structural cruising	130 mph (113 knots) CAS
Never exceed	164 mph (143 knots) CAS
Flaps extended	80 mph (70 knots) CAS

C.G. Range

LAND PLANE

(+101.3) to (+106.4) at 3,000 lb.
(+99.9) to (+106.4) at 2,800 lb.
(+96.5) to (+106.4) at 2,200 lb. or less
straight line variation between points given

FLOAT PLANE

(+101.3) to (+106.4) at 3,000 lb.
(+99.1) to (+106.4) at 2,700 lb.

SKI INSTALLATION

Federal installation drawing 11R1241. Federal AWB-3500A main skis and AWT-3500 tailwheel ski including 20 lbs. fixed ballast on tail wheel ski. Eligible with hydraulic conversion on ground and in flight. Weight and balance to be checked with ski in retracted positions.

(+101.3) to (+104.3) at 3,000 lb.
(+99.9) to (+104.3) at 2,800 lb.
(+96.5) to (+104.3) at 2,200 lb.
Straight line variation between points given.

H-391 and H-391B Data/Specification (Sheet 2). FAA, Wichita ACO.

Appendix 1: Data Specification Sheets

> NOTE: This Data/Specification is intended for general historical reference only, and is not intended for actual aircraft use. Anyone needing access to specific Aircraft Type Data Sheets should query the latest revision level offered by the FAA.

Empty Weight C.G. Range	None
Maximum Weight	LANDPLANE (H-391 and H-391B, S/N 001 through 031) 2,800 lbs. (Eligible for 3,000 lbs. When incorporating Helio modification 21, main landing gear assemblies 391-040-451-12 and -13, and tailwheel assembly 391-040-4101.) H-391B - S/N 032 and up: 3,000 lbs. FLOATPLANE (H-391B only, S/N 001 through 031) 2,800 lbs., When Helio modification No. 21 incorporated S/N 032 and up: 3,000 lbs.
Number of Seats	4 (2 at +103.5, 2 at +136. S/N 066 and on eligible for 5th seat at +165).
Maximum Baggage	200 lb. (+163)
Fuel Capacity	Model H-391: 60 gal. Total, 52.5 gal. Usable (two 30 gal. Tanks in wings at +113) Model H-391B: S/N 001 through 087 (except 075), 61 gal. total, 58.2 gal. usable (two 30 gal. tanks in wings at +113. 1 gal. header tank in fuselage) S/N 088 and up, 60.7 gal. total, 58.2 gal. usable (two 30.35 gal. tanks in wing at +113 no header tank).
Oil Capacity	Model H-391: 12 quarts (+37), Model H-391B: 12 quarts (+37)

H-391 and H-391B Data/Specification (Sheet 3). FAA, Wichita ACO.

Appendix 1: Data Specification Sheets

NOTE: This Data/Specification is intended for general historical reference only, and is not intended for actual aircraft use. Anyone needing access to specific Aircraft Type Data Sheets should query the latest revision level offered by the FAA.

Control Surface Movements	LANDPLANE		
	Stabilator (trailing edge)	Up 19°	Down 8°
	Stabilator trim tab (±2°)	Up 36°	Down 20°
	Stabilator anti-blalance tab	Within ±2° of neutral - measured from stabilator chord line	
	Aileron (±1°)	Up 20°	Down 20°
	Rudder (±1°)		
	S/N 001 thru 049	Right 30°	Left 30°
	S/N 050 & on	Right 30°	Left 25°
	Flaps		Down 40°
	FLOATPLANE		
	Stabilator (trailing edge)	Up 17°	Down 8°
	Anti-balance tab (trailing edge)	Within ± 2 ° of neutral - measured from stabilator chord line	
	Rudder (±1°)	Right 30°	Left 20°

Serial Nos. Eligible   Model H-391 - 1 only
                              Model H-391B - 001 and up

Certification Basis   Part 3 of the Civil Air Regulations effective November 1, 1949, as amended to May 16, 1953. Type Certificate 1A8 issued August 5, 1953. Application for Type Certificate dated May 1, 1951.

Production Basis   P.C. 311 (reissued December 5, 1962).

H-391 and H-391B Data/Specification (Sheet 4). FAA, Wichita ACO.

Appendix 1: Data Specification Sheets

> NOTE: This Data/Specification is intended for general historical reference only, and is not intended for actual aircraft use. Anyone needing access to specific Aircraft Type Data Sheets should query the latest revision level offered by the FAA.

Datum
60 in. forward of fuselage station 0. (Station 0 is at upper attachment of engine mount to fuselage). For weight and balance purposes, Station 100.25 is the centerline of wing spar (midway between two rows of bolts in wing root fitting on bottom side of wing).

Equipment
The basic required equipment as prescribed in the applicable airworthiness regulations (See Certification Basis) must be installed in the aircraft for certification. The equipment portion of Aircraft Specification 1A8, Revision 18, dated July 7, 1969, or the equipment list provided with each airplane should be used for equipment references on Helio Models H-391, H-391B, H-395, H-395A, H-250, and H-295 (prior to serial number 1458). Refer to the applicable equipment list for Model H-295, serial number 1458 and on, Model H-700, and Model H-800. In addition, the following FAA approved Airplane Flight Manuals and Airplane Flight Manual Supplements are required.

FAA Approved Airplane Flight Manual dated February 9, 1956 (H-391B, S/N 001 through 031; dated November 3, 1956 (H-391B, S/N 032 and up and for those S/N 001 through 031 modified per Helio Modification 21

NOTE: See the latest online FAA Type Data Sheet entries for specific Airplane Flight Manual Supplements, Notes and other information as subject to the most current revision level.

NOTE: See Department of Transportation, FAA Federal Register for all pertinent information in regards to Airworthiness Directives.

H-391 and H-391B Data/Specification (Sheet 5). FAA, Wichita ACO.

Appendix 1: Data Specification Sheets

Helio Model H-395 & H-395A
Data/Specification

Note: A plus (+) or a minus (-) sign preceding the weight of an item indicates that the net weight will change with the installation of that item.

Model H-395 (USAF L-28A or U-10B), 5 PCL-SM (Normal Category, Approved November 17, 1958)

Model H-395A, 4 PCL-SM (Normal Category, Approved June 29, 1959)

NOTE: This Data/Specification is intended for general historical reference only, and is not intended for actual aircraft use. Anyone needing access to specific Aircraft Type Data Sheets should query the latest revision level offered by the FAA.

Engine	(H-395)	Lycoming GO-480-G1D6	
	(H-395A)	Lycoming GO-435-G2B2-6	
Fuel	(H-395)	100/130 minimum grade aviation gasoline	
	(H-395A)	80/87 minimum grade aviation gasoline	
Engine Limits	(H-395)	Takeoff	3,400 RPM (295 HP)
		All other operations	3,000 RPM (280 HP)
	(H-395A)	Takeoff	3,400 RPM (260 HP)
		All other operations	3,000 RPM (240 HP)

Propeller (H-395) Hartzell controllable prop (S/N 075, 502 through 514, 516 through 530) hub HC-93Z20-1B1, blades 10151C or 10151C-5
Diameter: not over 101", not under 95"
Pitch settings at 30" Sta: low 11.8°, high 30.8°
Prop governor, Hartzell B-3
Prop spinner and mount, Hartzell 836-15

Hartzell controllable prop (S/N 531 and up)
hub HC-B3Z20-1B1, blades 10151C or 10151C-5
Diameter: not over 101", not under 95"
Pitch settings at 30" Sta: low 11.8°, high 30.8°
Prop governor, Hartzell B-3
Prop spinner and mount, Hartzell 836-15

(H-395A) (S/N 515, 1002 through 1005) Hartzell controllable propeller, hub HC-82X20-1A or HC82X20-1B, blades 10133D
Diameter: not over 101", not under 95"
Pitch settings at 30" Sta: low 13°, high 31°
Prop governor, Hartzell B-1 or B-3
Prop spinner, Hartzell C-888 dome with C-807-2 bulkhead

(S/N 1006 and up) Hartzell controllable propeller, hub HC-A2X20-1, blades 10133D
Diameter: not over 101", not under 95"
Pitch settings at 30" Sta: low 13°, high 31°
Prop governor, Hartzell B-1 or B-3
Prop spinner, Hartzell C-888 dome with C-807-2 bulkhead

H-395 and H-395A Data/Specification (Sheet 1). FAA, Wichita ACO.

> **NOTE:** This Data/Specification is intended for general historical reference only, and is not intended for actual aircraft use. Anyone needing access to specific Aircraft Type Data Sheets should query the latest revision level offered by the FAA.

Airspeed Limits

LAND PLANE

Maneuvering (2,800 lb.)	94 mph (82 knots) CAS
Maneuvering (3,000 lb.)	98 mph (85 knots) CAS
Max. structural cruising	150 mph (134 knots) CAS
Never exceed	189 mph (164 knots) CAS
Flaps extended	80 mph (69 knots) CAS

FLOAT PLANE - with Edo Model 249-2870 floats.
H-395A (S/N 515, 1002 and up) Float Installation per Helio modification no. 31.

Maneuvering	95 mph (83 knots) CAS
Min. structural cruising	130 mph (113 knots) CAS
Never exceed	164 mph (143 knots) CAS
Flaps extended	80 mph (70 knots) CAS

C.G. Range

LAND PLANE

(+101.3) to (+106.4) at 3,000 lb.
(+99.9) to (+106.4) at 2,800 lb.
(+96.5) to (+106.4) at 2,200 lb. or less
straight line variation between points given

FLOAT PLANE

(+101.3) to (+106.4) at 3,000 lb.
(+99.1) to (+106.4) at 2,700 lb. or less

SKI INSTALLATION

Federal installation drawing 11R1241. Federal AWB-3500A main skis and AWT-3500 tailwheel ski including 20 lbs. fixed ballast on tail wheel ski. Eligible with hydraulic conversion on ground and in flight. Weight and balance to be checked with ski in retracted and extended positions.

(+101.4) to (+104.3) at 3,000 lb.
(+99.9) to (+104.3) at 2,800 lb.
(+96.5) to (+104.3) at 2,200 lb.

Straight line variation between points given.

H-395 and H-395A Data/Specification (Sheet 2). FAA, Wichita ACO.

Appendix 1: Data Specification Sheets

> **NOTE:** This Data/Specification is intended for general historical reference only, and is not intended for actual aircraft use. Anyone needing access to specific Aircraft Type Data Sheets should query the latest revision level offered by the FAA.

Empty Weight C.G. Range	None
Maximum Weight	LANDPLANE 3,000 lbs. FLOATPLANE 3,000 lbs.
Number of Seats	5 (2 at +103.5, 2 at +136. 1 at +165)
Maximum Baggage	200 lb. (+163)
Fuel Capacity	60.7 gal. total, 58.2 gal. usable (two 30.35 gal. tanks in wings at +113) (No header tank)
Oil Capacity	10 quarts (+37)

Control Surface Movements

LANDPLANE

Stabilator (trailing edge,(±0)) Up 19°   Down 8° from neutral
　　　　　　　　　　　　　Neutral position is trailing edge down 2.5°.
Stabilator trim tab (±2 °)   Up 36°   Down 20°
　　　　　　　　　　　Measured from stabilator chord line
Stabilator anti-blalance tab Within ±2° of neutral - measured
(±2)　　　　　　　　　from stabilator chord line
Aileron (±1 °)   Up 20°   Down 20°
Rudder (±1 °)   Right 30°   Left 25°
Flaps (±1 °)   　　　　Down 40°

FLOATPLANE

Stabilator (trailing edge)   Up 17 °   Down 8 °
Anti-balance tab
　(trailing edge)   Within ± 2 ° of neutral - measured
　　　　　　　　　from stabilator chord line
Rudder   Right 30°   Left 20°

Serial Nos. Eligible	Model H-395 - 075, 502 through 514, 516 and up Model H-395A - 515, 1002 and up USAF U-10B airplanes are eligible for a civil airworthiness certificate when converted in accordance with Helio Drawing 395-000-050.
Certification Basis	Part 3 of the Civil Air Regulations effective November 1, 1949, as amended to May 16, 1953. Type Certificate 1A8 issued August 5, 1953. Application for Type Certificate dated May 1, 1951.
Production Basis	P.C. 311 (reissued December 5, 1962).

H-395 and H-395A Data/Specification (Sheet 3). FAA, Wichita ACO.

> NOTE: This Data/Specification is intended for general historical reference only, and is not intended for actual aircraft use. Anyone needing access to specific Aircraft Type Data Sheets should query the latest revision level offered by the FAA.

Datum
: 60 in. forward of fuselage station 0. (Station 0 is at upper attachment of engine mount to fuselage). For weight and balance purposes, Station 100.25 is the centerline of wing spar (midway between two rows of bolts in wing root fitting on bottom side of wing).

Equipment
: The basic required equipment as prescribed in the applicable airworthiness regulations (See Certification Basis) must be installed in the aircraft for certification. The equipment portion of Aircraft Specification 1A8, Revision 18, dated July 7, 1969, or the equipment list provided with each airplane should be used for equipment references on Helio Models H-391, H-391B, H-395, H-395A, H-250, and H-295 (prior to serial number 1458). Refer to the applicable equipment list for Model H-295, serial number 1458 and on, Model H-700, and Model H-800. In addition, the following FAA approved Airplane Flight Manuals and Airplane Flight Manual Supplements are required.

FAA Approved Airplane Flight Manual dated February 9, 1956 (H-391B, S/N 001 through 031; dated November 3, 1956 (H-391B, S/N 032 and up and for those S/N 001 through 031 modified per Helio Modification 21

NOTE: See the latest online FAA Type Data Sheet entries for specific Airplane Flight Manual Supplements, Notes and other information as subject to the most current revision level.

NOTE: See Department of Transportation, FAA Federal Register for all pertinent information in regards to Airworthiness Directives.

H-395 and H-395A Data/Specification (Sheet 4). FAA, Wichita ACO.

Appendix 1: Data Specification Sheets

Helio Model H-250
Data/Specification

<u>Note:</u> *A plus (+) or a minus (-) sign preceding the weight of an item indicates that the net weight will change with the installation of that item.*

Model H-250, 6 PCL-SM (Normal Category, Approved November 6,1964)

> NOTE: This Data/Specification is intended for general historical reference only, and is not intended for actual aircraft use. Anyone needing access to specific Aircraft Type Data Sheets should query the latest revision level offered by the FAA.

Note: The model H-250 is essentially the same as the model H-395 except for engine, increased gross weight, and minor structural changes.

Engine	(H-250)	Lycoming O-540-A1A5
Fuel	(H-250)	100/130 minimum grade aviation gasoline
Engine Limits	(H-250)	For all other operations, 2,575 RPM (250 HP)
Propeller and Propeller Limits	(H-250)	Hartzell controllable prop Hub HC-92WK-1D, blades W8847 Diameter: not over 88", not under 86" Pitch settings at 30" Sta: low 12°, high 28.5° Prop governor, Hartzell F-6-8 (S/N 2501 through 2520) Hartzell F-6-8L (S/N 2521 and up). Propeller spinner and mount, Hartzell C-2513-3

Airspeed Limits

<u>LAND PLANE</u>

Maneuvering (2,800 lb.)	94 mph (82 knots) CAS
Maneuvering (3,000 lb.)	98 mph (85 knots) CAS
Max. structural cruising	150 mph (134 knots) CAS
Never exceed	189 mph (164 knots) CAS
Flaps extended	80 mph (69 knots) CAS

H-250 Data/Specification (Sheet 1). FAA, Wichita ACO.

> **NOTE:** This Data/Specification is intended for general historical reference only, and is not intended for actual aircraft use. Anyone needing access to specific Aircraft Type Data Sheets should query the latest revision level offered by the FAA.

Airspeed Limits (continued)

FLOAT PLANE - with Edo Model 249-2870 floats.
H-395A (S/N 515, 1002 and up) Float Installation per Helio modification no. 31.

Maneuvering	95 mph (83 knots) CAS
Min. structural cruising	130 mph (113 knots) CAS
Never exceed	164 mph (143 knots) CAS
Flaps extended	80 mph (70 knots) CAS

C.G. Range

LAND PLANE

(+101.3) to (+106.4) at 3,000 lb.
(+99.9) to (+106.4) at 2,800 lb.
(+96.5) to (+106.4) at 2,200 lb. or less
straight line variation between points given

FLOAT PLANE

(+101.3) to (+106.4) at 3,000 lb.
(+99.1) to (+106.4) at 2,700 lb. or less

SKI INSTALLATION

Federal installation drawing 11R1241. Federal AWB-3500A main skis and AWT-3500 tailwheel ski including 20 lbs. fixed ballast on tail wheel ski. Eligible with hydraulic conversion on ground and in flight. Weight and balance to be checked with ski in retracted and extended positions.

(+101.4) to (+104.3) at 3,000 lb.
 (+99.9) to (+104.3) at 2,800 lb.
 (+96.5) to (+104.3) at 2,200 lb.

Straight line variation between points given.

H-250 Data/Specification (Sheet 2). FAA, Wichita ACO.

Appendix 1: Data Specification Sheets 185

> **NOTE:** This Data/Specification is intended for general historical reference only, and is not intended for actual aircraft use. Anyone needing access to specific Aircraft Type Data Sheets should query the latest revision level offered by the FAA.

Empty Weight C.G. Range	None
Maximum Weight	3,400 lbs.
Number of Seats	6 (2 at +103.5, 2 at +136, 1 at +162)
Maximum Baggage	340 lb. (+162) when 2-passenger aft sling seat is unoccupied
Fuel Capacity	60.7 gal. total, 58.2 gal. usable (two 30.35 gal. tanks in wings at +113)
Oil Capacity	12 quarts (+22)
Control Surface Movements	Stabilator (trailing edge,(±1)) Up 19° Down 10° from neutral *Neutral position is trailing edge down 2.5°.* Stabilator trim tab (±2 °) Up 36° Down 20° *Measured from stabilator chord line* Stabilator anti-blalance tab (±2) Within ±2° of neutral *measured from stabilator chord line* Aileron (±1°) Up 20° Down 20° Rudder (±1°) Right 30° Left 25° Flaps (±1°) Down 40°
Serial Nos. Eligible	Model H-250 - 2501 and up
Certification Basis	Part 3 of the Civil Air Regulations effective November 1, 1949, as amended to May 16, 1953. Type Certificate 1A8 issued August 5, 1953. Application for Type Certificate dated May 1, 1951.
Production Basis	P.C. 311 (reissued December 5, 1962).

H-250 Data/Specification (Sheet 3). FAA, Wichita ACO.

> NOTE: This Data/Specification is intended for general historical reference only, and is not intended for actual aircraft use. Anyone needing access to specific Aircraft Type Data Sheets should query the latest revision level offered by the FAA.

Datum   60 in. forward of fuselage station 0. (Station 0 is at upper attachment of engine mount to fuselage). For weight and balance purposes, Station 100.25 is the centerline of wing spar (midway between two rows of bolts in wing root fitting on bottom side of wing).

Equipment   The basic required equipment as prescribed in the applicable airworthiness regulations (See Certification Basis) must be installed in the aircraft for certification. The equipment portion of Aircraft Specification 1A8, Revision 18, dated July 7, 1969, or the equipment list provided with each airplane should be used for equipment references on Helio Models H-391, H-391B, H-395, H-395A, H-250, and H-295 (prior to serial number 1458). Refer to the applicable equipment list for Model H-295, serial number 1458 and on, Model H-700, and Model H-800. In addition, the following FAA approved Airplane Flight Manuals and Airplane Flight Manual Supplements are required.

FAA Approved Airplane Flight Manual dated February 9, 1956 (H-391B, S/N 001 through 031; dated November 3, 1956 (H-391B, S/N 032 and up and for those S/N 001 through 031 modified per Helio Modification 21

NOTE: See the latest online FAA Type Data Sheet entries for specific Airplane Flight Manual Supplements, Notes and other information as subject to the most current revision level.

NOTE: See Department of Transportation, FAA Federal Register for all pertinent information in regards to Airworthiness Directives.

H-250 Data/Specification (Sheet 4). FAA, Wichita ACO.

Appendix 1: Data Specification Sheets

Helio Model H-295 Data/Specification

Note: A plus (+) or a minus (-) sign preceding the weight of an item indicates that the net weight will change with the installation of that item.

Model H-295 (USAF U-10D), 6 PCL-SM (Normal Category, Approved April 15,1965)

NOTE: This Data/Specification is intended for general historical reference only, and is not intended for actual aircraft use. Anyone needing access to specific Aircraft Type Data Sheets should query the latest revision level offered by the FAA.

Note: The model H-295 is essentially the same as the model H-395 except for seating/gross weight.

Engine	(H-295)	Lycoming GO-480-G1D6 - Slow speed (1.250:1) generator drive or Lycoming GO-480-G1A6 - High speed (2.577:1) generator drive
Fuel	(H-295)	100/130 minimum grade aviation gasoline
Engine Limits	(H-295)	Takeoff 3,400 RPM (295 HP) All other operations 3,000 RPM (280 HP)
Propeller and Propeller Limits	(H-295)	Hartzell constant speed prop, Hub HC-B3Z20-1, blades 10151C Diameter: 96", (1" in reduction permitted) Pitch settings at 30" Sta: low 11.8°, high 30.8° Prop governor, Hartzell B-3 Prop spinner, Hartzell 836-15R (supersedes Hartzell 836-15)

H-295 Data/Specification (Sheet 1). FAA, Wichita ACO.

> **NOTE:** This Data/Specification is intended for general historical reference only, and is not intended for actual aircraft use. Anyone needing access to specific Aircraft Type Data Sheets should query the latest revision level offered by the FAA.

Airspeed Limits	Maneuvering	103 mph (89 knots) CAS
	Max. structural cruising	160 mph (140 knots) CAS
	Never exceed	200 mph (174 knots) CAS
	Flaps extended	80 mph (69 knots) CAS

C.G. Range

LAND PLANE

(+103.8) to (+110.0) at 3,400 lb.
(+98.9) to (+110.0) at 2,760 lb.
(+97.0) to (+110.0) at 2,330 lb. or less
straight line variation between points given

FLOAT PLANE

Float installation per Helio drawing 250-000-015
(+102.0) to (+109.0) at 3,400 lb.
(+98.0) to (+109.0) at 2,600 lb. or less
Straight line variation between points given

Empty Weight C.G. Range — None

Maximum Weight

LANDPLANE

3,400 lbs.

Number of Seats — 6 (2 at +103.5, 2 at +136, 2 at +162)

Maximum Baggage — 340 lb. (+162) when 2-passenger aft sling seat is unoccupied

Fuel Capacity — 60.7 gal. total, 58.2 gal. usable (two 30.35 gal. tanks in wings at +113)

Oil Capacity — 12 quarts (+37)

H-295 Data/Specification (Sheet 2). FAA, Wichita ACO.

Appendix 1: Data Specification Sheets

> **NOTE**: This Data/Specification is intended for general historical reference only, and is not intended for actual aircraft use. Anyone needing access to specific Aircraft Type Data Sheets should query the latest revision level offered by the FAA.

Control Surface Movements	Stabilator (trailing edge,(±1°))	Up 19°	Down 8° from neutral Neutral position is trailing edge down 2.5°.
	Stabilator trim tab (±2 °)	Up 36°	Down 20° Measured from stabilator chord line
	Stabilator anti-blalance tab	Within ±2° of neutral Measured from stabilator chord line	
	Aileron (±1°)	Up 20°	Down 20°
	Rudder (±1°)	Right 30°	Left 25°
	Flaps (+0°, -2°)		Down 40°

Serial Nos. Eligible   1201 through 1233, 1278 and up; S/N 1234 through 1277 (USAF 66-14332 through 66-14375) eligible when converted in accordance with Helio drawing 295-000-020.

Certification Basis   Part 3 of the Civil Air Regulations effective November 1, 1949, as amended to May 16, 1953. Type Certificate 1A8 issued August 5, 1953. Application for Type Certificate dated May 1, 1951.

Production Basis   P.C. 311 (reissued December 5, 1962).

H-295 Data/Specification (Sheet 3). FAA, Wichita ACO.

> **NOTE:** This Data/Specification is intended for general historical reference only, and is not intended for actual aircraft use. Anyone needing access to specific Aircraft Type Data Sheets should query the latest revision level offered by the FAA.

Datum	60 in. forward of fuselage station 0. (Station 0 is at upper attachment of engine mount to fuselage). For weight and balance purposes, Station 100.25 is the centerline of wing spar (midway between two rows of bolts in wing root fitting on bottom side of wing).
Equipment	The basic required equipment as prescribed in the applicable airworthiness regulations (See Certification Basis) must be installed in the aircraft for certification. The equipment portion of Aircraft Specification 1A8, Revision 18, dated July 7, 1969, or the equipment list provided with each airplane should be used for equipment references on Helio Models H-391, H-391B, H-395, H-395A, H-250, and H-295 (prior to serial number 1458). Refer to the applicable equipment list for Model H-295, serial number 1458 and on, Model H-700, and Model H-800. In addition, the following FAA approved Airplane Flight Manuals and Airplane Flight Manual Supplements are required.
	FAA Approved Airplane Flight Manual dated February 9, 1956 (H-391B, S/N 001 through 031; dated November 3, 1956 (H-391B, S/N 032 and up and for those S/N 001 through 031 modified per Helio Modification 21
	NOTE: See the latest online FAA Type Data Sheet entries for specific Airplane Flight Manual Supplements, Notes and other information as subject to the most current revision level.
	NOTE: See Department of Transportation, FAA Federal Register for all pertinent information in regards to Airworthiness Directives.

H-295 Data/Specification (Sheet 4). FAA, Wichita ACO.

Appendix 1: Data Specification Sheets

Helio Model HT-295
Data/Specification

Note: A plus (+) or a minus (-) sign preceding the weight of an item indicates that the net weight will change with the installation of that item.

Model HT-295, 6 PCLM (Normal Category), approved December 18, 1973)

NOTE: This Data/Specification is intended for general historical reference only, and is not intended for actual aircraft use. Anyone needing access to specific Aircraft Type Data Sheets should query the latest revision level offered by the FAA.

Note: The model HT-295 is essentially a tricycle version of the standard H-295.

Engine	(HT-295)	Lycoming GO-480-G1D6
		Lycoming GO-480-G1A6
Fuel	(HT-295)	100/130 minimum grade aviation gasoline
Engine Limits	(HT-295)	Takeoff — 3,400 RPM (295 HP)
		All other operations — 3,000 RPM (280 HP)
Propeller and Propeller Limits	(HT-295)	Hartzell constant speed prop, Hub HC-B3Z20-1, blades 10151C
		Diameter: 96", (1" in reduction permitted)
		Pitch settings at 30" Sta: low 11.8°, high 30.8°
		Prop governor, Hartzell B-3
		Prop spinner, Hartzell 836-15R (supersedes Hartzell 836-15)
Airspeed Limits		Maneuvering — 103 mph (89 knots) CAS
		Max. structural cruising — 160 mph (140 knots) CAS
		Never exceed — 200 mph (174 knots) CAS
		Flaps extended — 80 mph (69 knots) CAS

HT-295 Data/Specification (Sheet 1). FAA, Wichita ACO.

Appendix 1: Data Specification Sheets

> NOTE: This Data/Specification is intended for general historical reference only, and is not intended for actual aircraft use. Anyone needing access to specific Aircraft Type Data Sheets should query the latest revision level offered by the FAA.

C.G. Range	**LAND PLANE** (+103.8) to (+110.0) at 3,400 lb. (+98.9) to (+110.0) at 2,760 lb. (+97.0) to (+110.0) at 2,330 lb. or less straight line variation between points given
Empty Weight C.G. Range	None
Maximum Weight	3,400 lbs.
Number of Seats	6 (2 at +103.5, 2 at +136, 2 at +162)
Maximum Baggage	340 lb. (+162) when 2-passenger aft sling seat is unoccupied
Fuel Capacity	60.7 gal. total, 58.2 gal. usable (two 30.35 gal. tanks in wings at +113)
Oil Capacity	12 quarts (+37)

HT-295 Data/Specification (Sheet 2). FAA, Wichita ACO.

Appendix 1: Data Specification Sheets 193

> **NOTE:** This Data/Specification is intended for general historical reference only, and is not intended for actual aircraft use. Anyone needing access to specific Aircraft Type Data Sheets should query the latest revision level offered by the FAA.

Control Surface Movements			
	Stabilator (trailing edge,(±1°))	Up 19°	Down 10° from neutral (Neutral position: trailing edge down 2.5°.)
	Stabilator trim tab (±2 °)	Up 36°	Down 20° (Measured from stabilator chord line)
	Stabilator anti-blalance tab	Within ±2° of neutral - (Measured from stabilator chord line)	
	Aileron (±1°)	Up 20°	Down 20°
	Rudder (±1°)	Right 30°	Left 40° (+0°, -2°)

Serial Nos. Eligible: 1701 and up.

Certification Basis: Part 3 of the Civil Air Regulations effective November 1, 1949, as amended to May 16, 1953. Type Certificate 1A8 issued August 5, 1953. Application for Type Certificate dated May 1, 1951.

Production Basis: P.C. 311 (reissued December 5, 1962).

HT-295 Data/Specification (Sheet 3). FAA, Wichita ACO.

Appendix 1: Data Specification Sheets

> NOTE: This Data/Specification is intended for general historical reference only, and is not intended for actual aircraft use. Anyone needing access to specific Aircraft Type Data Sheets should query the latest revision level offered by the FAA.

Datum	60 in. forward of fuselage station 0. (Station 0 is at upper attachment of engine mount to fuselage). For weight and balance purposes, Station 100.25 is the centerline of wing spar (midway between two rows of bolts in wing root fitting on bottom side of wing).
Equipment	The basic required equipment as prescribed in the applicable airworthiness regulations (See Certification Basis) must be installed in the aircraft for certification. The equipment portion of Aircraft Specification 1A8, Revision 18, dated July 7, 1969, or the equipment list provided with each airplane should be used for equipment references on Helio Models H-391, H-391B, H-395, H-395A, H-250, and H-295 (prior to serial number 1458). Refer to the applicable equipment list for Model H-295, serial number 1458 and on, Model H-700, and Model H-800. In addition, the following FAA approved Airplane Flight Manuals and Airplane Flight Manual Supplements are required.

FAA Approved Airplane Flight Manual dated February 9, 1956 (H-391B, S/N 001 through 031; dated November 3, 1956 (H-391B, S/N 032 and up and for those S/N 001 through 031 modified per Helio Modification 21

NOTE: See the latest online FAA Type Data Sheet entries for specific Airplane Flight Manual Supplements, Notes and other information as subject to the most current revision level.

NOTE: See Department of Transportation, FAA Federal Register for all pertinent information in regards to Airworthiness Directives.

HT-295 Data/Specification (Sheet 4). FAA, Wichita ACO.

Appendix 1: Data Specification Sheets

Helio Model H-700
Data/Specification

Note: A plus (+) or a minus (-) sign preceding the weight of an item indicates that the net weight will change with the installation of that item.

Model H-700, 6 PCLM (Normal Category), approved January 24, 1984)

> NOTE: This Data/Specification is intended for general historical reference only, and is not intended for actual aircraft use. Anyone needing access to specific Aircraft Type Data Sheets should query the latest revision level offered by the FAA.

Note: The model H-700 is essentially the same as the model HT-295 except for powerplant installation, increased gross weight, structural changes, and miscellaneous minor changes.

Engine	(H-700)	Lycoming TIO-540-J2B
Fuel	(H-700)	100/100LL minimum grade aviation gasoline
Engine Limits	(H-700)	2,575 RPM (350 HP) 49" M.P.

Propeller and Propeller Limits	(H-700)	Hartzell constant speed prop, Hub HC-E3YR-1RF, blades F9587A-10
		Diameter: 87"
		Pitch settings at 30" Sta: low 12.7°, high 31.0°
		Prop governor, Hartzell FA-13
		    Serial No. H-7 through H-10
		    Hartzell F4-30
		    Serial No. H-11 and up
		Prop governor, Hartzell A2295-1

H-700 Data/Specification (Sheet 1). FAA, Wichita ACO.

Appendix 1: Data Specification Sheets

> **NOTE:** This Data/Specification is intended for general historical reference only, and is not intended for actual aircraft use. Anyone needing access to specific Aircraft Type Data Sheets should query the latest revision level offered by the FAA.

Airspeed Limits	Maneuvering	93 knots
	Maximum structural cruising	133 knots
	Never exceed	168 knots
	Flaps extended - 40°	83 knots
	Flaps extended -15°	96 knots

C.G. Range

LAND PLANE

(+101.0) to (+108.5) at 3,800 lbs.
(+98.0) to (+108.5) at 2,600 lbs. or less
straight line variation between points given

Empty Weight C.G. Range

None

Maximum Weight

3,800 lbs

Number of Seats

LANDPLANE
6 (2 at +103.5, 2 at +136.0, 2 at +162.0)

Maximum Baggage

LANDPLANE
Total load aft of pilot's seat - 40 lb. per sq. ft.
10 lb. per sq. ft. in luggage compartment
See AFM for loadings.

Fuel Capacity

LANDPLANE
121.4 gal. total, 120.5 gal. usable (four 30.35 gal. tanks in wing at +113)

Oil Capacity

12 quart maximum, 10 quart normal (+37)

H-700 Data/Specification (Sheet 2). FAA, Wichita ACO.

Appendix 1: Data Specification Sheets

NOTE: This Data/Specification is intended for general historical reference only, and is not intended for actual aircraft use. Anyone needing access to specific Aircraft Type Data Sheets should query the latest revision level offered by the FAA.

Control Surface Movements	Stabilator (Leading edge, ±1°)	Up 10°	Down 21° from neutral Neutral position is trailing edge down 2.5°.
	Stabilator trim tab (±2°)	Up 30°	Down 28° Measured from stabilator chord line
	Stabilator anti-blalance tab	Within ±2° of neutral	Measured from stabilator chord line
	Aileron droop	0.87" (±.07")	
	Aileron (±1°)	Up 20°	Down 20°
	Rudder (±1°)	Right 30°	Left 25°
	Flaps (±1°)		Down 40°
	Interceptor retracted position	Below surface of wing, 0.38" to 0.50"	

Serial Nos. Eligible   H1 and up.

Certification Basis   Part 3 of the Civil Air Regulations effective November 1, 1949, as amended to May 16, 1953. Type Certificate 1A8 issued August 5, 1953. Application for Type Certificate dated May 1, 1951.

Production Basis   P.C. 311 (reissued December 5, 1962).

H-700 Data/Specification (Sheet 3). FAA, Wichita ACO.

> NOTE: This Data/Specification is intended for general historical reference only, and is not intended for actual aircraft use. Anyone needing access to specific Aircraft Type Data Sheets should query the latest revision level offered by the FAA.

Datum	60 in. forward of fuselage station 0. (Station 0 is at upper attachment of engine mount to fuselage). For weight and balance purposes, Station 100.25 is the centerline of wing spar (midway between two rows of bolts in wing root fitting on bottom side of wing).
Equipment	The basic required equipment as prescribed in the applicable airworthiness regulations (See Certification Basis) must be installed in the aircraft for certification. The equipment portion of Aircraft Specification 1A8, Revision 18, dated July 7, 1969, or the equipment list provided with each airplane should be used for equipment references on Helio Models H-391, H-391B, H-395, H-395A, H-250, and H-295 (prior to serial number 1458). Refer to the applicable equipment list for Model H-295, serial number 1458 and on, Model H-700, and Model H-800. In addition, the following FAA approved Airplane Flight Manuals and Airplane Flight Manual Supplements are required.

FAA Approved Airplane Flight Manual dated February 9, 1956 (H-391B, S/N 001 through 031; dated November 3, 1956 (H-391B, S/N 032 and up and for those S/N 001 through 031 modified per Helio Modification 21

NOTE: See the latest online FAA Type Data Sheet entries for specific Airplane Flight Manual Supplements, Notes and other information as subject to the most current revision level.

NOTE: See Department of Transportation, FAA Federal Register for all pertinent information in regards to Airworthiness Directives.

H-700 Data/Specification (Sheet 4). FAA, Wichita ACO.

Appendix 1: Data Specification Sheets

Helio Model H-800
Data/Specification

<u>Note:</u> *A plus (+) or a minus (-) sign preceding the weight of an item indicates that the net weight will change with the installation of that item.*

Model H-800, 4 PCSM (Normal Category), approved July 19, 1983)

NOTE: This Data/Specification is intended for general historical reference only, and is not intended for actual aircraft use. Anyone needing access to specific Aircraft Type Data Sheets should query the latest revision level offered by the FAA.

Note: The model H-800 is essentially the same as the model HT-295 except for powerplant installation, increased gross weight, structural changes, and miscellaneous minor changes.

Engine	(H-800)	Lycoming IO-720-A1B
Fuel	(H-800)	100/100LL minimum grade aviation gasoline
Engine Limits	(H-800)	2,650 RPM (400 HP)
Propeller and Propeller Limits	(H-800)	Hartzell constant speed prop, Hub HC-C3YR-1RF, blades F8475R Diameter: 86" Pitch settings at 30" Sta: low 11.8°, high 30.8° Prop governor, Hartzell FA-3A Prop spinner, Hartzell A2295-1

Airspeed Limits:
Maneuvering	93 knots
Maximum structural cruising	133 knots
Never exceed	168 knots
Flaps extended - 40°	83 knots
Flaps extended -15°	96 knots

C.G. Range

<u>LAND PLANE</u>

(+102.0) to (+109.0) at 4,000 lb. (Max. takeoff weight)
(+101.0) to (+109.0) at 3,800 lb. (Max. landing weight)
(+98.0) to (+109.0) at 3,200 lb. or less
straight line variation between points given

<u>FLOAT PLANE</u>
Edo-Aire 696-3500
(+104.0) to (+110.0) at 3,888 lb.
(+101.0) to (+110.0) at 3,200 lb. or less

Edo-Aire 582-3430
(+104.0) to (+110.0) at 3,800 lb.
(+101.0) to (+110.0) at 3,200 lb. or less

H-800 Data/Specification (Sheet 1). FAA, Wichita ACO.

> NOTE: This Data/Specification is intended for general historical reference only, and is not intended for actual aircraft use. Anyone needing access to specific Aircraft Type Data Sheets should query the latest revision level offered by the FAA.

Empty Weight C.G. Range	None

Maximum Weight	**LANDPLANE**
	4,000 lbs. takeoff
	3,800 lbs. landing
	
	FLOATPLANE
	Edo-Aire 696-3500
	  Water operations:
	    3,888 lbs. takeoff
	    3,800 lbs. landing
	
	  Land operations:
	    3,790 lbs. takeoff
	    3,600 lbs. landing
	
	Edo-Aire 582-3430
	  Water operations:
	    3,800 lbs. takeoff

Number of Seats	**LANDPLANE**
	6 (2 at +103.5, 2 at +136.0, 2 at +162.0)
	FLOATPLANE
	696-3500
	  4 (2 at +103.5, 2 at +136.0, restricted to 306 lb. total weight)
	582-3430
	  4 (2 at +103.5, 2 at +136.0, restricted to 213 lb. total weight)

Maximum Baggage	**LANDPLANE** Total load aft of pilot's seat - 40 lb. per sq. ft. 10 lb. per sq. ft. in luggage compartment See AFM for loadings. **FLOATPLANE** 40 lb. per sq. ft. rear seat and cargo area Combined loadings rear passenger seats - 218 lb. See AFM for loadings.
Fuel Capacity	**LANDPLANE** 121.4 gal total, 120.5 gal. usable (four 30.35 gal tanks in wing at +113) **FLOATPLANE** 696-3500 amphibious and 582-3430 floats 60.7 gal. total, 60.2 gal. usable at +113
Oil Capacity	19 quart maximum, 17 quart normal (+37)

H-800 Data/Specification (Sheet 2). FAA, Wichita ACO.

Appendix 1: Data Specification Sheets

NOTE: This Data/Specification is intended for general historical reference only, and is not intended for actual aircraft use. Anyone needing access to specific Aircraft Type Data Sheets should query the latest revision level offered by the FAA.

Control Surface Movements	Stabilator (Leading edge, ±1°)	Up 10° Down 21° from neutral
Neutral pos. is trailing edge down 2.5°.
	Stabilator trim tab (±2°)	Up 30° Down 28°
Measured from stabilator chord line
	Stabilator anti-blalance tab	Within ±2° of neutral
Measured from stabilator chord line
	Aileron droop	0.87" (±.07")
	Aileron (±1°)	Up 20° Down 20°
	Rudder (±1°)	Right 30° Left 25°
	Flaps (±1°)	Down 40°
	Interceptor retracted pos.	Below surface of wing, 0.38" to 0.50"
Serial Nos. Eligible	H1 and up.	
Certification Basis	Part 3 of the Civil Air Regulations effective November 1, 1949, as amended to May 16, 1953. Type Certificate 1A8 issued August 5, 1953. Application for Type Certificate dated May 1, 1951.	
Production Basis	P.C. 311 (reissued December 5, 1962).	

H-800 Data/Specification (Sheet 3). FAA, Wichita ACO.

Appendix 1: Data Specification Sheets

> **NOTE:** This Data/Specification is intended for general historical reference only, and is not intended for actual aircraft use. Anyone needing access to specific Aircraft Type Data Sheets should query the latest revision level offered by the FAA.

Datum	60 in. forward of fuselage station 0. (Station 0 is at upper attachment of engine mount to fuselage). For weight and balance purposes, Station 100.25 is the centerline of wing spar (midway between two rows of bolts in wing root fitting on bottom side of wing).
Equipment	The basic required equipment as prescribed in the applicable airworthiness regulations (See Certification Basis) must be installed in the aircraft for certification. The equipment portion of Aircraft Specification 1A8, Revision 18, dated July 7, 1969, or the equipment list provided with each airplane should be used for equipment references on Helio Models H-391, H-391B, H-395, H-395A, H-250, and H-295 (prior to serial number 1458). Refer to the applicable equipment list for Model H-295, serial number 1458 and on, Model H-700, and Model H-800. In addition, the following FAA approved Airplane Flight Manuals and Airplane Flight Manual Supplements are required.

FAA Approved Airplane Flight Manual dated February 9, 1956 (H-391B, S/N 001 through 031; dated November 3, 1956 (H-391B, S/N 032 and up and for those S/N 001 through 031 modified per Helio Modification 21

NOTE: See the latest online FAA Type Data Sheet entries for specific Airplane Flight Manual Supplements, Notes and other information as subject to the most current revision level.

NOTE: See Department of Transportation, FAA Federal Register for all pertinent information in regards to Airworthiness Directives. |

H-800 Data/Specification (Sheet 4). FAA, Wichita ACO.

Appendix 1: Data Specification Sheets

Helio Model H-500
Data/Specification

Note: A plus (+) or a minus (-) sign preceding the weight of an item indicates that the net weight will change with the installation of that item.

Model H-500, 6 PCLM (Normal Category), approved June 11, 1963)

NOTE: This Data/Specification is intended for general historical reference only, and is not intended for actual aircraft use. Anyone needing access to specific Aircraft Type Data Sheets should query the latest revision level offered by the FAA.

Engine	2 Lycoming O-540-A2B (Carb. Setting No. 10-4404)
Fuel	91/96 minimum grade aviation gasoline
Engine Limits	All other operations 2,575 RPM (250 HP)
Propellor and Propellor Limits	Hartzell HC92ZK-2B/8447 Pitch settings at 30 in. Sta: low 11.4°, high 82.7° (feathered) Diameter: not over 84 in., not under 82 in.
Airspeed Limits	Maneuvering Vp 116 mph (101 knots) CAS Max structural cruising Vno 189 mph (164 knots) CAS Never exceed Vne 212 mph (184 knots) CAS Flaps extended Vfe 92 mph (80 knots) CAS Minimum control Vme 59 mph (51 Knots) CAS
C.G. Range	(+106.0) to (+113.0) at 4,500 lbs. (+101.2) to (+113.0) at 3,800 lbs. Straight line variation between points given

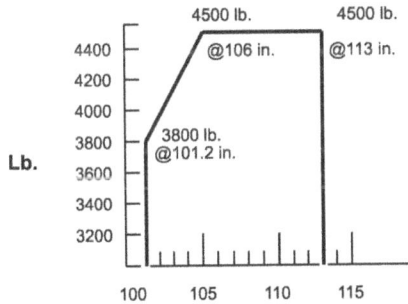

C.G. Position - Inches Aft of Datum

H-500 Data/Specification (Sheet 1) FAA, Wichita ACO.

Appendix 1: Data Specification Sheets

> **NOTE:** This Data/Specification is intended for general historical reference only, and is not intended for actual aircraft use. Anyone needing access to specific Aircraft Type Data Sheets should query the latest revision level offered by the FAA.

Empty Weight C.G. Range	None
Datum	Longitudinal reference Station 0 located 90.79 in. Ahead of leading edge of wing proper (without slats). Horizontal reference is 38.75 in. Below centerline of and parallel to fuselage lower longeron.
Leveling Means	Two leveling studs at lower corner of right door frame.
Maximum Weight	4,500 lbs.
Number of Seats	6 (2 at +103.5, 2 at +136.0, 2 at +164.5)
Maximum Baggage	425 lbs. (+136.0) with middle seat removed 425 lbs. (+164.5) with rear seat removed
Fuel Capacity	120 gal. (4 tanks, 2 in each wing, each tank 30 gal. At +123.0)
Oil Capacity	6 gal. (3 gal. each engine at +65.0)

Control Surface Movements		
	Wing flaps	Up 0°±1-1/2° Down 40°±1-1/2°
	Aileron	Up 20° ±1° Down 20°±1°
	Aileron trim tab (optional - left side only)	Up 19°±1° Down 19°±1° (measured from aileron chordline)
	Stabilator (trailing edge)	Up 25°±1° Down 8°±1° from neutral. Neutral is 2.5° down from horizontal reference.
	Stabilator trim tabs	Measured from horizontal stabilator chordline. Tab trailing edge up (+) Tab trailing edge down (-)
	Stabilator neutral, flaps up	+ 19.1°±2° pilot's trim indicator full nose down - 31.7°±2° pilot's trim indicator full nose up
	Stabilator trailing edge full up, flaps up	+ 37.9°±2° pilot's trim indicator full nose down - 30.4°±2° pilot's trim indicator full nose up
	Stabilator trailing edge full down, flaps up	+ 4.0°±2° pilot's trim indicator full nose down - 44.3°±2° pilot's trim indicator full nose up
	Stabilator anti-balance tabs	Same tabs as trim tabs - measured in same manner

H-500 Data/Specification (Sheet 2) FAA, Wichita ACO.

Appendix 1: Data Specification Sheets

NOTE: This Data/Specification is intended for general historical reference only, and is not intended for actual aircraft use. Anyone needing access to specific Aircraft Type Data Sheets should query the latest revision level offered by the FAA.

```
Trim indicator neutral
Stabilator neutral          + 0°
Stabilator T.E. full up     + 42.9°
 25° from neutral
Stabilator T.E. full down   - 20.0°
 8° from neutral

Flap interconnect effect on
  Stabilator trim tabs
  Flaps down 30°, pilot's
  trim indicator in takeoff
  position, stabilator
  trailing edge down 8°
  trim tab trailing edge    - 28° ±2°

Rudder              Right  25°±1°    Left  25°±1°
Rudder trim tab     Right  25°±2°    Left  25°±2°
                    Measured from rudder chordline
```

Serial Nos. Eligible	2 and up
Certification Basis	CAR 3 dated May 15, 1956, plus amendments 3-1 through 3-5 thereto. Type Certificate No. A2EA issued June 11, 1963. Date of application for Type Certificate July 28, 1961.
Production Basis	None. Prior to original certification of each aircraft, an FAA representative must perform a detailed inspection for workmanship, materials, and conformity with the approved technical data, and a check of flight characteristics.

H-500 Data/Specification (Sheet 3) FAA, Wichita ACO.

Appendix 1: Data Specification Sheets

> <u>NOTE</u>: This Data/Specification is intended for general historical reference only, and is not intended for actual aircraft use. Anyone needing access to specific Aircraft Type Data Sheets should query the latest revision level offered by the FAA.

Equipment   The basic required equipment as prescribed in the applicable airworthiness regulations (see Certification Basis) must be installed in the aircraft for certification.

(a) Shoulder harness and seat belts must be installed for all seats.
(b) FAA Approved Flight Nanual, Helio Model 500, dated June 11, 1963.

<u>NOTE</u>: See the latest online FAA Type Data Sheet entries for specific Airplane Flight Manual Supplements, Notes and other information as subject to the most current revision level.

<u>NOTE</u>: See Department of Transportation, FAA Federal Register for all pertinent information in regards to Airworthiness Directives.

H-500 Data/Specification (Sheet 4) FAA, Wichita ACO.

Appendix 1: Data Specification Sheets

Helio Model HST-550 Data/Specification

Note: A plus (+) or a minus (-) sign preceding the weight of an item indicates that the net weight will change with the installation of that item.

Model HST-550, 10 PCLM (Normal Category), approved August 26, 1965)

> NOTE: This Data/Specification is intended for general historical reference only, and is not intended for actual aircraft use. Anyone needing access to specific Aircraft Type Data Sheets should query the latest revision level offered by the FAA.

Engine	United Aircraft of Canada, Ltd. PT6A-6A (turboprop)
Fuel	JP-1, JP-4, and JP-5 fuels conforming to P&WA Spec. No. 522
Oil	(Engine and Gearbox) UACL PT-6 Engine Service Bulletin No. 1 lists approved brand oils.
Engine Limits	Static Sea Level Ratings

	Shaft H.P.	Jet Thrust	ESHP	Gas Gen. RPM	Propeller Shaft Speed	Max. Perm. Turbine Inlet Temp. °C	Max. Torque PSIG
Takeoff (2 min.)	550	70	578	38,100-101.5	2,200	994	42.5
Max. continuous	500	62	525	38,100-101.5	2,200	952	38.5
Starting trans. (2 sec.)						1,038	
Max. reverse (1 min.)	500			38,100-101.5	2,000	994	42.5

At low altitude and low ambient temperature, the engines may produce more power at takeoff than the airplane has been certified for. Under these conditions, the placarded torquemeter limitations should not be exceeded.

Oil Temperature	Minus 40° F To 185°F maximum continuous Minus 40° F To 195°F not to exceed 5 minutes

Propellor and Propellor Limits	Hartzell Model HC-B3TN-3yT-10173C
	Diameter: 101 in. (2 percent reduction allowable for repairs)
	Pitch settings at 30 in. Sta:
	    Low 16°
	    Feathered 78°
	    Reverse -17°

Airspeed Limits (CAS)	Maneuvering Vp 121 mph (105 knots) Max. structural cruising Vno 201 mph (175 knots) Never exceed Vne 226 mph (197 knots) Flaps extended Vfe 109 mph (80 knots)

HST-550 Data/Specification (Sheet 1) FAA, Wichita ACO.

208   Appendix 1: Data Specification Sheets

> **NOTE:** This Data/Specification is intended for general historical reference only, and is not intended for actual aircraft use. Anyone needing access to specific Aircraft Type Data Sheets should query the latest revision level offered by the FAA.

C.G. Range	At gross weight 127.70 in. to 137.80 in.
	At reduced weight 3,298 lb. 123.30 in.
	Straight line variation between points given
Leveling Means	For leveling the airplane, use the floorboards under the pilot's or co-pilot's seat.
Empty Weight C.G. Range	None
Max. Weight	5,100 lbs.
Minimum Crew	One pilot in the left front seat.
Number of Seats	10 (2 at +103.5, 3 at +131(aft facing), 3 at +171, 2 at +209)
Maximum Baggage	Total cargo load on floor not to exceed 2,153 lbs. See AFM.
Fuel Capacity	120 gallons (total usable in tip tanks - 51 gallons each)
	61 gallons (total usable in 2 auxiliary tanks - 30.5 gallons each)
	61 gallons (total usable in 2 main tanks - 30.5 gallons each)
Oil Capacity	1.5 gallons (total usable in engine integral tank.)

Control Surface Movements

Wing Flaps	Up 0°	Down 40°
Aileron ±1°	Up 20°	Down 20°
Stabilator (trailing edge) (±1°)	Up 25°	Down 8°
	Neutral is 2.5° down from horizonta reference.	
Stabilator trim tabs (±2°)	Measured from horizontal stabilator chordline.	
	Tab trailing edge up (+)	
	Tab trailing edge down (-)	

Stabilator neutral, flaps up	± 19.1°	pilot's trim indicator full nose down
	- 31.7°	pilot's trim indicator full nose up
Stabilator trailing edge full up	+ 37.9°	pilot's trim indicator full nose down
	+ 30.4°	pilot's trim indicator full nose up
Stabilator trailing edge full down	+ 4°	pilot's trim indicator full nose down
	- 44.3°	pilot's trim indicator full nose up
Stabilator anti-balance tabs (±2°)	Same tabs as trim tabs measured in same manner	

HST-550 Data/Specification (Sheet 2) FAA, Wichita ACO.

Appendix 1: Data Specification Sheets

> NOTE: This Data/Specification is intended for general historical reference only, and is not intended for actual aircraft use. Anyone needing access to specific Aircraft Type Data Sheets should query the latest revision level offered by the FAA.

        Tabs(±2°)
          Trim indicator neutral
          Stabilator neutral   + 0°
          Stabilator T.E. full up
          25° from neutral   + 42.9°
          Stabilator T.E. full down - 20.0°
          8° from neutral

          Flap trim interconnect tab
          Flaps full down   + 40° +2° -1°

          Rudder   Right 25°   Left 25°
          Rudder trim tab Right 25°   Left 25°
                            Measured from rudder chordline

Serial Nos. Eligible   1 and up

Certification Basis   Application for type certificate dated October 8, 1963. Part 3 of the Civil Air Regulations dated May 15, 1956, as amended by 3-1 through 3-8. Special Conditions for CAR 3 turbine-powered aircraft submitted with February 11, 1964. FAA letter to Helio and amended by September 9, 1964. FAA letter to Helio Type Certificate No. A4EA issued August 26, 1965.

Production Basis   S/N -001 through -004. None. Prior to original certification of each aircraft, an FAA representative must perform a detailed inspection for workmanship, materials, and conformity with the approved technical data, and a check of flight characteristics. For aircraft S/N -005 and on. Production Certification 311 is applicable.

HST-550 Data/Specification (Sheet 3) FAA, Wichita ACO.

> NOTE: This Data/Specification is intended for general historical reference only, and is not intended for actual aircraft use. Anyone needing access to specific Aircraft Type Data Sheets should query the latest revision level offered by the FAA.

Datum — Longitudinal reference Station 0 located 114 in. forward of leading edge of wing proper (slats in). 115.83 in. forward of leading edge of wing with slats extended.
Horizontal reference is 38.75 in. below centerline of and parallel to fuselage lower longeron.

Equipment — The basic required equipment as prescribed in the applicable airworthiness regulations (see Certification Basis) must be installed in the aircraft for certification.

In addition, the following items of equipment are required:

(a) Shoulder harness and seat belts must be installed for first row of seats.
(b) FAA Approved Flight Nanual, Helio Model HST-550, dated August 26, 1965, revised November 9, 1965.

NOTE: See the latest online FAA Type Data Sheet entries for specific Airplane Flight Manual Supplements, Notes and other information subject to the most current revision level.

NOTE: See Department of Transportation, FAA Federal Register for all pertinent information in regards to Airworthiness Directives.

HST-550 Data/Specification (Sheet 4) FAA, Wichita ACO.

Appendix 1: Data Specification Sheets

Helio Model HST-550A
Data/Specification

Note: A plus (+) or a minus (-) sign preceding the weight of an item indicates that the net weight will change with the installation of that item.

Model HST-550A, (USAF AU-24A), 10 PCLM (Normal Category), approved August 1, 1969)

NOTE: This Data/Specification is intended for general historical reference only, and is not intended for actual aircraft use. Anyone needing access to specific Aircraft Type Data Sheets should query the latest revision level offered by the FAA.

Engine	United Aircraft of Canada, Ltd. PT6A-27 (turboprop)
Fuel	JP-1, JP-4, and JP-5 fuels conforming to P&WA Spec. No. 522
Oil	(Engine and gearbox) synthetic type confprming to CPN Spec 202 as revised. UACL Engine Service Bulletin No. 1 lists approved brand oils.
Engine Limits	Static Sea Level Ratings

	Shaft H.P.	Jet Thrust	ESHP	Gas Gen. RPM	Propeller Shaft Speed	Max. Perm. Turbine Inlet Temp. °C	Max. Torque PSIG
Takeoff (2 min.)	680	90	715	38,100-101.5	2,200	725	53
Max. continuous	500	70	528	38,100-101.5	2,200	695	38.5
Starting trans. (2 sec.)						1,090	
Max. reverse (1 min.)	620			38,100-101.5	2,100	725	53

At low altitude and low ambient temperature, the engines may produce more power at takeoff than the airplane has been certified for. Under these conditions, the placarded torquemeter limitations should not be exceeded.

Oil Temperature	Minus 40°F to 210°F maximum continuous

Propellor and Propellor Limits	Hartzell Model HC-B3TN-3/T-10178CH
	Diameter: 101 in. (2 percent reduction allowable for repairs)
	Pitch settings at 30 in. Sta:
	    Low 14°±1°
	    Feathered 87°±1°
	    Reverse -12°±1°

Airspeed Limits (CAS)	Maneuvering Vp 124 mph (108 knots) Max. structural cruising Vno 194 mph (169 knots) Never exceed Vne 218 mph (190 knots) Flaps extended Vfe 109 mph (95 knots)

HST-550A Data/Specification (Sheet 1) FAA, Wichita ACO.

Appendix 1: Data Specification Sheets

> **NOTE:** This Data/Specification is intended for general historical reference only, and is not intended for actual aircraft use. Anyone needing access to specific Aircraft Type Data Sheets should query the latest revision level offered by the FAA.

C.G. Range	At gross weight 127.70 in. To 137.80 in. At reduced weight 3,624 lb. 121.90 in. Straight line variation between points given
Leveling Means	For leveling the airplane, use lower surface of wing carry through structure which is 4.5° nose up to W.L. zero
Empty Weight C.G. Range	None
Max. Weight	5,100 lbs.
Minimum Crew	One pilot in the left front seat.
Number of Seats	10 (2 at +103.5, 3 at +144.0, 3 at +176, 2 at +209)
Maximum Baggage	Total cargo load carried on the floor not to exceed 2,153 lbs.
Fuel Capacity	60 gallons (total usable in 2 auxiliary tanks - 29.5 gallons each) 60 gallons (total usable in 2 main tanks - 29.5 gallons each)
Oil Capacity	1.5 gallons (total usable in engine integral tank.)

Control Surface Movements

Wing Flaps	Up 0°	Down 40°
Aileron ±1°	Up 20°	Down 20°
Stabilator (trailing edge) (±1°)	Up 25°	Down 8°
	Neutral is 2.5° down from horizonta reference.	

Stabilator trim tabs (±2°)   Measured from horizontal stabilizer chordline.
Tab trailing edge up   (+)
Tab trailing edge down (-)

Stabilator neutral, flaps up	± 19.1°	pilot's trim indicator full nose down
	- 31.7°	pilot's trim indicator full nose up
Stabilator trailing edge full up	+ 37.9°	pilot's trim indicator full nose down
	+ 30.4°	pilot's trim indicator full nose up
Stabilator trailing edge full down	+ 4°	pilot's trim indicator full nose down
	- 44.3°	pilot's trim indicator full nose up
Stabilator anti-balance tabs (±2°)		Same tabs as trim tabs measured in same manner

HST-550A Data/Specification (Sheet 2) FAA, Wichita ACO.

Appendix 1: Data Specification Sheets 213

NOTE: This Data/Specification is intended for general historical reference only, and is not intended for actual aircraft use. Anyone needing access to specific Aircraft Type Data Sheets should query the latest revision level offered by the FAA.

Tabs(±2°)

Trim indicator neutral
Stabilator neutral, 0°
Stabilator T.E. Full up +42.9°
25° from neutral
Stabilator T.E. Full down -20.0°
8° from neutral

Flap down interconnect tab
Flaps full down +40° +0° -2°
Rudder Right 25° ±2° Left 25° ±2°
Rudder trim tab Right 25° ±1° Left 10°±1°
Measured from rudder chordline

Additional Requirements/Limitations: HST-550A Airplanes for 5,800 lbs Gross Weight Certification. The airplane must incorporate the modifications listed on Helio Aircraft LTD. Drwg. No. 550-000-051

Airspeed Limits (CAS)	Maneuvering	Vp 111 mph
	Max. structural cruising	Vno 159 mph
	Never exceed	Vne 199 mph
	Flaps extended	Vfe 95 mph
C.G. Range	At gross weight	130.5 in. To 137.8 in.
	At 3,624 lbs. or less	121.9 in. To 137.8 in.
	Straight line variation between points given	
Max. Weight	5,800 lbs.	
Fuel Capacity	120 gallons (total usable in 2 tip tanks - 51 gallons each)	
	60 gallons (total usable in 2 auxiliary tanks - 29.5 gallons each)	
	60 gallons (total usable in 2 main tanks - 29.5 gallons each)	

HST-550A Data/Specification (Sheet 3) FAA, Wichita ACO.

Appendix 1: Data Specification Sheets

> NOTE: This Data/Specification is intended for general historical reference only, and is not intended for actual aircraft use. Anyone needing access to specific Aircraft Type Data Sheets should query the latest revision level offered by the FAA.

Serial Nos. Eligible	Serail Numbers -001 and up Prior to civil certification, AU-24A airplanes must be modified in accordance with Helio Drawing 550-000-050 which may be obtained from the manufacturer.
Datum	Longitudinal reference Station 0 located 114 in. forward of leading edge of wing proper (slats in). 115.83 in. forward of leading edge of wing with slats extended. Horizontal reference is 38.75 in. below centerline of and parallel to fuselage lower longeron.
Certification Basis	Application for type certificate dated October 8, 1963. Part 3 of the Civil Air Regulations dated May 15, 1956, as amended by 3-1 through 3-8. Special Conditions for CAR 3 turbine-powered aircraft submitted with February 11, 1964. FAA letter to Helio and amended by September 9, 1964. FAA letter to Helio Type Certificate No. A4EA issued August 26, 1965.
Production Basis	S/N -001 through -004. None. Prior to original certification of each aircraft, an FAA representative must perform a detailed inspection for workmanship, materials, and conformity with the approved technical data, and a check of flight characteristics. For aircraft S/N -005 and on. Production Certification 311 is applicable.
Equipment	The basic required equipment as prescribed in the applicable airworthiness regulations (see Certification Basis) must be installed in the aircraft for certification. NOTE: See the latest online FAA Type Data Sheet entries for specific Airplane Flight Manual Supplements, Notes and other information subject to the most current revision level. NOTE: See Department of Transportation, FAA Federal Register for all pertinent information in regards to Airworthiness Directives.

HST-550A Data/Specification (Sheet 4) FAA, Wichita ACO.

Appendix 2: Helio Aircraft Models and Production Totals

MODEL	FAA APPROVAL (or registration)	YEARS PRODUCED	CONFIRMED SERIALS (or commentary)	TOTAL AIRCRAFT
Helioplane-Two	(N939OH)	1949	Proof of Concept Aircraft	1
Helioplane-Four	(N74151)	1950	Experimental Prototype	1
Courier Protos		1950–1952	Pre-Production Prototypes	3
H-391		1952	001 (one of the pre-production prototypes modified to be Army YL-24, S/N 52-2540)	(1)
H-391B	S/N 001 (N242B) used as company demo aircraft T.C. #1A8	1954–1959	001–102 S/N 001-005 Fleet Mfg. Canada; S/N 006–102 Pittsburg, KS. 1 aircraft, #FML-004 (CF-18F), built completely by Fleet	102
H-392 Strato Courier		1957	(Converted H-391B)	1
H-395 Super Courier		1958–1964	502–639	138
			U-10A (29 A/C): 58-7026–7028 (Former L-28) 63-13166–13185 (ARMY)	(3 A/C) (20 A/C)
			U-10B (58 A/C): 62-5907–5920 63-8091–8098 63-8099–8110 63-13090–13113 (Air Guard)	(14 A/C) (8 A/C) (12 A/C) (24 A/C)
H-395A		1959	049, 515 & 1002–1008 (049 converted H-391B, 515 converted H-395)	9
H-500 Twin Courier	T.C. #A2EA	1962	(Also parts for 10 A/C) U-5A-HE	7
H-250 Courier Mk II H-250A Caballero		1964–1966	2501–2541	41
HST-550 (U-10X)		1965	Experimental Prototype	(1)
HST-600		1965	Experimental Prototype	1
HST-600B		1966	Experimental Prototype	1

Appendix 2: Helio Aircraft Models and Production Totals

H-295 Super Courier 1200 Series		1965–1969	1201–1295 U-10D (44 A/C): 66-14332–14345 66-14369–14369 66-14370–14375 (ARMY)	**95** (14 A/C) (24 A/C) (6 A/C)
H-295 Super Courier 1400 Series		1969–1974	1401–1479	**79**
HST-550A Stallion	T.C. #A4EA	1969–1972	001–016 S/N 002–016 to USAF AU-24A-HE 72-1319–1333)	**16**
H-370		1969	Experimental Prototype	**1**
HT-295 Tri-Gear	ST.C. SA 138SW	1973–1974	1701–1719 Approx. 19 a/c converted to tri-gears for CAP	**19**
H-800		1983–1984		**9**
H-700		1984		**7**
H-21A Rat'ler		1984	Experimental Prototype	**1**

Prepared by Frank Rowe (Sources: company files and interviews)   **Total:**   **523 Production Aircraft**

Notes

Unless otherwise noted, all specifications, performance data, and manufacturing/sales descriptions are derived from Helio Aircraft Corporation company files/archives.

All Type Certificate (T.C.) data derived from FAA/U.S. government files.

1. Chasing the Sun

1. *General Aviation Accident Analysis Book* (Frederick, MD, AOPA Air Safety Foundation, Emil Buehler Center For Aviation Safety, 1991), 12–15, 17–19.
2. David Thurston, *Design for Safety*, 2d ed. (New York, TAB Books/McGraw-Hill, 1995), 6–7.
3. *General Aviation Accident Analysis Book*, 19.
4. "Tanager Wins Grand Prize in Safe Airplane Contest," *Aviation*, January 11, 1930, 69–70.
5. William G. Brown, *Aviation*, February 8, 1930, 236–237.
6. Peter M. Bowers, *Curtiss Aircraft 1907–1947* (Annapolis, MD, Naval Institute Press, 1987), 219.
7. Leonard Bridgman, *Jane's All the World's Aircraft, 1955–1956* (New York, McGraw-Hill, 1957), 245.
8. "Department of Commerce Light Airplane Specifications," *Aviation*, July 1934.
9. Otto Koppen, "Helio Courier Oral History," videotape interview by Jungle Aviation and Radio Service, Inc., Waxhaw, NC, 1987.
10. Cy Caldwell, *Aero Digest*, October 1938.

2. Dawn of the "Tennis Court Airplane"

1. "New Slow-Flying Plane Developed," *Aviation Week*, May 16, 1949, 51–52.
2. Ibid.
3. Ibid.
4. Ibid.
5. Karl H. Bergey, "Special Aspects of Structural Design for Safety of Light Aircraft," SAE Technical Paper No. 610251, in *Aircraft Crashworthiness /PT-50*. (Warrendale, PA, Society of Automotive Engineers, 1995), 23–27.
6. Richard G. Snyder, "Civil Aircraft Restraint Systems: State-of-the-Art Evaluation of Standards, Experimental Data and Accident Experience," SAE Technical Paper No. 770154, in *Aircraft Crashworthiness/PT-50* (Warrendale, PA, Society of Automotive Engineers, 1995), 145.
7. Koppen, interview.
8. Ibid.
9. "New Slow-Flying Plane Developed," 51–52.
10. Ibid.
11. Koppen, interview.
12. Ibid.
13. Ibid.
14. Ibid.
15. Ibid.
16. Ibid.
17. Ibid.
18. Ibid.
19. Ibid.
20. Ibid.
21. Lynn L. Bollinger, Letter to Philip S.

Hopkins, Director, Smithsonian Institution, August 27, 1963.
22. J. Mac McClellan, "Helio All-Star Short Fielder," *Flying*, March 1984, 60.
23. Koppen, interview.
24. Ibid.

3. Geared for Success

1. Lynn L. Bollinger, Helio Aircraft Company Press Release, Sunday, May 15, 1949.
2. Alexander McSurley, "Aeronca Will Produce Helioplane," *Aviation Week*, March 20, 1950.
3. "Aeronca-Helioplane Deal Pending," *Aviation Week*, November 28, 1949, 15–16.
4. Lynn L. Bollinger, *Report to Stockholders*, Helio Aircraft Corporation, May 15, 1950, 8.
5. Ibid., 6–7.
6. Ibid., 9.
7. Ibid., 9–10.
8. James Gilbert, "The Helio Stallion," *Flying*, July 1966, 105.
9. Ibid.
10. Lynn Bollinger, *Special Action Report to Stockholders* (General Aircraft Corporation, June 15, 1974), 3.
11. Bob Casebeer (former vice president/manufacturing, Helio Aircraft Company), videotape interview by Jungle Aviation and Radio Service, Inc., Waxhaw, NC, 1987.
12. Bollinger, *Special Action Report to Stockholders*, 3.
13. Ibid.
14. Koppen, interview.
15. Helio Aircraft Corporation, Norwood, Massachusetts, H-391B Sales and Marketing Brochure.
16. Bollinger, *Special Action Report to Stockholders*, 2–4.
17. John Fricker, "Flying The V/STOL Courier," *Aeronautics and Astronautics*, March 11, 1960.
18. Robert F. Buckhorn, *The People's Lawyer* (New York: Prentice Hall, 1972), 111.
19. James T. Bruce and John B. Draper, "Crash Safety In General Aviation Aircraft," *Air Facts, Etc.*, January 1970, 77.

4. Litterbugs and Black OPS

1. A. J. Craig, *Evaluation of the Performance, Stability and Control of the Helio Courier Airplane* (Report Number 264, Final Report), University of Wichita, Department of Engineering Research (Wichita, KS, February 1957), 45–46.
2. Ibid., 40.
3. Ibid., 29.
4. U.S.A.F. Release, *For Aviation/Space Writers Conference*, 1962.
5. Lt. Col. John L. Rowan, *Informal Evaluation of the Cessna Model 185 and L-28A (Helio Courier Model 395) Airplanes*, ATBG-SEC-AVN 663, United States Army Aviation Board, Fort Rucker, Alabama, July 27, 1962.
6. Report 1320-G-2-A, *United States Army U-10A Helio Courier*, Technical Description, U.S. Army Special Warfare Center/Aviation, 1–3.
7. News Release, "Air Force Psywar Adds Personal Touch to Messages (Bien Hoa)," United States Air Force, Directorate of Information, Headquarters, Seventh Air Force, Tan Son Nhut Air Base, Republic of Vietnam, February 1968.
8. Christopher Robbins, *Air America* (New York, G. P. Putnam's Sons, 1979), 69.
9. Warren Hinckle and William W. Turner, *Deadly Secrets, The CIA-Mafia War Against Castro and the Assassination of J.F.K.* (New York, Thunder's Mouth Press, 1992), 74.
10. Robbins, 104.
11. Ibid., 109.
12. Ibid., 116.
13. Ibid., 229.
14. Ibid., 303–304.
15. Ibid., 306.
16. Ibid.

5. Above and Beyond

1. Robert B. Kimnach, *1967 Annual Report*, Helio Aircraft Company.
2. Lynn L. Bollinger, *Special Action Report to Stockholders*, 6–7.
3. Bob Devine (former vice president and chief of engineering, Helio Aircraft Company), taped interview, July 5, 1995.
4. Ibid.
5. Robert I. Stanfield, "Pilot Report: STOL Capabilities Mark Twin Helio," *American Aviation*, February 1965, 35.
6. Ibid.
7. H580 Marketing Brochure, Helio Aircraft Company.
8. David A. Brown, "Modified Helio U-5 Proposed for COIN," *Aviation Week and Space Technology*, June 22, 1964, 21.

9. Bollinger, *Special Action Report to Stockholders*, 2–4.
10. Stephan Wilkinson, "Pilot Report: The Helio Stallion," *Flying*, April 1971, 52.
11. Don Downie, "Helio's Stallion/Pilot Flight Check," *AOPA PILOT*, April 1973.
12. Paul E. Davis (former technical representative/Cambodia, Helio Aircraft Company), taped interview, September 23, 1995.
13. Downie, "Helio's Stallion."
14. Wilkinson, "Pilot Report," 100.
15. Casebeer, interview.
16. Wilkinson, "Pilot Report," 101.
17. Neil Sandler, "Fairchild Industries' AU-23A Peacemaker," (*NATO's Fifteen Nations*, December 1975–January 1976), 102.
18. Ibid.
19. Ibid.
20. General Otto Glasser (Former Deputy Chief of Research and Development), *Transcript: House Subcommittee on Department of Defense Hearing*, Chaired by Rep. George H. Mahon, October, 1971.
21. Davis, interview.
22. Ibid.
23. Ibid.
24. Ibid.
25. Helio Advertising Film.
26. General Aircraft Corporation, *Special Report to Stockholders (High Points at 1972 Annual Meeting)*, July 20, 1972.

6. Twilight of the Courier

1. Thurston, 130.
2. Phil Buttram, "Happy Helios," *Pilot News*, Vol. 12 No. 12, May 1984, 9B.
3. Steve Koppes, "Helio Launches First Plane in 8 Years," *Pittsburg (KS) Morning Sun*, March, 26, 1983.
4. Ibid.

7. Couriers of the Word

1. Ecclesiastes 10:20
2. Jamie Buckingham, *Into the Glory* (Plainfield, New Jersey, Logos International, 1974), 33.
3. Ibid., 33–34.
4. Ibid., 73.
5. Ibid., 63.
6. Terry Heffield (engineer, JAARS), taped interview, JAARS, Inc. Waxhaw, North Carolina, August 8,1995.
7. Buckingham, 64.

8. Epilogue

1. Saville R. Davis, "Two Men and an Idea: A Plane for Really Safe Civilian Flying," *Christian Science Monitor*, May 16, 1949 (second edition).

Bibliography

Andre, John. *U.S. Military Aircraft Designations and Markings since 1909.* Hinckley, Leics., United Kingdom: Midland Counties Publications, 1979.
Bateson, Richard P. *Aircraft Profile, Fieseler Fi-156 Storch.* London: Profile Publications Ltd., 1971.
Bergey, Karl H. "Special Aspects of Structural Design for Safety of Light Aircraft" (SAE Technical Paper No. 610251). In: Chandler, *Aircraft Crashworthiness (PT-50).*
Black, Charles L. "Report on the Helioplane." *Flying,* April 1950.
Boyne, Walter J. *The Aircraft Treasures of Silver Hill.* Toronto, ON: McClelland & Stewart, 1982.
Brown, David A. "Modified Helio U-5 Proposed for COIN." *Aviation Week and Space Technology,* June 22, 1964.
_____. "Helio Changes Improve Cruise, Climb Rate." *Aviation Week and Space Technology,* August 31, 1964.
_____. "Turbo-Porter Displays Exceptional STOL." *Aviation Week and Space Technology,* October 5, 1964.
_____. "New Twin STOL Stresses Controllability." *Aviation Week and Space Technology,* April 1, 1968.
Bruce, James T., and John B. Draper. "Crash Safety in General Aviation Aircraft." *Air Facts, Etc.,* January 1970.
Buckhorn, Robert F. *The People's Lawyer.* New York: Prentice-Hall, 1972.
Buckingham, Jamie. *Into the Glory.* Plainfield, N.J.: Logos International, 1974.
Bulban, Erwin J. "New Helioplane." *Aviation Week,* July 12, 1954.
Buttram, Phil. "Happy Helios." *Pilot News,* May 1984.
Casebeer, Bob. Videotape interview by Jungle Aviation and Radio Service, Inc., Waxhaw, NC, 1987.
Chandler, Richard F., ed. *Aircraft Crashworthiness (PT-50).* Warrendale, PA: Society of Automotive Engineers, 1995.
Clark, Bill. *Illustrated Buyers Guide to Used Airplanes.* 3rd ed. Blue Ridge Summit, PA: TAB Aero Books, 1992.
Conrad, John W. "Helio Courier/In-the-Air Test." *Air Progress,* July 1992.
Cook, Charles Leroy. "C/STOL Super Courier." *Private Pilot,* July 1971.
Craig, A.J. *Evaluation of the Performance, Stability and Control of the Helio Courier Airplane* [and related progress reports]. Wichita, KS: University of Wichita, Dept. of Engineering Research, February 1957.
Davis, Ed. "Classic Courier/In-the-Air Test." *Air Progress,* November 1994.
Davis, Paul E. Taped interview. September 23, 1995.

Davis, Saville R. "Two Men and an Idea: A Plane for Really Safe Civilian Flying." *Christian Science Monitor*, May 16, 1949 (second edition).
DeHaven, H. *Development of Crash Survival Design in Personal, Executive and Agricultural Aircraft*. Ithaca, N.Y.: Cornell University Medical College, 1953.
Devine, Bob. Taped interview. July 5, 1995.
Downie, Don. "Helio's Stallion/Flight Check." *AOPA Pilot*, April 1973.
Francillon, René. *The Air Guard*. Austin, TX: Aerofax Inc., 1982.
_____. *Vietnam, The War in the Air*. New York: Arch Cape Press, 1987.
Frawley, Gerald. *International Directory of Civil Aircraft 95/96*. Fyshwick, Australia: Aerospace Publications, 1995.
Fricker, John. "Flying The V/STOL Courier." *Aeronautics and Astronautics*, March 11, 1960.
Friedman, W.S. "The Paraplane." *Flying*, September 1949.
General Aviation Accident Analysis Book. Frederick, MD: AOPA Air Safety Foundation, Emil Buehler Center For Aviation Safety, 1991.
Gilbert, James. "Pilot Report: The Maules." *Flying*, April 1965.
_____. "Pilot Report: Fairchild Hiller Turbo Porter." *Flying*, December 1965.
_____. "Pilot Report: The Helio Stallion." *Flying*, July 1966.
Grable, Ron. "High-Steppin' Helio." *Plane & Pilot*, July 1993.
Green, William. *Aircraft of the World*. New York: Doubleday and Co., 1965.
Haddaway, George E. "The Associated Explorer." *Flight*, April 1955.
Heffield, Terry. Taped interview by Jungle Aviation and Radio Service, Inc., Waxhaw, NC, 1987.
Hibben, Roderick D. "Helio's Stallion." *Aviation Week and Space Technology*, June 1, 1964.
Hinckle, Warren, and William W. Turner. *Deadly Secrets, The CIA-Mafia War against Castro and the Assassination of JFK*. New York: Thunder's Mouth Press, 1992.
Hoekstra, Harold D. *Safety in General Aviation*. Alexandria, VA: Flight Safety Foundation, Inc., 1971.
Horne, Thomas A. "Helio's Macho Machines." *AOPA Pilot*, January 2001.
Horonjeff, Robert. *Planning and Design of Airports*. 2nd ed. New York: McGraw-Hill, 1975.
Hughes, Albert D. "Low and Slow Via Helioplane." *Skyways*, July 1950.
Kohlman, David L. *V/STOL Airplanes*. Ames: Iowa State University Press, 1981.
Kissick, Jim. "Helio Super Courier." *Rotor and Wing*, April 1969.
Koppen, Otto. *Helio Courier Oral History*. Videotape interview by Jungle Aviation and Radio Service, Inc., Waxhaw, NC, 1987.
Leeker, Dr. Joe F., "The Aircraft of Air America — Helio H-395 Super Courier & Helio H-500 Twin Courier," [Data Base], Air America Archives/McDermott Library, University of Texas at Dallas, June 3, 2004.
Mahan, Ernst. *The History of McNally Pittsburg*. Wichita, KS: McCormick-Armstrong Co., Inc., Publishing Div., 1972.
Martin, Patrick. *Tail Code, The Complete History of USAF Tactical Aircraft Tail Code Markings*. Atglen, PA: Schiffer Publishing, Ltd., 1994.
McClellan, J. Mac. "Helio All-Star Short Fielder." *Flying*, March 1984.
Naugle, R.G. "Can We Slow Down the Lightplane." *Flying*, March 1950.
"New Slow-Flying Plane Developed." *Aviation Week*, May 16, 1949.
O'Leary, Michael. *U.S. Sky Spies since World War I*. Poole, Dorset, United Kingdom: Blandford Press, 1986.
Osborne, Robert R. "The Tanager and Some of Its History, A Technical Description and a Chronological Discussion of the Incorporation of the Design Features." *Aviation*, February 8, 1930.
Page, Ron, and William Cummings. *Fleet, The Flying Years*. Erin, ON: Boston Mills Press, 1990.
Robbins, Christopher. *Air America*. New York: G. P. Putnam's Sons, 1979.
Ross, John C. "Is This the Revolutionary Light Plane." *Flying*, June 1949.
Rowe, Frank Joseph, and Craig Miner. *Borne on the South Wind, A Century of Kansas Aviation*. Wichita, KS: Wichita Eagle and Beacon Publishing Co., 1994.

Sandler, Neil. "Fairchild Industries' Au-23A Peacemaker." *NATO's Fifteen Nations*, Dec. 1975 — Jan. 1976.
Shortt, A. J. *Helio H-391B Courier*. [Lecture transcript.] National Aviation Museum, Ottawa, Ontario, Canada, January 27, 1978.
Simpson, R.W. *Airlife's General Aviation, A Guide to Post-War General Aviation Manufacturers and Their Aircraft*. Shrewsbury, United Kingdom: Airlife Publishing, Ltd., 1991.
Smith, Gene. "Those STOL Helios." *Air Progress*, December 1968, January 1969.
_____. "Working Warhorse." *Air Classics*, November 1985, page 60–82, Challenge Publications, Chatsworth, CA.
Snyder, Richard G. *Civil Aircraft Restraint Systems: State of the Art Evaluation of Standards, Experimental Data and Accident Experience* (SAE Paper 770154). Ann Arbor: University of Michigan, 1977.
Stanfield, Robert I. "Pilot Report: STOL Capabilities Mark Twin Helio." *American Aviation*, February 1965.
Stites, Charles E. "Helio Stallion Number One." *Private Pilot*, August 2003.
Thurston, David. *Design for Safety*. 2nd ed. New York: TAB Books/McGraw-Hill, 1995.
Underhill, Peter. "Harrier for the Common Man." *Private Pilot*, December 1995.
U.S. Government Technical Manual 1U-10A-21: *Aircraft Inventory Record, Master Guide: USAF & Army Series U-10A, U-10B & U-10D Aircraft*, 7/9/70.
U.S. Government Technical Manual 1U-10A-33-1-1/2(2S/2) & 1U-10A-33-1-2: *Non-Nuclear Munitions Basic Information/Loading Procedures and Supplement, USAF & Army Series U-10A, U-10B & U-10D Aircraft*, 4/1/71.
U.S. Government Technical Manual T.O. 1U-10A-4: *Illustrated Parts Breakdown, USAF & Army Series U-10A, U-10B & U-10D Aircraft*, 2/1/71.
Weeghman, Richard B. "The Helio Courier H-295." *Flying*, August 1969.
_____. *Aviation Consumer Used Aircraft Guide*. Vol. II. 5th ed. Norwalk, CT: Belvoir Publications, 1991.
Warner, Edward P. "The Tanager." *Aviation*, February 8, 1930.
Werner, Steve. *The Plane & Pilot International Aircraft Directory*. Blue Ridge Summit, PA: TAB Aero Books/McGraw-Hill, 1995.
Wilkinson, Stephan. "Pilot Report: The Helio Stallion." *Flying*, April 1971.

Index

Adams, Gary 66
Advisory Group for Aerospace Research & Development (AGARD) 87
Aero Digest 26
Aerofoto Mexicana Compañía (CAM) 74
Aeromatic Propeller 32
Aeronautica Macchi: AM-3C 135
Aeronautical Research Foundation 30
Aeronca Aircraft Corporation 22, 50, 51, 53, 54; Model C-2 7, 9; Model Sedan 50; Model Tandem 50
Aeronca Engines 9
Agricultural Aviation Convention (Las Vegas, Nevada) 157
Air Commerce Act of 1926 30
Air Products (Ercoupe) 18
Air Taxi 142, 143
Aircraft Acquisition Corporation (AAC) 66
ALAR (Lisbon, Portugal) 116, 143
Allison Engines 111; Allison, 250-B15 111, 112, 142, 144
ALON (AirCoupes) 18
Alvis (Engines) 23
American Eagle Aircraft: American Eagle Eaglet 7
AOPA Air Safety Foundation 2
Arado 232B 25
Argus (Engines): 240 HP 20
Armstrong, Dale 58, 59
Associated Explorer 25
Astoria, New York 30
Autogyro 7–8
Aviation Week & Space Technology 96, 98

Avro 7; Model Lancaster Bomber 54
Bedford, Massachusetts 61, 66, 111, 113
Beech Aircraft Company 1, 30, 65; Bonanza 30, 135; Travel-Air 30; Twin Bonanza 30
Belk, Henderson 166
Bell Helicopter, Huey 138
Bellanca (Aircraft): YO-50 21, 22
Bender Oil Operations 64
Bering Strait 93
Berliner, Henry 16
Bleriot, Louis 9
Boeing aircraft: B-47 54, 57, 58; L-15 Scout 23–25; YC-14 14
Boeing-Wichita 67, 137, 148
Bollinger, Dr. Lynn L. 28, 29, 31, 36, 37, 40, 43, 48–54, 57, 58, 59, 61, 64, 74, 108, 119, 123, 143, 144, 150, 171
Boston, Massachusetts 54, 66
Boston Metropolitan Airport 60
Bostwick Prospecting Company 64
Brent, Clarence 148
Brooks, Harry 30
Brownwood, Texas 95
Bruce, James T. 84
Brunner-Winkle 5
Buckingham, Jamie 170
Buffalo, New York 54
Buhl Aircraft Company 7
Bureau of Air Commerce 14, 16
Burnelli, Vincent 5
Buttram, Phil 147

Caldwell, CY 26
CAMCORP (Consolidated Asset Management Corporation) 66
Canadair, LTD 55, 56
Canton, Massachusetts 27, 43, 60
Caribbean Traders, Inc.: Model Husky Mk. II 25
Casebeer, Bob 83, 130, 150
Castro, Fidel 100
Caton, Lawrence, W 59
Centaur 101(Acme) 25
Central Intelligence Agency (CIA) 86, 94, 98, 100–105, 108, 113, 160
Central Intelligence Agency, aircraft: Beech-Volpar Model Turbo18 100; Cessna Model L-19/O-1 "Birdog" 100; Curtiss Model C-46 "Commando" 100; DeHavilland Model DHC-4/CV-2 "Caribou" 91 100; DeHavilland Model Otter 100; DeHavilland Model U-6A Beaver 97, 100; Douglas Model DC-3/C-47 "Dakota"/"Skytrain" 93, 95, 100; Fairchild Model C-119 "Flying Boxcar" 96; Fairchild Model C-123 "Provider" 93, 138, 140; Grumman Model Hu-16 "Albatros" 96; Martin Model B-26B "Marauder" 93; North American Model T-28B "Trojan" 93, 138
Central Intelligence Agency, aviation entities: *Holding Companies*: Pacific Corporation 100; *Non Operating Companies*: Air Ventures 100, Atlantic General Enterprises, Inc. 100, Aviation Investors, Inc. 100, Consultair Associates 100, King-Hurley

225

Research Group 100; *World-Wide Air Operations*: Air America, Inc 100–103, Air Asia Company, LTD 100 103, 104, Civil Air Transport, LTD 100, Southern Air Transport 100
Central Intelligence Agency, black operations 98 102, 103; Pathet Lao 100, 102; Meo Tribesmen 100–103
Central Intelligence Agency, locations: *Burma*: Shan Hills 102; *Cambodia* 103; *China* 103; *Cuba*: Havana 100; *Formosa*: Tainan 103; *Golden Triangle* 102; *Indochina* 105; *Laos* 100–103, Ho Chi Minh trail 101, Long Tieng 101, Plain of Jars 101, Vientiane 101; *Thailand* 103, Udorn 103; *North Vietnam* 103
Cessna Aircraft Company 1, 25, 65, 87, 106, 160, 168; Model A-37B "Dragonfly" 138; Model 140 29; Model 170A 25, 26, 52; Model 170B 53; Model 185 83, 90; Model 188 "Agwagon" 158; Model 206 166; Model 208/208B "Caravan"/"Grand Caravan" 147, 149, 155, 156; Model 309 (A, B &C) 25, 26; Model 310 83; Model T-41 "Mescalero" 138
Charlotte, North Carolina 166
Chicago, Illinois 51
Cierva: Model C.4 7
Cierva, Juan de la 7–8
Civil Aeronautics Board (CAB) 65
Civil Air Patrol 83
Civil Aviation Authority (CAA) 34, 35, 43, 46, 49, 50, 61, 65, 69, 74
Civil Aviation Board (CAB) 2, 18, 19
Clifford, Defense Secretary Clark M. 135
Coles, Percy 57
Collier Trophy 8
Commerce, Department of 14
Conrad, John, W. 160
Consolidated Aircraft Company 54
Continental Engines 11; 65 HP 17; 260 HP 12; C-85 32; C-145-4 32
Controlled Materials Plan 54
Convair (Consolidated-Vultee Aircraft Corporation): Model L-13 24–26
Cornell University Medical College 29

Corser Ventures 66
Corsini, Gene 148
Cox, Jim 148, 155, 158
Craig, A.J. 87
Crash safety in general aviation aircraft 84
Cross Anchor, South Carolina 66
Cunningham-Hall 5
Curtiss-Wright Corporation: Model Tanager 5–7
Custer, Willard 12
Custer Channel Wing 11–12, 14; Model CCW-1 12; Model CCW-5 12

Davis, Ed 1, 49
Davis, Paul 125, 139–142
Davis, Saville R. 27
Davis-Monthon Air Force Base 137, 138
Dedham, Massachusetts 20
DeHaven, Hugh 2, 29, 37
DeHavilland Aircraft Company 7, 55; Model DHC-2 Beaver 55, 57; Model DHC-2 Turbo Beaver 121, 133; Model DASH-7 108, 146
Detroit, Michigan 51
Devine, Bob 109
DeVoucalla, George 170
Doole, George 104
Douglas Aircraft Company: Model AC-47 "Spooky" Gunship 133; Model C-47 "Skytrain" 138; Model DC-3 145
Downie, Don 106, 127, 129
Draper, John B. 84
Droste, Louis 115
Dulles International Airport 122

Earhart, Amelia 8
Eberts, Herman L. 55
Edmonton, Alberta, Canada 56
Eglin Air Force Base, Florida 136, 138
El Segundo, California (GAC Research Facility) 146
ERCO (Engineering & Research Corporation) 16
Ercoupe (ERCO) 14, 16–19, 26, 29, 65; Model 310 16; Model 415C 16
Everest, Dave 34

Fairchild Aviation Corporation 30, 53, 134, 138; Model AU-23A "Peacemaker" Pilatus Turbo Porter 121, 125, 133–138; Model Turbo Porter (Navy-OV-12A) 135; Model PC-6 134; Model PC-6A Turbo Porter 134

Fairchild Flight Analyzer 87
Federal Aviation Administration (FAA) 61, 65, 78, 84, 107, 108, 113, 142, 145, 146; Airworthiness Directives (AD) 148, 149; Certification 123–125, 128; FAA/ICAO Standards 65; FAA PART 23, 116, 148; Supplementary Type Certificate (STC) 167, SA217ICE 149
Fieseler-Flugzeugbau 20; Model F5 20; Model Fi-156 Storch 20, 21, 25, 26
Flaperons 39
Fleet, Major Reuben Hollis 54
Fleet Manufacturing, LTD 5, 50, 54–57, 59, 66, 215; Fleet-Built Helio Couriers 53, 57; Model 1 54; Model 2 54; Model 80 Canuck 54; Model PT-23/PT-26 54
Focke-Wulf 7
Ford, Henry 19, 30
Ford Flivver 19, 30, 34
Ford-Leigh Safety Wing 5
Ford Motor Company 30
Ford Tri-motor 30
Forney Manufacturing Company (Ercoupes) 18
Fort Bragg, North Carolina 86
Fort Erie, Ontario, Canada 54, 56
Fort Eustis, Virginia 87
Fort Rucker, Alabama 90
Franklin (Engines): Flat Six 25
Fricker, John 71
Frise-Type Aileron 42, 43

Garrett AiResearch Engines 26; TPE 331-1 134; TPE 331-2-1 121; TPE 331-1-101F 134 137; T76-G-6/8 118, 119
Garside, Joseph 31
Gaston, Ralph 59
General Aircraft Company 66; Model Skyfarer 18, 20, 30, 31
General Aircraft Corporation *see* Helio business entities
General Electric 14
Geneva Agreement of 1954 101
Gerlach, Heinrich 21
Glasser, General Otto (Chief of Research and Development) 136
Goldhush, Allan 66, 147
Goodyear Cross-wind Landing Gear 32, 68, 70, 127, 128
Grable, Ron 1, 147
Gran Sasso 21
Great Depression 7
Greene, Betty 163
Griffin, Bob 166
Guggenheim, Harry F. 4

Index

Guggenheim Safe Aircraft Competition 4, 7, 14

Haddon, Carl 16
Hagerstown, Maryland 134
Hammond, Dean 15,
Hammond Aircraft Corporation: Model Y 15 16
Handley-Page 5–7; Slats 35, 106, 126, 152, 154, 155
Hanscom Air Force Base 61, 113
Harvard University 27; Business School 54; Stadium 39
Hastings, Joe 59
Hastings, Merrill G. 59
Hawks, Frank 8
Hayes International Corporation (Birmingham, Alabama) 143
Heffield, Terry 167
Helicopter 37, 38, 62, 64, 87, 89, 91, 93, 94, 100, 102, 106, 136, 143, 144, 147, 150, 166; H/E (Helicopter/Equivalent) 65
Helio/Helio Courier 26, 27, 30, 36, 43, 50, 51, 54, 55, 57, 59–61, 64–67, 72, 73, 84, 86–89, 92–94, 98–105, 106–109, 111, 116, 133, 135–137, 142, 144, 145, 147, 48, 150, 155–157, 160, 161, 163, 165–167, 169–171
Helio Aircraft Company/Corporation 48, 49, 51–52, 57–60, 64–66, 89, 98, 103–105, 107, 108, 121, 123–127, 145; design requirements/goals 28, 29, 31, 32
Helio aircraft design, airframe construction 31 32, 43, 46, 54, 114, 118, 126, 111; center cabin safety truss 20, 32, 67, 68, 126, 148, 149; wing 36, 44, 126
Helio aircraft design, airframe systems/controls & components 29 35–43, 113; ailerons 36, 39, 42, 43; control force augmenting device 124; flaperons 39; flaps 36, 39, 43, 69, 71, 127; interceptor 39, 40, 42, 126, 128; landing gear 32, 68, (composite) 148, 149, (cross-wind) 68, 70, 83, 127, 128, (tricycle), 83–84; leading-edge slats (automatic) 35, 36, 40, 41, 126, 129; noise abatement 27, 28, 30, 39, 111; rudder 19, 36, 45, 127, (rudder/aileron interconnect) 36, (split rudder) 39; stabilator 44; Stick Force Augmentation System (SFAS) 124, 125, 128;

vertical tail 44, 45; wing 36, 40–43, 44
Helio aircraft models: AU-24A-HE 107 109, 111, 123, 130–142, (Type Data Specifications) 210–214; GAC-100 108, 110, 111, 144–146; Helio Courier 1, 3, 4, 20, 28, 29, 31, 37, 39, 43, 53, 55, 56, 58, 59, 62, 65; Helio Courier Mark II 1, 78–80; Helioplane 39, 51, 53; Helioplane-Four 43–46, 50–53, 86, 215; Helioplane-Two 36, 39, 43, 44, 45, 46, 49, 50, 215; Helio Proof-of-Concept Aircraft 31, 33, 34, 35; Helio Plane Prototype 37, 38, 43–46; H-21A "Rat'ler" 150, 151, 157–159, 216; H-250 67, 78–80, 148, 151, 154, 171, 215; H-250A "Caballero" 78–80, 215, (Type Data Specifications) 189–193; H-295 Super Courier, 1200 Series 49, 67, 78–84, 89, 91, 106, 107, 109, 121, 148, 150–152, 154, 216, (Type Data Specifications) 194–198; H-295 Super Courier, 1400 Series 45, 67, 80–81, 107, 142, 216, (Type Data Specifications) 194–198; HT-295 Tri-Gear Super Courier 67, 83–85, 148, 151, 154, 216, (Type Data Specifications), 199–202; H-370 Propjet Courier 110–113, 142, 216; H-391 46–48, 76, 86, 148, 151, 154, 215; H-391B 46, 49, 50, 53–55, 59, 61–64, 67–74, 76, 87, 89, 109, 148, 151, 154, 166, 215, (Type Data Specifications) 174–178; H-392 Strato Courier 67, 74–76, 215; H-395/L-28A Super Courier 67, 76–78, 80, 89–91, 100, 109, 148, 151, 154, 167, 170, 215, (Type Data Specifications) 179–183; H-395A Courier 67, 77–79, 89, 148, 151, 154, 215, (Type Data Specifications) 184–188; H-500 (U-5A) Twin Courier 104, 105, 109–111, 113–116, 118, 121, 143, 215, (Type Data Specifications) 203–206; H-500B ("CHASQUI") 113; HST-550 Stallion (U-10X) 110, 111, 119–123, 215, (Type Data Specifications) 207–209; HST-550A Stallion 106–116, 119, 122–131, 142, 143, 147, 149, 155, 171, 216, (Type Data Specifications) 210–214;

HST-600 Stallion 121, 215; HST-600B 215; H-580 Twin Courier 108–111, 116, 117, 143; H-600 151, 152; H-634 Stallion Twin 108, 110, 111, 142–144; H-700 67, 109, 147–155, 157, 171, 216; H-800 40, 67, 109, 148–155, 157, 171, 216; H-1100 151, 155–157; H-1201 110, 111; H-1320 (U-5X), Twin Stallion 110, 111, 118–120; H-1650T Super-COIN Transport 110, 111, 119; H-2000 "Freightliner" 149, 151, 155–157; U-10 83, 86, 90, 91–98, 100, 106, 118, 131, 166; U-10A 86, 90–92, 94, 215; U-10B, 91, 92, 95, 96, 167, 215; U-10C 91; U-10D 91, 92, 94, 216; YL-24 46, 48, 86, 87, 215
Helio business entities: General Aircraft Corporation 66, 104, 108, 144–146; Helio Aircraft Corporation (Division of General Aircraft Corporation) (GAC) 109, 144–146; Helio Aircraft del Peru 113, 116; Helio Aircraft, Inc. 66; Helio Aircraft, LLC 171; Helio Aircraft, LTD 66, 148; Helio Courier, LTD 66; Helio Enterprises, LLC 66; Helio Precision Products 66; John Roberts LTD 66, 47, 148; Mid States Division of Helio Aircraft Corporation 66; Mid States Manufacturing Corporation 57–59, 66; Midwest Aircraft Corporation 66
Helio business plan/marketing 28, 51–54, 61–64, 107–109, 145–148, 150, 155, 156
Helio flight characteristics: C/STOL 35, 38, 39, 47, 49, 54, 61, 64, 65, 86, 88, 90, 98–101, 107, 129, 143; lateral control, 39, 40, 43, 88; performance, stability and control (evaluation), 87–89; safety 2, 27–29, 30–32, 34, 36, 37, 41, 48, 49, 52, 66–68, 86, 90, 107, 14, 50, 157, 165, 168; slow speed flight 1, 36, 37, 53, 165; stall/spin 27, 35, 36, 89, 106, 113 (H-500), 123–125
Helio litigation 104–105, 108, 147; U.S. Court of Claims, Washington, D.C. 104
Helio maintenance/service plan 51, 53
Helio manufacturing: facility (layout) 60; manufacturing partnerships 54–60

Helio powerplants & transmission/drive systems *see* Allison Engines; Continental Engines; Lycoming Engines; Pratt & Witney Engines; Propellers
Helio Type Certificates: *1A8* 46 51, 75, 185, 190, 195, 200, 207, 210; *A2EA* 113, 205; *A4EA* 121, 213
Holland Furnace Company 64
Holshouser, Robert 59
Hoover, Herbert 8
Hopkins, Phillip 40
Horton, Ben J. 57
House and Senate Armed Services Committee 135
House Subcommittee on the Department of Defense 136
Hubbard, A.W. 57
Hubbard, M.W. 58
Hughes, Albert D. 27

Interceptor 40–42
International Research and Development Corporation 64
Island Creek Coal Company 64

JAARS, INC. 67, 160–164, 166–168, 170
JAARS Aviation 160–170
JAARS facilities: Aviation 166–167; General Training 166; Mexico Museum 166; Museum of the Alphabet 166; Printing Operations 166; Radio Lab 166
JAARS outreach locations: Africa 166, 169; Oceania 166; Southeast Asia 165, 166, 168; South America 161, 162, 163, 164, 166
JAARS programs 161, 162, 163, 165
John F. Kennedy Center for Military Assistance 86
John Roberts LTD *see* Helio business entities
Junkers Model Ju-52/3m 25

Kaman Aircraft Corporation 119, 32
Kamov (Nikolay Il'ich) 8
Kellet 7
Ken Mar Airpark, Wichita, Kansas 87
Kent, Washington 66
Kesselring, Albert 21
Kimnach, Robert B. 107–108
Kissick, Ed 49
Koppen, Dr. Otto 19, 20, 27–31, 33–37, 39, 40, 43, 48–50, 54, 59, 61, 109, 150, 171

Korean War 53, 54, 58, 65
Ky, Air Marshal Nguyen, Cao 137

Lanier, Edward M. 11
Lanier Model Vacuplane (Paraplane) 9, 11, 14, 26
Larmont Aviation (Spartanburg, South Carolina) 167
Lateral Control Roll Augmenter 40
Lawler, John 50
Letton, Raymond 57
Litterbugs 86, 95, 96, 102
Lockheed Aircraft Corporation 57; Model AC-130A "Spectre" Gunship 133; Model C-130 "Hercules" 137
Luftwaffe 21
Lycoming Engines 12, 19, 21; *295 HP R-680–9* 21; *125 HP* 23; *300 HP* 25; *GSO-480-A1A6* 74, 75; *GSO-480-B1A6* 134; *GO-480* 152; *GO-480-G1A6* 199; *GO-480-G1D6* 76, 77, 81, 83, 84, 91, 179, 194, 199; *GO-480-G1F6* 121; *GO-435-C2* 47, 68, 70; *GO-435-C2B* 174; *GO-435-C2B2* 174; *GO-435-C2B2–6* 174; *GO-435-C2B6* 68, 73, 77, 78, 91, 184; *GSO-540-B1A* 91; *IO-540-G1A5* 109, 117; *IO-540-C2C* 113, 115; *IO-720-A1B* 148, 149, 154, 155, 157, 159; *O-540* 152; *O-540-A1A5* 78, 79, 189; *O-540-A2B* 109, 113, 115, 203; *TIO-540-J2B* 148, 52, 153

Mafia 103
Mahon, Representative George H., D-TEX 136
Marietta, Georgia 57
Marsh, Verne 59
Massachusetts Institute of Technology (MIT) 19, 27, 30, 61; Athletic Field 39
Maugsch, Victor 20
Maule Aircraft Company 65
McClellan, J. Mac 147
McDonnell-Douglas: Model YC-15 14
McNally-Pittsburg Company 50, 57, 59, 60
Menasco Engines 16
Mewes, Reinhold 20
Mexican Civil Aeronautics Department 75
Mid States Division *see* Helio business entities
Mid States Manufacturing Corporation *see* Helio business entities

Middleton, Ohio 50
Military operations/programs/competitions: Air Commando/Special Operations 97; Black Operations 86; Counter Insurgency (COIN) 111; Credible Chase 135 136, 138; Desert Strike 94; Farmgate 93; Laos 86, 94; Lima Sites 94; Military Assistance Programs 135; Military Equipment Delivery Team–Cambodia (MEDTC) 139; Mule Train 93; Pave Coin 135; Project Flycatcher 139; Psychological Warfare 93–97; Ranch Hand 93; River Patrol Operations (Riverine) 135; Special Warfare 91; Tactical Air Navigation (TACAN) 94
Military theatres and locations: *Cambodia (Republic of Khemer)* 138 139, 141, (Battambang) 141, (Kompong Chhnang) 141, (Phnom Penh) 139, 141, (Pochentong) 141, (Ream), 141; *Laos* 139; *Southeast Asia* 93, 95–97, 101, 102, 134, 140, 141, 147; *Vietnam* 93, 97, 136, 137, 139, (Bien Hoa) 95, (Mekong Delta) 95, 135, (Mekong River) 139, 141, (South Vietnamese) 95, (Tan Son Nhut Air Base) 95, (Vietnam War) 93, (Vietcong) 95; *Thailand* 138, 139
Missionary outreach, aircraft: Aeronca 160; Bell 166; Cessna 160; Consolidated PBY Catalina 163; Douglas Model DC-3 160 163; Grumman Duck 163; Hiller 166; Luscombe 160; Piper 160; Stinson 160; Taylorcraft 160; Turbine Islanders 160
Missionary programs: Church of the Prophecy 160; JAARS, Inc. 160–170; Mission Aviation Fellowship (MAF) 160 161; Moody Bible Institute 164
Mitchell Field, Long Island 5
Mitsubishi Model Mu-2 39
Montgomery, Larry 109, 125, 127–129, 163, 166, 167
Mooney Aircraft 18
Musgrove, Maj. Don W. 95
Mussolini, Benito 21

NACA 50; 23012 Airfoil 36, 26; 4418 Airfoil 11, 113
Nader, Ralph 83–84
Nader's Raiders 84
National Advisory Committee

Index

for Aeronautics (NACA) 30, 36, 39
National Air & Space Museum, Smithsonian Institution 40, 46
National Guard 25; Air National Guard (ANG) 91–93, 97
National Transportation Safety Board (NTSB) 2
New York Port Authority 64
Nol, General Lon 138, 141
Noordyun Aircraft of Canada 12
North American Aviation: Model AT-6 Texan 128; Model F-86 Sabre Jet 55; Model P-51 Mustang 36
North American Rockwell 135; Model OV-10A "Bronco" 135
Norwood, Massachusetts 27, 31, 43, 46, 54–56, 59, 60, 66

Ochoa, Claudio Robles 75
Office of Naval Research 25
Office of Transportation Research and Development Command (TRADCOM) 87
Operation Eiche 21
Orlando, Florida 162
Osborne, Robert 7

Pacific Airmotive Corporation (PAC)/PUREX Corporation 145
Paradynamics, Inc. 64
Pentagon 89
Peruvian Ministry of War 64
Petroleum Helicopters, Inc. 64
Phillips, Jack 27, 34
Pilatus Flugzeugwerke A.G. 134
Pilot error 3
Piper Aircraft Company 1, 65; Model Cub 22–23, 36, 147; Model Super Cruiser 162; Model Vagabond 31, 32
Pitcairn 7
Pitcairn, Harold 8
Pittsburg, Kansas 50, 57–61, 66, 87, 113, 137, 147, 215; Atkinson Airport 128, 129, 158
Pittsburg Memorial Auditorium 57
Pittsburg State University (PSU) 57
Pol Pot Regime 141
Pratt & Whitney (United Aircraft of Canada, LTD, Engines): PT6A 157; PT6A-6 121 22, 25, 34, 207; PT6A-27 123, 125, 129, 131, 138, 142, 149, 155, 156, 210; PT6A-40, 146; Wasp 21; Wasp-Junior 25
Prestwick Pioneer 22
Princeton University 84

Propellers: Aeromatic 32–34 44; Hartzell 47, 73, 75, 77–79, 81, 84, 122, 142, 150, 53, 55–157, 176, 181, 186, 191, 196, 201, 203, 207, 210; Magic Formula 34–35
Prouty, Fletcher 100

Ranger (Engines): V-12 21
Rawdon Aircraft Company 87
Reading, Pennsylvania Air show 111
Rearwin Aircraft Company: Model Junior 7
Reconstruction Finance Corporation Loan 50
Red China 93, 109
Republic Aviation: Model F-84 Thunderjet 55
Republic of Vietnam Air Force (RVNAF) 136
Rheinstrom, Charles A. 31
Robbins, Christopher 86, 100–104
Rocket Assisted Take-off (RATO) 17
Rommel, Field Marshall Erwin 21
Ross, John C. 27
Rounds and Porter Lumber Company 64
Royal Khemer Air Force 138–142
Royal Thai Air Force 138
Ryan (Aircraft): Model YO-51 "Dragonfly" 21–23 26

Safety/General Aviation 68; restraints 30
St. Louis, Missouri 61, 62
San Diego, California 165
Schiff, Barry 1
Schroeder-Wentworth 5
Seibel Helicopter Company 87
Sihanouk, Prince Norodom 138
Skorzeny, Otto 21
Slip 19
Smith, Gene 1, 106
Smithline, Lawrence N. 59
Souphanouvong, Prince 101
Southern Peru Copper Company 64
Souvanna Phouma, Prince 101
Soviet Union 93
Sparks, Jay 86
Stabilator 44
Stall Proof 36
Stearman, Lloyd 16
Stearman-Hammond Aircraft: Model Y-1S 16
Stearman Trainer 128, 158
Stein Lumber Company 64
Stinson 22; Model L-5 22;

Model YO-49 21 22; Model YO-49A 21; Model L1 Vigilant 21
STOL 22 25, 35, 38, 39, 54, 61, 64, 65, 67, 71, 86, 87, 89, 106, 107, 113, 16, 121, 123, 124, 129, 131, 135, 136, 137, 143, 144, 146, 147, 148, 155, 156, 158, 160
Stout, William, B. 30
Struck, Luis 75
Summer Institute of Linguistics (SIL) 162
Supplementary Type Certificate (STC): SA138SW 83

Taylor Brothers "Chummy" 5
Taylorcraft 22 23; Model L-2 22; Model E-2 7
Tennis Court Airplane 38 39
Teterboro Airport 64
Texas Instruments Corporation 130
Thurston, David 150
Townsend, William Cameron 160–163, 165, 166
Tully, Arthur H., Jr. 28
Tulsa, Oklahoma 165
Turbomeca Astazou II, Turbine 134
Turner, Thomas 136
Tuscon, Arizona 66

Union Carbide Nuclear Company 64
United States Air Force 54, 87, 89–93, 95, 96, 98, 107, 109, 132, 134, 136, 138, 216; Air Guard 96, 97, 215; Foreign Military Sales Program 138
United States Army 86, 87, 89–93, 96, 98, 107, 215, 216; Army Aviation Board, 90; Special Forces 91, 93, 160; Special Warfare Center 90
United States Border Patrol 64
United States Fish and Wildlife Service 25
United States General Accounting Office 135
United States Government 54, 65, 104– 105, 107, 108
United States Navy 87 135
University of Miami 9
University of Wichita 87, 89; Department of Engineering 87
U.S.S. *Kearsarge* 165
Utley, R.C. 48

Vedenyev M14 Radial Engine (Russian) 171
Vidal, Eugene 14

Waltham, Massachusetts 61
Waterman, Cliff, Jr. 58
Waxhaw, North Carolina 160, 166, 169
Weeghan, Richard 1
Weick, Fred E. 14, 16, 18
Weick Aircraft: Model W1/A 13–15
Western Newspaper Union 64

Weston, Massachusetts 30
White, Russell 59
Wichita, Kansas 27, 30
Wiggins, E.W. Airways 31
Wilkinson, Stephan 106, 124, 125, 129, 130
World War II 54
Wright, T.P. 7
Wright Brothers 53

Wright Field 21
Wycliffe, John 162
Wycliffe Bible Translators 160–163

Zerbach, Darius 66
Zoche Aero-Diesel 169, 170

www.ingramcontent.com/pod-product-compliance
Ingram Content Group UK Ltd.
Pitfield, Milton Keynes, MK11 3LW, UK
UKHW050533150426
5217IPUK00026B/1919